Only Make Believe

Only Make Believe

My Life in Show Business

HOWARD KEEL
with Joyce Spizer

BARRICADE
BOOKS

Fort Lee, New Jersey

Published by Barricade Books Inc.
185 Bridge Plaza North
Suite 308-A
Fort Lee, NJ 07024

ISBN 1-56980-292-0

Printed in the USA

Dedication

For
Grace
Rosemary
Helen
Kaija & Kirstine
Judy & Leslie
And most of all
Gunnar

Contents

Acknowledgments

My thanks to:

Jim Gammon who lent me my first computer and kept comin' over and trying to help me.

Bill Nadeau who forced me to buy another computer.

Judy who bought me a brand new computer for my 80th!

Post-it notes

Bic Pens and paper

Magic Markers and more paper

To Scotch tape and more, much more paper

And to trash cans

And especially Gunnar, my son, who pulled this out of me.

I Was Born a Coal Miner's Son

★　　★　　★　　★　　★

The only thing I knew about "Dallas" was that it was some little soap opera my wife, Judy, watched on Friday nights. I baby-sat our daughter, Leslie, answered the telephone, and didn't allow anyone to interrupt her watching that show. My manager called and told me Leonard Katzman wanted to see me. Who the hell was Katzman?

As writer-producer-director, Leonard was "Dallas," and he had the balls that would eventually spin that soap opera around the world. He mastered the taming of J.R. and Bobby and pulled the sex appeal out of every lady on that show.

So I found myself sitting in his waiting room when his secretary, Louella Caraway, said, "Here's the script. Do you want to read it?"

I replied, "I don't read."

She looked at me.

I was introduced to Lenny and liked him right away. He said, "Are you busy next week?"

He didn't know how busy I wasn't. "No, sir."

"We'd like you to shoot Monday and Tuesday."

"What's the part like, and who is he?"

He told me what he wanted, and I agreed. We shook hands, and that was the beginning of a long, lovely friendship.

This 1981 scene revived my career that had begun on an MGM stage in 1949 when I starred in *Annie Get Your Gun*. My whirlwind movie-Broadway-British stage-TV life included the first 3-D movie, *Kiss Me Kate,* the first film shot in CinemaScope, *Kismet*, and the most-watched movie classic, *Seven Brides for Seven Brothers*.

How did I get here?

* * *

No one told me I'd need balls to live the life I've lived. Not to worry, I got 'em. I'm a quick study in the school of hard knocks that began, to correct the tabloid reports of my birth date, April 13, 1919, in Gillespie, Illinois. I was born Harry Clifford Keel in a four-room house at 908 South Madison Street where I lived until I was sixteen years old.

Towering elm trees and multicolored maples lined Gillespie's sleepy little streets. Three thousand residents knew it was a great place to raise their kids. The town boasted a more-than-adequate public school system consisting of the Little Brick School, the Maple Street School, the Big Brick School, and a community high school that served surrounding smaller towns, as well.

In Gillespie, you prayed for your sins or you paid for your crimes. Five churches: the Catholic, Lutheran, Methodist, Episcopalian, and Baptist, prayed for your soul. A central police and fire station maintained order. Two railroads crossed each other just north of Main Street: the electric Illinois Railroad and the steam engine Big Four.

The Illinois, mainly a freight system for coal and merchandise with only a couple of two-car passenger trains, ran right down Main Street. The Big Four was hardly used at all.

Commerce included farms and coal mines. One of those mines known as the Little Dog sat on the north side of town.

Weekends for the town sportsmen included drinking, football, basketball, track, baseball, soccer, and a bit of tennis. And my favorite, the movies. The Colonial and the Lyric, our two motion-picture houses, sat on either end of the three-block-long downtown business center.

Charles Homer Keel, my father, was a coal miner with a serious drinking problem and a raging temper. My mother, Grace Osterkamp, was a paperhanger. They were a curious combination. My mother often hung wallpaper to keep the family solvent.

As far as we can tell, my dad had to marry my mother. My brother, Bill, was born June 26, 1913. Their wedding certificate listed their marriage date as October 29, 1912.

I was six years younger than Bill, and from day one, we never got along. I was naturally more curious. He was the older, spoiled one. I looked up to him as my big brother, and he really looked down on me.

The first thing I remember about my youth was being locked up in a chicken coop with my cousin, Oren Osterkamp, when I was three and Oren was two. We had been running around making a mess of the alfresco arrangements at Oren's father's wedding to his step-mother.

I was a curious little brat, and being older than Oren, I was the leader of the pack. This is when I made the first major mistake of my life. I underestimated my mother's speed and strength. She stood an imposing six feet tall. Using her long arms and strong hands, she swooped us up by the seat of our pants, placed us in the chicken coop, and locked the door behind her. We sat on a chicken roost and got comfortable to watch the whole affair. What better accommodations could two unwanted guests expect?

My mother's parents, Fred and Mathilda Osterkamp, owned a third-generation milk farm in Gillespie. Coal miners washed the coal in the Osterkamp lake. This process caused the water level to drop lower and lower because the coal would get thicker and thicker. We kids would often dive into the lake and be up to our elbows in black mud.

I went to church for a while because I loved to hear the choir, but I quit at about the age of six or seven. I knew Gillespie hosted several different religions, but my grandmother, Mathilda Osterkamp, prayed to one called "The Never Dies." For hours, the minister would pontificate its philosophy that people never died and went to heaven or hell, but rather that they lived forever. She and I listened to those sermons. But I wanted to hear the music.

My grandfather, Fred Osterkamp, stood about 6 feet 6 inches to 6 feet 8 inches tall. He scared the shit out of me. He had this bushy mustache, and when he spoke, his voice boomed across the room. One night, I had to sleep with him because we had houseguests. I was so scared, I didn't move one inch all night. The next day, he told the family I was a good sleeper.

I was five. It was my first day of school at the Little Brick School, and I fell in love with a beautiful little girl named Othella Brown. It was to be my secret for the next three years. Then and there, I made a life-changing decision. I would love girls the rest of my life.

During the winter of my second grade, I was running around the school acting silly and fell on a piece of ice, injuring my left elbow. I stayed in school for the rest of the day, and eventually mom and dad picked me up and took me to see a doctor.

The doctor said the arm had been badly sprained and suggested all I'd have to do was carry a heavy bucket of sand around and it would eventually straighten out. That's exactly what I did. I carried that damned bucket around for months, and the elbow hurt like hell the entire time . . . and it never did straighten out!

The day after the accident, I walked around school, and Othella saw me and said she was sorry about my arm. Immediately my love for her grew by leaps and bounds. I believed that she really liked me.

Then, in the third grade, we both missed seven times eight in the multiplication table. I knew it! We were destined to be in love for the rest of our lives. Then CALAMITY struck! Her family moved to St. Louis, and I never saw her again. It was my first real heartbreak.

The arm was to become the bane of my existence because I couldn't fight with Frances Skelley as we walked home from school.

I never thought I'd be good at any sport because my left arm couldn't take the pressure. This truly distorted my sense of self-confidence and started my ego on a downhill spiral. My anger took an uphill approach. Both ego and anger clashed as my life's major conflicts.

I would run away from fights. Then one day when I was about eleven, there was this one kid that kept pushing me around. I said, "That's it."

I fought the damn kid for a half-hour or so and pounded him into the ground. I stood and walked away. Everything changed after that.

The last time my mother spanked me, I was about eight years old. We had a pond in town, and I wanted to go fishing there with some other kids. I said, "Come on. Let's go fishing."

Mom said, "No. You have errands to do."

I thought, hey, I'm going fishing. And I did.

A man walked down to the fishing hole and asked if Harry Keel was anywhere around.

One of the kids said, "Yes, he's right here."

I said, "Shh. I'm not here."

The man said, "His mom wants to see him right now."

I popped up from the gully to find my mother sitting in the car. "Hi, Mom," I said. "I just started walking home with this kid and stopped by here for a second."

She didn't believe me, but I thought it was quite original. She opened the car door, pulled me inside, and drove home. She ordered me into the house and told me to pull down my pants. There I stood, naked. She took a big strap and whopped me three or four times. I never ever disobeyed her like that again. Oh, I had my mouth washed an awful lot because I used to cuss a lot. Still, do. Instead of saying "bullshit," I could get away with "bull horns." But I couldn't get away with "dang it" or "ding it." She knew what I was thinking.

More embarrassing than standing naked in front of my mom were the weekly baths. I bathed in an old tin tub with no privacy. Mom warmed well water and poured it in there. I hated the humiliating baths.

★ ★ ★

My second love was my sixth-grade teacher, Miss Ehlert. She was attractive and sensitive to all her students. I don't think I was her only secret lover. Under her tutelage, I did my best in grade school. She helped me get over my first love, Othella Brown. When I love, I love hard.

Around this time my brother, Bill, and I began studying the trombone, though we were not destined to become the Dorsey Brothers. I played by ear and quickly learned how to play "My Country 'Tis of Thee."

The teacher taught us chords and sharps and flats, but I preferred playing by ear, although I could read half, quarter, and whole notes. I would sit and listen to the chap beside me, then simply play the same notes. I played in the band that way until my junior year in high school.

★ ★ ★

I remember spending a nickel to see *Phantom of the Opera*. The movie scared the hell out of me, but I was a tough little kid. I had a bum arm, couldn't play sports, my brother hated me, I was angry as all get out, and my ego lay safely at the bottom of the toilet.

Our family's deepest depression lay ahead and events that followed would change me forever.

Whose Life Changed Forever When I Was Eleven

★ ★ ★ ★ ★

I never really got to know my dad very well and have few memories of him. He was a very strong man and weighed 235 pounds. He joined the navy in St. Louis, Missouri, on April 1, 1909. At twenty-five years old, according to his enlistment record, he stood 5 feet 8½ inches tall, with blue eyes, brown hair, and a ruddy complexion. He traveled the world when Teddy Roosevelt sent the great White Fleet on a so-called "goodwill" tour. Dad mustered out, returned to Gillespie, and went to work in the coal mines. His drinking problem had been pretty well established by the time he mustered out. He cussed like the sailor he'd been, too.

My family's history, filled with intrigue and undercurrents, was constantly fed by my dad's drinking. My mother was a member of the Women's Christian Temperance Union, and that did not enhance our family harmony. She was so strict, we couldn't have root beer in the house. It was also against the Methodist rules to gamble or play cards. All these things kept our lives in continual turmoil.

Dad, who was about forty-two at the time, smoked a pipe and used tobacco called Miners and Puddlers. He began to have a problem with his teeth that gave way to chronic pain. The teeth were in such bad shape that the dentist extracted all of them in one sitting. Then dad had problems holding the pipe in his mouth. So he wrapped black tape around the top of the pipe and held it between his gums.

The relationship between Bill and me continued to deteriorate. Being six years younger, I was a constant pain in the you-know-what to him. He would twist my arm because he knew it hurt. Each day, I faced aggravation and torment from him. With a bum left side, I didn't have much defense, although we'd have quite impressive battles. My only offense was to kick him as hard as I could, usually on the shinbones. Then I'd run as fast as I could, but generally not fast enough. He'd run me down, grab my left arm, and twist it, and then kick the hell out of me. I decided to keep clear of him as much as possible. I never liked or trusted my brother after that.

One day, Bill and a guy named Palmer said they were going swimming. I wanted to tag along. They said, "No, you're not going to go with us."

I hopped on the car, and Bill tried to sling me off, oscillating the steering wheel back and forth. He was beyond mean. I believe that single event gave me the strength to succeed and to try so hard throughout my life.

I became a loner, and it'd soon be more lonely at home.

★ ★ ★

On Bill's birthday, when I was eleven, he spent the night at a friend's house. My father staggered home roaring drunk. He had a bottle in one back pocket and a big .45-caliber German Luger in the other. My father was loaded, got into an argument with my mother, and chased her out the back door. I ran after him and snatched the bottle out of his pocket, but he caught my hand and grabbed it back. When they returned to the house, my parents continued to argue.

Without any warning, dad removed a glass from the kitchen cabinet, uncorked the bottle, and poured the contents into the glass. He said, "I'm going to kill myself" and drank down the whole glass in one swallow.

He immediately began to moan and groan in pain. Mother and I were shocked. We couldn't believe what was happening. All she said was, "Why, Homer Keel, what have you done to yourself?"

Even in his pain, he reached for his Luger, and my terrified mother ran out of the house. My father lurched around in agony and ended up in the front bedroom. I could hear him, but I didn't know what to do. I ran toward my uncle's house for help. Then I remembered I had left our little dog, Wiggles. I guess I was afraid dad would kill her, and I went back for her.

When I entered the kitchen, I could hear my father in pain in the front bedroom. I snatched up Wiggles, and we took off for my uncle's. By the time help arrived, my father was dead! The authorities later determined that the bottle contained carbolic acid.

The father that I needed, but never knew, was gone. It was June 26, 1930. I was beyond consolation, young, and lost. I crawled inside my anger and locked the whole world out. I cried for days. I don't remember anything about the funeral or receiving any consolation from neighbors or family.

This tragedy had a terrible effect on my life. It wasn't until years later that I sat down and tried to figure out what had caused my father to do what he did. He was forty-five years old. For a long time, I thought I would die when I was forty-five. I was so glad to have that birthday pass without incident.

After my dad took himself out, my mother took in a roomer with two pluses: Farina was a nice guy, and he worked in the movie theater. I would polish all his shoes and keep them clean, and he'd give me a nickel and dime. That's how I earned money for the movies.

Grief continued to weigh heavily on me, and I looked for distractions. I started smoking by the time I was twelve or thirteen. By my junior year in high school, I smoked every chance I got and whenever I could afford them. I liked Lucky Strikes or Camels—but I'd smoke whatever I could get my hands on. I would wake up in the morning and light up.

I was more mischievous and filled with devilment than harmful. Someone taught me to smoke, and naturally I trained others. One of my favorite pastimes was to turn over outhouses. It was a lot of fun until the police caught me and some other guys one night and threatened to put us in jail.

After my father was gone, our lives were more difficult. The Big Depression hit close to home. My mother was a paperhanger by trade, but now people had no money except for essentials. She washed, ironed, cleaned, and did just about any other work she could

11

find. From 1932 through 1934, I would often stand in line and get flour so mom could make bread that we sold at the grocery store.

I slopped and cleaned up after cats and dogs for the people who could afford to pay me. When things couldn't get much worse, mother became seriously ill with tuberculosis and would have died except for the kindness of a local doctor who saved her.

Grandmother Mathilda and Grandfather Fred Osterkamp supplemented our diet with fresh vegetables from their farm.

★ ★ ★

When I entered the seventh grade at the Big Brick School, one of my three teachers was Miss Ehlert. She took me aside and told me how sorry she was and tried to help me understand my loss. She was truly a wonderful woman. I hope she's still alive to read this and know what an impact she made on my life.

By the eighth grade, I starred as the class under-achiever. I was the loneliest student, withdrawn and filled with anger. One day I was being obnoxious, and a teacher, Miss Hogget, clouted me along side of my head and knocked me clear out of my seat. She had MY complete attention for the rest of the year!

Throughout my youth, I continued to press my self-destruct button and never learned much of anything except to develop my anal vision when Miss Hogget was around. That's a lesson I learned from one tough lady.

By my high school freshman year, I had decided I would study to become a doctor. I found out that Latin was required and immediately lost interest. No Dr. Keel!

I walked home from school one afternoon and met a group of guys who were tossing a football around. They had screwy names like Popes Anderson, Beast Hunter, Harko Smith, and Panky Picket. Popes and I became fast friends. He was on the football team, had a strong body, and ran like a deer. He also had a great sense of humor. He was seventeen. I was thirteen.

I was just beginning to grow and stretching out very fast. My feet were getting bigger and bigger, while I became skinnier and skinnier. I was certainly no match for Popes. He was like the big brother that I badly needed, but didn't have. I felt very secure around him. He was a straight arrow, a tough guy, and a great fighter.

Wanting to follow Popes, I thought about a career in football. I suited up for every game, but was the only guy on the squad that didn't play that year. With my bum arm, Coach Red Nickolet urged me to find another outlet.

I took a class with coach called manual training. It involved drafting, drawing, and measuring. I was very good at it. Of all my classes, I enjoyed this one the most. Coach had a rule if you had an "A," you didn't have to take the final exam; if you had a "B," you took the exam.

Coach gave me my paper with a big black mark on it and said, "You're wrong."

I looked at him and said, "I'm not wrong. I'm right. You look at it and see."

He changed it and gave me an "A." I grew an inch and a half that day. I thought FUCK YOU, YOU ASSHOLE.

Having mastered that, I moved on toward other obstacles life had in store for me.

Beast Hunter, a stocky little guy and another of my

buddies, was like a little brother to me. He was tough for his size, quiet, and very bright.

During the summer that I turned fourteen, Popes, Beast, and I hopped the freights that rolled through the center of town. We rode them to Staunton, about nine miles south, hopped off, and went to band concerts on Thursday nights. Popes had a girl there he was making time with, but Beast and I never did score. No girl would even look at us, but we had a lot of laughs trying all evening. Then we'd hop a northbound freight around 11 o'clock for home.

One day, we decided to hook the ITS, the Illinois Traction System. We rode it north to South Pekin, just south of Peoria, Illinois. Popes and Beast, who were eighteen by now, thought they could get jobs at the local Caterpillar factory. What dreamers.

Mother gave me permission to go along. She knew Popes and trusted him to look after me. We caught the first freight going north in the late afternoon and rode all night to South Pekin. By the time we arrived, we decided that Popes might have the best chance of getting hired, and if he did, then Beast would try. Off he went, and we waited around all day.

Popes returned and told us they weren't hiring anyone.

Oh well, we tried. Although we had traveled north on the ITS, we thought it'd be wiser to go home on the CNW, the Chicago North Western, which was primarily a coal hauler.

We reached the train yard around five in the afternoon and climbed a tall fence to get in. The bulls (the railroad police) saw us. We scrambled back over the

14

fence and laid low for a while till we saw a freight heading south. We scaled the fence again and ran like hell. The freight was moving at a healthy speed. Popes and Beast jumped on, but I couldn't make it. By this time, the bulls were hot on our tails. I just knew that I'd be spending time in jail.

Popes jumped off the train and yelled at me, "Get on that train, or I'm going to kick the shit out of you."

I tried again and caught the north end of a train going south, which was all wrong. There were only two rungs up the side of the car, and you couldn't climb to the top. I could feel my feet hit the rails, and it scared the hell out of me. I thought somehow I'd pull myself up, and somehow I did. I grabbed the second rung and put my foot into the step below. I held on outside for several miles, then the train slowed down enough, on a slight hill, and I jumped off and got in that dirty coal car with Popes and Beast. I shook like some dog shitting peach stones. After six hours, we passed the coal washer east of Gillespie, jumped off, and walked the last two miles home. I slept for a day and a half. What an experience for a skinny kid of fourteen.

A short time later, Popes joined the navy. After indoctrination, he returned to Gillespie. I tried to start the old crazy dialogue, and he said, "Look, I'm no longer the crazy guy I was. I'm a man now, and I suggest that you stop acting like a juvenile and grow up."

That shook me up! He married his high school sweetheart, and they moved to California.

★ ★ ★

For my fifteenth birthday, mom bought me my first hat, a new sweater, and a pair of pants. That weekend Beast

Hunter, Panky Picket, and I went to a dance in Benld, just two miles south of Gillespie. Chicago gangsters hid there when it got too hot for them in the Windy City.

The Progressive Miners of America, a coal miner's union, owned a two-story building where the dances were held. When we arrived in Benld, Beast managed to get a bottle of bourbon and some Coca-Cola. By the time we arrived at the eight o'clock dance, it was nine-thirty, and we felt no pain. We bounced off the walls as we climbed a flight of stairs to the second floor. I checked my hat in the cloakroom and staggered into the dance hall.

Panky danced, but Beast and I struck out. We kept asking, and the girls kept refusing. Now Beast was short and chunky. By this time, I was 6 feet 2 inches and skinny. I mean skinny, about 125 pounds. Beast and I were turned down time and time again.

Finally Beast announced that we were being turned down because I didn't know how to dance. He would teach me the current dances, so we went to the cloakroom for lessons. We both were really crocked by this time, and the lady in charge of the cloakroom was in hysterics watching us. When it was obvious to Beast that teaching me was futile, he went bananas. He knocked down a whole row of clothes, grabbed my hat, and threw it out the window, which really peed me off.

I retreated to the window and saw my new hat lying in the middle of the street. A good Samaritan, who was almost as drunk as me, picked it up and brushed it off.

I yelled down at him. "Hey! That's my hat."

After he saw me hanging out the window, he tried time and again to toss it up to me. After nearly falling out several times trying to catch it, I sobered to the conclusion that I should go down and fetch it myself.

At the top of the stairwell, I took about two steps when my heel slipped out from under me. I fell on my ass and bounced all the way down the stairs. Once I picked myself up, the ass of my pants was torn loose, and the good Samaritan had taken off with my hat. There I was, no hat and my pants all torn in the rear. I was drunk and pissed off. I pressed my "self-destruction button" and said, "Fuck it, I'm going to walk home."

The boys picked me up, threw me into the backseat, and drove me to a corner by the Red and White Grocery store in Gillespie. They sat me down, told me to clean up my act, and go home. Instead I threw up, then lay in front of the store and slept.

Around daylight, I felt a little better and walked about three-and-a-half blocks home. On the way, I thought about what my mom would say if she saw me. She was so against booze. I decided to sneak in the back door and get into my room, which was in the rear of the house. I tiptoed in, walked across the kitchen in the dark, struck a chair, and fell on my ass, making one hell of a noise.

I looked up, and there stood mom looking down at me. She started to cry and went to her bedroom. I don't think I ever felt so much hatred for myself as I did that moment. She had gone through so much hell with dad's AND my brother's drinking problems that to let her see me in that condition at fifteen was too much.

She eventually forgave me, and I never drank again until I was on my own.

★ ★ ★

17

I walked about a mile and a half to school each day and took all the shortcuts through yards and alleys that I could. One route took me by the home of a family named Gibbons. They had a son named Chuck who was a year ahead of me in school. A tall redhead, Chuck always dressed sharp and was quite the ladies' man. He was a good student, politically "in" at school, and an all-around good guy. As a football and basketball player, he was quite the jock, too.

One morning as I cut through his yard, he popped out of his house and said, "Hold on, and I'll walk to school with you."

We talked about school and life. He asked me, "Are you a junior?"

I replied, "Yes."

"Do you have a girl?"

"Nope."

He asked me about sports, and I said, "I'm too skinny, and I have a bad left arm. So they never pick me. But I play slide trombone in the school band."

Then he asked me, "What's wrong with your teeth?"

"What do you mean?"

We stopped, and he said, "Smile. Your teeth are green! Don't you ever wash your teeth?"

And I said, "What for?"

"To keep them clean! You'll never get a girl with dirty teeth like that! You've got nice teeth, but they're dirty."

"My mother always told me to wash my teeth, but I never have time. I just rinse them out with water."

Chuck said, "You've got to brush them! You've got a nice smile, but your teeth look like hell, so brush them."

He paused. "You going to the Junior-Senior Prom?"

"Heck no."

"You don't have a girl, do you?"

"There's one girl in one of my classes that I like, but she'd never go with me."

"Why don't you ask her?"

"No way. She's a nice, quiet girl from a good family. She'd never go with me. She's probably got a date anyway."

Chuck said, "You wash your teeth tomorrow and come by. Dad and I will give you a ride to school."

From that time on, Chuck took me in hand, taught me what to wear to look sharp, and I began to shy away from my old habits and take a more positive look at myself. The school had an open dress code. A pair of blue-and-white-striped overalls and turtleneck sweaters were very stylish. Shoes, regardless of brand, had to be clean.

Chuck introduced me to the P. C. Gibbons' Pool Hall, a great place for guys like me who needed definition and guidance. P.C. was a wonderful old man who lived by a strict code: clean clothes, clean mouth, and no drinking. The pool table had to be respected and clean, especially with regard to temper tantrums. If a ball was hit so hard it left the table, you didn't play for weeks.

Every Saturday morning, P.C. had the very best pool players teach us everything from how to handle the pool stick to the rudiments of good play. I never missed one free session. I soon developed into a very good pool player. I had mastered the trombone, reading music, playing sports, and now pool.

I reserved my own pool cue for twenty-five cents and

played five cents a game as often as I could afford it. I cleaned up dog shit around the neighborhood and ran errands to earn maybe ten cents spending and gambling money. I didn't lose many games and gained a little more respect for myself.

As the Junior-Senior Prom drew near, Chuck and his girl, Virginia, kept after me to invite Elizabeth, the girl I liked. I put off asking her. I just couldn't get up enough courage. They told me she didn't have a boyfriend and all I'd have to do was ask her. But Ole Hairbreadth Harry was just too scared. Ole Harry went to the prom stag, and there was Elizabeth by herself, too. I pressed the old self-destruct button, ate with the others, and left alone.

How could I be so dumb and cowardly? I hated myself about that incident for a long time. I should have written to her and apologized. I found out later she liked me and wanted me to ask her. I still regret it, but I probably did her a favor because I left for California that summer.

Maybe she'll read the book. She'll know who she is, if she's still alive.

* * *

By my sixteenth birthday on April 13, 1935, my mother had taught me to drive our 1929 Model-A Ford. It was a nice old four-door, green with a black top. I quickly mastered handling it.

My buddy, Chuck, wanted to go to Staunton to visit a girl he knew, and I asked mom if I could take him. She agreed and let me drive the car for the first time without her.

We picked up Chuck's girl, dropped by a soda fountain for a Coke, and talked. Chuck always had great taste in women. This young girl was very nice and had a great sense of humor.

He suggested, "Why don't you drop us off at her home and pick me up in about half an hour?"

I left them off and cruised down one of the main drags at a good pace when I passed a movie house that had just let out. A lot of young people mingled in front talking when I heard a spurt of a siren behind me. It sounded like a couple of kids putting me on. I yelled out the window at them, put the pedal to the metal, and tooled off. The siren then roared to life as the police car pulled me over at the next block.

They said I was being a young smart ass, took me to the police station, and locked me up. After a while, I talked them into going to the home where Chuck was and bringing him to the station. They wanted eight dollars to bail me out.

Chuck didn't have that kind of money, and neither did I. Chuck got them to give him my car so he could drive home and get his father to help us. He drove about sixteen miles to pick up his dad. It was about 10:30 at night, and by the time he returned, it was around midnight.

I thought his father would be sore at me, but he wasn't. He paid the fine and chewed out the cops for treating me the way they did. He told them he didn't care what I had done, they had no right to put me in jail. He was a nice man and very intelligent. I can't tell you how glad I was to get out because I had seen my father thrown in jail a couple of times, and it hadn't been easy to watch.

I was scared and still had to face my mother. What a thing to happen to me on the very first night I had the car. I show off and wind up in jail.

Moving to California: A Risky Move

★ ★ ★ ★ ★

When the Civilian Conservation Corps was established, my brother, Bill, joined it. After a short stint in Washington State, he transferred to Fallbrook, California, to develop Live Oak Park. There he met Hilda Lenfers and married her. She worked for a packing house where she picked lemons and oranges. He wrote us and said we should come out to California. That's where the work was.

We drove to Granite City, Illinois, and visited with my Aunt Rea and Uncle Don. Rea was mother's sister. They were wonderful people who I loved and adored.

I got my voice from Aunt Rea, who had a beautiful contralto that matched her handsome face. Many people said she could have been another Madam Schuman-Heink. But she met Uncle Don, and they fell in love and married. Uncle Don had been gassed in World War I and couldn't breathe very well, but he studied and put himself through law school.

We all agreed that relocating to the West Coast would be positive and made plans for the big move.

Our home in Gillespie had four rooms, a closed-in back porch, and a basement. My mother sold the whole thing, house and furnishings, for $400. We packed the 1929 Model-A Ford with little sacks containing our meager belongings and took off for California. A young man named Thompson rode with us and shared expenses.

We didn't realize that being the middle of July, it'd be hotter than hell. There'd been a drought, and the entire Midwest was a dust bowl.

We followed Route 66 through the heat and dust all the way to California driving across Missouri, Oklahoma, Texas, New Mexico, Arizona, and Nevada, into California, then Highway 395 to Fallbrook.

It was fairly decent driving until we reached New Mexico. There, for about 250 miles, we hit washboard roads where we could only drive twenty miles an hour. The ruggedness shook our poor old Ford clear across the state. It's a wonder that the car didn't fall apart. No matter how hot it was or how much dust we drove through, that little ole '29 Model-A just kept pinging along. It only had four cylinders, but it was loaded with courage and determination. We made the trip in five or six days.

We reached Las Vegas a little before noon. It was 110 degrees in the shade as the saying goes, but it was true that day. There wasn't much development in Vegas in 1935, just a little park with some shade trees surrounded by a couple of stores and a few honky-tonk bars. I never dreamed that nineteen years later, I'd return as a headliner at the Last Frontier Casino.

Later that day, we reached Route 395, and around nine o'clock, we hit a cool breeze and stopped the car. We couldn't figure out where it was coming from. We heard a zip, zip, zip sound and discovered farmers were irrigating a huge orange grove. We sat there on the side of the road for about fifteen minutes and cooled down.

We found an early relative of a motel with six cabins and moved in. Our one-room cabin had a tiny kitchen and no indoor bathroom.

Fallbrook High School, with its 150 students, had been named the Model Rural District High School of the United States at that time. Its sports included baseball, basketball, and tennis, but no football.

Mother found a job right away as a cook in the El Camino Real Hotel. I enrolled in school and learned I'd have to take both civics and history again. I had passed civics in Gillespie, but was kicked out of the history class because of my charming shenanigans. It really peed me off that I had to take a full year of both courses, and the old self-destruct button started right off. Fortunately, it didn't last long.

I found new buddies right away. Robert Stone, John Blakemore, Marion Clemmens, Kermit Cave, and Jack Glasscock were seniors. They were all good students and nice guys with a good sense of humor.

Bob Stone invited me to his home where I met his sister, Ginny, and their mother. This family was very nice to me during my stay in Fallbrook. They were my security blankets at a time when I needed one.

Bob became president of the senior class. He played all sports, and under his tutelage, I learned a lot. Although I never thought I was very good at sports.

He and Ginny taught me to dance, and I loved that. With girls, that is! We used to visit a lovely home where the Kingsbury girls lived, and we'd dance all afternoon.

It was a huge ranch, and the two sisters were very attractive. Bob and I would switch dance partners back and forth. Don't get me wrong, at this stage of my life, there was no hanky-panky. Just dancing. The girls were well-educated, classy young ladies. The Kingsbury family were down-to-earth, nice people. They were extremely wealthy, but never trumpeted that. They always made us feel welcome, and I felt honored to be in their company.

By this time, at 6 feet 3 inches tall, I was weighing about 135 pounds. Not much to look at, but I could dance, and my teeth were clean. I had the same pair of patched pants and shoes and the same pair of overalls. I was not what you would call Dapper Dan, but I was learning a lot about life.

I don't think I impressed my mother very much. She simply tried to put up with me and keep me straight.

Johnny Blakemore was a ruggedly handsome guy from Monrovia, California. He'd come from a strong family background, but I think he was sent down to Fallbrook for some unknown reason. We had good fun together. He dated Helen Pierce, a nice girl who was not only very bright, but was the most attractive girl in school. She was crazy about Johnny, and they later married.

Marion Clemmens was a good student and quite a prankster, full of the Old Nick! He and I got into a little trouble at school when school officials became suspicious about our grades in civics class. The superintendent at the graduation ceremony made a speech about cheating in life, and we sat there pleased as punch that we wouldn't have to face him again. As far as I was concerned, I'd do anything to get me out of school.

Kermit Cave was a good friend, but too smart to get

very involved in our cutups. His family seemed quite strict with him.

Jack Glasscock had a thick Arkansas accent. We called him "Ole Brittle Prick," which he accepted with good humor. I never got to know Jack very well, which was probably best for him.

* * *

I had an accident in shop class and cut off the tip of my right forefinger. The doctor treated me and sent the bill to the school. The superintendent said the school didn't have to pay the ten dollars. That was a lot of money for mom, and I told him so.

He remained stern. "The school will not pay for it."

Ole Hairbreadth Harry kicked in. I said a few words about what I thought of the superintendent and the school and got expelled for a few days, but the school paid the medical bill. Mission accomplished!

There was an English teacher named Miss McKeever who I liked. She was a nice lady and a fine teacher, a lot like Miss Ehlert, warm, intelligent, and caring with a good sense of humor.

The senior school book carried two pages of predictions ten years hence for the thirty-two graduating students. In our senior photo, I stood beside a 7-foot-1-inch kid. My prediction was short and sweet: Harry Keel. Address: 1144 Sing Sing on the Hudson . . . a reference not to my singing, but to Sing Sing Prison in New York.

Having spent most of a night in jail in Staunton, Illinois, I was not exactly big time, but I had learned my lesson.

* * *

Bill continued to influence me in a negative way. Even though I told him I didn't know how to fight, he volunteered me for a boxing event.

Bill said, "Oh come on, this is just a little sparring match."

I fought a tough kid named Bob Cludgage, and he was whipping me badly.

I thought, "Holy shit. I'm getting beat. I need to do something." I hauled off and punched him and knocked him right flat on his ass. He couldn't get up. I became the BIG BOY.

The next fight I had was with a strong guy about twenty-two years old. He hit me in the gut so hard I almost died. I collapsed, and that was my last official fight.

From then on, I used my brain and bullied my way through things. Don't get me wrong, I'm a good scrapper and can take a lot of verbiage. Just don't push me.

My first positive sense of accomplishment occurred after graduation. I needed a job and visited the local lumberyard in Fallbrook.

A nice young man who worked there said, "No jobs here, but I have a load of lumber to take to the top of Mount Palomar. I need someone to help me. There's lots of steep curves and grades, and the mountain road isn't paved. I'll be leaving here this afternoon. Would you like to go?"

We took off in a big Chevrolet truck with a couple of tons of lumber on it. We left Fallbrook around 3:30 P.M. and started up the grade at five o'clock. The curves were so sharp that we would start the turn, stop the truck, back up a bit, pull forward, stop, back up, stop, pull for-

27

ward, then back up again. We would repeat this process until he could safely make the turn. He did the forward work. My job was to guide him when he backed up. It was a very slow and dangerous procedure and took us nine hours to climb the grade.

We delivered the first load of lumber for the building of the huge Mount Palomar Observatory. It was my job to see that the lumber didn't slide down the mountain. We felt like a couple of pioneers. Thank God, the Chevy was built like a "Rock." I made two dollars for that back-breaking job.

Mother decided to visit my Uncle George and Aunt Grace in Burbank and see about work there. She took the train and left the old Ford with me. Hilda, my sister-in-law, helped me get a job at the packing house.

They would bring in seven-foot-high stacks of boxes of lemons, and my job was to lift them down from the top and pour them onto a moveable sorting board. When I tried to lift the first one, my left arm collapsed, and I spilled the entire box of lemons on the floor. The women all laughed, but they helped me pick up the lemons and place them on the conveyor belt.

I caught the second box on my chest, then dumped the lemons on the belt. This went on for a while until my chest became so scratched up, it bled through my shirt and hurt like hell. My old temper took over. I pressed my self-destruct button and walked off the job. I hated myself for not being able to do the job and letting Hilda down after she arranged it for me. That damned elbow just would not take it.

I wasn't destined for manual labor.

Losing My Virginity,
Made the Trip Worthwhile

★ ★ ★ ★ ★

Mom called from Los Angeles to say that her brother, Uncle George Osterkamp, had purchased a new car that had to be picked up in Detroit. He wanted us to help Aunt Grace make the journey. I hopped in the old Ford and went pinging down the road to L.A.

In Huntington Beach, the car started knocking. I checked under the hood, then crawled under the engine, and found a hole in the oil pan. As fortune would have it, the car stalled near an oil field. I looked around, found a pool of dirty oil and a stick, took rags and wrapped them around the stick, and plugged up the hole.

Then I spotted an old can, took the dirty oil, and filled up the crankcase. I hopped in the old crate, turned the engine over, and it started right away. We went pinging right on up to Burbank.

That little episode again helped to build my self-confidence. I even felt a little cocky when I told everyone the story.

Uncle George decided that the old Model-A was done for and fixed up an old Dodge to make the trip east. Aunt Grace, mom, and my two cousins, Jordan and David, who were eight and eleven years old, and I took off for Detroit. My cousins were fistfuls and fought with each other most of the trip.

The car ran great until we reached Wyoming. It was summer. We had remembered our move from Gillespie when it was hot and decided to take the northern, cooler route. Ho! Ho! We were on a hundred-mile stretch between two small cities, Rock Springs and Rawlings. Right in the middle of this hot, lonely road, fifty miles each way to civilization, and the Dodge broke down.

I checked the gas, looked at the engine to see if any wires had come loose, kicked the tires, and said, "Well, doesn't that frost your balls."

There I was stuck with my mom, my aunt, and the two little monsters in the middle of nowhere. The temperature was as hot as I was and no help in sight. I told them that I'd try and catch a ride to Rock Springs to the garage where we had gassed up and find a mechanic to help us. We were short of money, but mom gave me her watch to barter with.

A good Samaritan gave me a ride to the garage and told the mechanic that I needed help.

He said, "No way."

I showed him the watch, and he just laughed. I got hot and raised up my 6-foot-3-inch frame and said, "I'm going to stay right here until you help us."

I followed his ass all over that garage. No matter what he did, I hounded him.

Finally he said, "All right. When I get through here, I'll go see what I can do."

Around 4:30 P.M., he closed the shop and drove me to the family. After he repaired the timer, I gave him the watch, and he gave mom a bill for fifty dollars saying, "Pay me when you can. That kid of yours is something else. He just badgered me until I had to do something."

He turned out to be a nice guy. Later, Aunt Grace and mom mailed him a check, and he sent a bill marked PAID IN FULL and returned the watch, too.

* * *

We eventually arrived in Gillespie, and Aunt Grace caught a train to Detroit, picked up the new Ford, which I drove all the way to California. The car, a 1936 V8 Ford, was great! I was in high cotton behind the wheel.

The first morning after we returned to Burbank, Uncle George thrust a newspaper in my hands and said, "Look in the want ads!" I had to find a job and, at seventeen, didn't have a clue how to go about it.

I think he was sore at me for driving the new car all the way home. I don't blame him. I was a bit of a shit, but I was fed up with the whole damn adventure. He didn't sit down with me and make suggestions or advise me at all.

It was during this period that Bill found out I was still a virgin, and he took me to a house. He told me to pick out a hooker. I chose one a little older than me, probably around twenty-one. Now I hadn't had a bath for three or four days. This girl said, "Okay, get your clothes off."

I took all my clothes off, but kept my socks on.

She said, "Take your socks off. You don't fuck with

31

your socks on."

"Okay!" I pulled them off, and it was all over in a matter of seconds. Bam!

★ ★ ★

I began my long search for work. Everything that appealed to me seemed to require previous experience and schooling, neither of which I had. I knew I had to do something because the family didn't have room for me anymore. I wasn't even a good baby-sitter.

I found a want ad for waiters and busboys. In Fallbrook, I had helped mother clean up the kitchen and washed and dried dishes, so I felt I qualified for this job at a restaurant chain called the White Log Taverns.

I took the streetcar to Los Angeles, found the place, told them my qualifications, and was hired on the spot. It was three in the afternoon, and I had to report to work by five o'clock at the corner of Eighth and Hoover. I made it on time, met the boss, put on the White Log Taverns' uniform, apron and cap, and started to work. I did a very good job for him that night, and at 1:00 A.M., we were replaced by another shift.

My boss asked me where my home was, and I said, "I don't have one."

He couldn't believe it when I told him, "I'm new in L.A., and I didn't have time to find one."

He asked me where I was going to stay that night. I told him I didn't know. He looked at me completely dumbfounded then said, "Look, I have a room, and you can sleep on the floor. Maybe tomorrow you can get a room for yourself."

Which is exactly what I did.

My boss was very happy with my work ethic. After

only a couple of days, he told his district manager how well I was doing. The district manager took him at his word and moved me to a new location at Melrose and Bronson, right in front of Paramount Studios. I found a nice room only a couple of blocks away for three dollars a week.

Saturday was my night off. I rode the streetcar and saw the sights. For only a dime, I could ride to Santa Monica, Long Beach, and return to L.A. It was great. One Saturday night, I went to a dance hall called the Palomar on Sunset Boulevard and Vermont Avenue and paid fifty cents to get in. It was a beautiful palatial hall, and the Phil Harris Band played that night. Such a magical evening!

I was still quite shy about asking a girl to dance, so I stood in front of the orchestra and listened to Phil Harris sing his fabulous songs. I especially liked "That's What I Like About the South." I clapped and clapped until he looked down at me and winked.

At that moment, I became a great fan. Later in life, we became good friends. What a guy!

The following Saturday night, they told me I had to work. "This is my night off! I have something to do."

They said, "You either work, or you're fired!"

I said, "You can't do that. I quit!" Ole Hairbreadth Harry and his temper self-destructed again.

I went to the Palomar, but Phil Harris wasn't there. So I went to a couple of movies in Hollywood instead.

Now I was out of a job and would soon be out of money. The next day, I met a young fellow from Texas who seemed like a nice enough guy. He said he didn't have a place to stay, and he'd give me a couple of bucks if I'd let him stay at my place. That was okay with me.

The next morning, he told me he was going down to the shoeshine stand, shoot craps, then take off. "Would you like to come along and watch?"

I said, "Sure."

The game was in high gear when we arrived. The police followed us through the front door and raided the joint. They rounded everybody up, including my new-found friend. "Hey," I said. "That's my friend. I have to stay with him."

One of the cops looked at me and offered me some great advice. "Kid, get your ass out of here. They're going to jail."

That scared the hell out of me, and I took off like a frightened jack rabbit. I later discovered that "my friend" had stolen my senior sweater. What a jerk I was! Now I was down to my pants with the patches, my shoes, and overalls.

* * *

I was walking down Melrose a couple of blocks to a hot dog stand when a young guy who parked cars next door to the stand said he was quitting his job and did I need one. It only paid nine dollars per six-day week, 7:00 A.M. to 7:00 P.M., but beggars can't be choosers. I was on my knees financially, so I took it. I later found out there wasn't even time off for lunch. Another hard lesson learned.

My mom saw me one Saturday, and after work, we went to Sears and Roebuck. They measured me for a nice suit, then checked my credit, and decided that I couldn't possibly make the payments on a sixteen-dollar suit. What a bummer.

I was good at parking cars and taking care of them, but never received any tips. Fred MacMurray used to park there. I'd brush off his car and keep it in a special place, but no tips! I called him on it a couple of years later when I starred in *Callaway Went Thataway* with him. Fred was tight in certain ways and a real softy in others.

During the Christmas holidays, my old pal, Robert Stone, arrived in Los Angeles and asked me to join him at the Pasadena Auditorium and dance. The next day, we'd park cars at his uncle's place for the Rose Bowl and make five dollars each.

It was bitterly cold that year, and all I owned were an old sweater and my patched pants. Bob lent me his cousin's camelhair overcoat. I tried it on, and it fit rather well. Away we went to the dance.

I actually walked up to a girl and asked her if she'd like to dance, and amazingly enough, she said yes. We danced the night away to the Alvino Ray Orchestra and the King Sisters, who were great. I sweated a blue streak, but I kept dancing. I told the girls I danced all the time wearing a coat. I even had a bet that I could dance until midnight without taking it off. It was New Year's Eve, and after they played "Auld Lang Syne," Bob and I walked to his uncle's home. I caught a hell of a cold, but I parked cars, picked up my five dollars, thanked Bob and his uncle, and caught a bus home.

Right after New Year's, I had a chance to go to see my mother at UCLA where she worked as a cook at Hilgard Hall. She introduced me to a young man named Tommy Thompson, who was working his way through school in the personnel department at Douglas Aircraft. He and mother were great friends. Because he knew I wasn't making much money, he took me to Douglas. I lied about my age because I was only seventeen. They hired me at fourteen dollars a week for the night shift working 4:30 P.M. to 12:30 A.M. in the fuselage department.

I found a new place to live in Ocean Park, a couple of blocks from the beach, for two dollars a week. It had a wash basin in the closet and a john down the hall. This was January, and it was too cold to swim. During the day, I'd stroll along the beach, and once in a while, it was warm enough to swim and lay on the beach near Lick Pier. Life was good.

My first job at Douglas was as a helper to a skin fitter in the fuselage department. The young man I worked with was quite a character, but he was a good teacher and quickly taught me the skill of skin fitting. We finished the last of the DC-2s, and then started on the DC-3s. By the end of two months, I was a very good skin fitter and worked by myself. The work was interesting, and I enjoyed it.

On weekends, I'd spend a lot of time at the Casino Gardens watching the dancers and listening to the bands. On one side, they had a beautiful restaurant where patrons could dine. On the other side, I would pay ten cents a dance.

The bands were excellent: Tommy Tucker, Spud Murphy, and Stan Kenton. Once in a while, they would radio broadcast coast to coast, and the announcer would say, "Dance and romance at the beautiful Casino Gardens in Ocean Park, California."

For a young punk like me, it was a very exciting time.

I had worked at Douglas for seven months when one night I pulled a real "butch," as we called them when we screwed up. I drilled a whole group of holes in the wrong place. If it was a serious mistake, engineers would come to the shop and repair it. Mine was that serious. It made me so angry with myself that I quit. Embarrassment and temper again! I had no patience and no tolerance for mistakes, especially my own.

For the next several weeks, I stretched out on the beach, body-surfed once in a while, and worked on developing a tan. I even put on about fifteen pounds. One day, I was on the beach near Lick Pier when a very attractive woman approached and asked me if I could teach her to body-surf.

I, of course, said, "Sure! Let's go."

We surfed for a while, and she kept clinging to me in the water. Without warning, she planted a kiss on me that was a humdinger. She was the kind of woman that I had never experienced before, and Ole Omar the Tentmaker was getting pleasantly excited. She suggested going to her room and having some fun.

Well! I stayed the entire night, and she taught me a lot of things that I'd never known before. She had a great body and drove me crazy exploring it. I had never before had that kind of fun, and I couldn't get enough of her. God, she was wild and fantastic. She kept insisting on more fun, until finally, she fell asleep.

I crawled out of her bed, dressed, and returned to my hotel. I slept all the following day. When I woke up, showered, dressed, and got a bite to eat, me and Omar went looking for her. I walked the length of the pier and along the beach in both directions, but I never saw her again.

It was like a dream every young man should have. She was my sex tutor, and I wanted more lessons. God, she was electrifying. She remains one of my favorite fantasies.

I'm a Quick Study, but Omar's a Problem

★ ★ ★ ★ ★

I met Lester Haugland, who helped me get a job on the day shift at North American Aircraft in the empennage department installing vertical and horizontal stabilizers.

Pete and Willie, who also worked for North American, and I would ride to work together. The company was located at Mines Field, which is now known as Los Angeles International Airport.

That fifteen-dollar-a-week salary enabled Willie and me to share a room in the Dome Hotel on the beach in Ocean Park, right next door to Casino Gardens. It had twin beds and a bath with a shower. Wow, coming up in the world. That cut my expenses in half.

I became such a good mechanic that they put me on the rudder assembly for the O-47A, an observation plane, then in charge of that rudder assembly. The inspectors got to the point where they would just stamp my work OK without inspecting it. Even when the army guys walked through, the company inspector would OK the assembly. I was proud of that. They even gave me a ten-cent-an-hour raise.

* * *

What's a fella to do when the area around Omar starts itching really badly? I had been scratching my genital area for a few days when I asked one of my pals if they knew what it was.

He said, "You probably have a dose of the crabs."

I didn't have a clue what he was talking about. He explained the situation to me, and I asked him what I could do to get rid of them. He suggested that I soak a rag with diluent, which is a paint thinner, and that would do them in.

I went into the paint shop, next door to the assembly line, and soaked a rag with paint thinner. In the rest room, I gave my crotch a thorough going over with the rag. I pulled up my pants and returned to the jig to work on the rudder assembly.

No sooner had I put my ass on the stool than my genitals exploded and burned like fire. I took off to the rest room like a striped-ass ape, turned on the cold water, and soaked my crotch. Eventually my genitals stopped burning.

I killed the mechanized dandruff, but my whole genital area, including my scrotum, peeled. I had the cleanest balls, etc., in the whole world. They were tender for a while and not used again for some time.

When I decided the time was right, I met a very attractive young woman at the Casino Gardens, and she suggested that we share a sandwich. Over the snack, she slipped me the key to her hotel room, which was across the street and two flights up.

A man approached our table and told me to stay away from his wife. She told me he was crazy, that he wasn't her husband, and encouraged me to follow her.

I waited a few moments, then entered the hotel lobby and walked past the desk clerk, who wanted to know my business there. I knocked on her door, and she greeted me sans clothes and eager to make love. I pulled off my clothes, and we were just getting to know each other when BAM! The hotel room door flew off the hinges, and this guy said, "YOU SON OF A BITCH! You're with my WIFE."

I scrambled and rounded up my clothes when it became apparent he wanted to fight me. I grabbed my pants with one hand and with the other, hit him one time clear through the door. He landed on his butt in the hallway, dazed and mad.

By that time, I had on my underwear and shirt and was trying to pull on my pants as I ran down the two flights of stairs, four risers at a time. At the lobby, the desk clerk hollered at me, "Who's going to fix that door?"

I tore ass around the corner to the staircase behind the hotel and raced to my upstairs apartment. For the rest of the night, I shook like some dog shitting peach stones. I never saw her again.

There was a carnival saying during that time, "Hey Rube!" All the big gambling houses, amusement rides, and bars in the area were tough. They always had big guys hanging around who we called "Rube," guys who unofficially kept and protected the peace. Luckily, I never had to call on anyone to defend me. I never saw the woman's husband again, either.

I can dance. Can I sing?

★ ★ ★ ★ ★

One evening at the Casino Gardens, I saw a pretty girl standing with someone who looked like her mother. I asked if she'd like to dance. She looked at her mother, who gave her approval. The girl's name was Sadie McCullough. She was a lovely girl and a great dancer. I spent the balance of the evening with both of them, and we agreed to meet again the following Friday.

All that week, I thought only of Sadie. When Friday arrived, Sadie walked into the ballroom, and I was in heaven.

On certain Friday nights, they held amateur singing contests. We danced while Tommy Tucker's band played one of my favorite songs, "That Old Feeling," and I quietly sang it to her.

She said, "Hey, you sing very well. You should enter the singing contest tonight."

I told her I couldn't do that, but she insisted. "You can. Do it for me."

I thought for a moment. "Okay, just for you."

When they announced that the singing contest was coming up next, I walked to the bandstand and told them, "I'd like to enter the contest and sing 'That Old Feeling.'"

"What key?"

I told them I didn't know about keys, but I sang it to my girlfriend when the band was playing. They said, "Okay, that's it."

My turn came quickly enough, and surprisingly, I wasn't nervous. I sang very well and won the contest. I was eighteen years old.

As I walked toward Sadie, Miss Arnell, Tommy Tucker's band singer, told me, "Young man, you have a really fine voice. You should study."

I couldn't believe my ears. I thanked her and told Sadie what she had said. We blessed that moment with a stolen kiss behind the Casino Gardens. I really loved her and thought she cared for me. We agreed we'd meet again the following Friday.

It rained steadily for the next week including Friday. I waited and waited for Sadie, but she and her mother never showed. I was so depressed, I bought a half-pint of bourbon, went upstairs to the men's room, and killed the whole thing—straight down. I gagged like hell, and it's a wonder I survived that night.

I left the casino and staggered up the stairs to my room where I reached in my pocket for the key and fell flat on my face. When Willie came home, he dragged me into the room and threw me on the bed. Boy, did I have a hangover the next day.

I thought with all the rain, there was probably a lot

of flooding, and Sadie couldn't make it. For some stupid reason, I never wrote down her phone number. I waited again the following Friday, but still no Sadie. I saw her again a couple of months later on a Sunday afternoon at the Casino Gardens with a big, good-looking guy about twenty-four or twenty-five years old.

Sadie approached me, and I asked her who the guy was.

She said, "I just go out with him once in a while."

He had a car, and I never saw her again. It really hurt me because I had quite a case on Sadie.

* * *

Sometimes I'd grab a sandwich at a drugstore across the street from the Dome Hotel. A couple of fun guys, Arthur Shields and Walter Waffle, worked behind the counter, and we had a good time bantering back and forth. They said, "Why don't you come over on weekends at night and help us out?"

I said, "Great."

The following weekend when I showed up, they put me right to work. Things were going fine at my end of the counter when a nice little old Jewish lady sat down and ordered a sandwich. The guys told me she was very sweet, but warned me not to give her a glass of water. That seemed strange, but I didn't question it.

She finished her sandwich and said, "Could I have a glass of vater, please?"

I ignored her, but every time I passed her, she would ask, "Could I have a glass of vater, please?"

This continued for some time. I would glance at the guys who smiled and repeatedly shook their heads.

But I felt sorry for her and finally gave her a glass of water. She took out her teeth, both uppers and lowers, washed them in the water, put them in her mouth, paid her bill, left a tip, said, "T'ank you very much," and walked out. I looked at the guys. They shrugged with that I-told-you-so look on their faces.

I broke them up with, "Vhat else?"

The two weekends that I worked there were a laugh a minute and a wild learning experience. After work, Arthur, Walter, and I would go to the casino and shoot the breeze. Walt hated his last name and later took his mother's maiden name, "Young."

One night they said, "Why don't you come to our place where we room in L.A.? It's on Roosevelt Avenue, south of Venice Boulevard. We'll have lunch and then listen to the USC and UCLA football game."

That's where I met Mom Ryder, who served a delicious lunch. At that time, UCLA had never beaten USC, and we were all pulling for the underdog. UCLA had the ball on the one-yard line, four downs to put it across and win the game, and they couldn't deliver. USC held them to a tie. When we poured a couple of drinks to build up our spirits, Mom Ryder sat down at the piano.

Walt said, "Come on, Harry, and sing a song."

Mom Ryder asked me if I sang.

Being a little high, I said confidently, "Yeah, I can sing."

She asked me what songs I knew, and I answered, "In the Still of the Night." She fumbled around, we found a key, and I sang.

"You have a fine voice. You should study," she told me.

And I said, "Where do I go?"

She arranged for me to go to a musical conservatory in Boyle Heights in East Los Angeles. I took my first lesson for twenty-five cents. Twelve other singers of all voice ranges joined me. They would go up and down the scale in all sorts of keys while I shouted away. I could hardly talk when the class was finished, let alone sing.

After I learned a couple of other songs, Mom Ryder arranged for me to sing at Bert Rovere's Paris Inn Cafe in downtown L.A. I sang well, and he said he'd hire me as a singing busboy while I took singing lessons from a famous teacher named Tamarcio.

I immediately quit my job at North American and went to work at Bert Rovere's. I bused tables from 11:00 A.M. to 3:00 P.M., returned at 5:00 P.M. and worked until closing, which could be around 2:00 A.M. What a job.

Right off the bat, the waiters found out that I had quit a good-paying job at North American and told me that I was out of my mind. But I was determined to learn to sing. For three nights, I sang "Without a Song," "Chloe," "In the Still of the Night," and "Night and Day." But I still hadn't met with this Tamarcio guy, and I was getting a little ticked off.

It was about 1:00 A.M., and I picked up two pitchers of water, one in each hand, when the head busboy told me to get the lead out. I threw the pitchers against the wall and said, "You can take the pitchers and this job and you know where you can put them!" I left and never went back for my paycheck.

I called my friend, Walt Young, and hired on at Douglas Santa Monica. I worked there a few days, putting flotation lines in the last few TBDs, Torpedo

Bomber Douglas. These planes were way too slow and later became shooting ducks for the Japanese in the Battle of Midway.

When I finished the ill-fated TBDs, I transferred to Douglas El Segundo and put brackets in the fuselage of the DB-7 bombers. I was a very good mechanic by this time and over a period of two years, had assembled a high-quality tool kit that I was very proud of.

I gave up all thoughts of serious singing and decided it was time to get serious about my aircraft work. I told my lead man, Bill Hitt, when I completed one assembly that I wanted something else to do. Inside of two months, he taught me how to install every bracket in the fuselage. The department supervisor moved Bill up to assistant supervisor, and they gave me Bill's job.

At the age of twenty, I was a lead man supervising twenty men and so proud of myself I could bust. I saw to it that no man laid down on the job. The DB-7 contract ran out in about a year, and I was made an assistant supervisor on the graveyard shift on the fuselage of the SBD, the dive bomber that was so successful in the Battle of Midway.

Does life get any better than this?

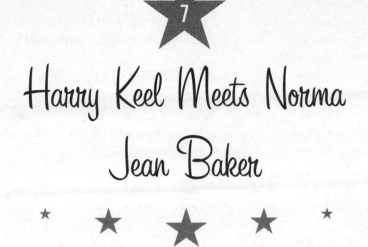

Harry Keel Meets Norma Jean Baker

By this time, I had a new Chevrolet coupe and a pleasant room in Westwood Village near my mother. She was the housekeeper for wonderful people named Howells, and I would pop in on her several times a week. One day, I walked in the back door of the house, and there stood a beautiful girl about thirteen years old. My mother introduced me to her. Her name was Norma Jean Baker. She was a very sweet and inquisitive, sensual young woman, standing about 5 feet 5 inches tall.

Naturally, I returned the following Sunday, and this innocent-looking creature was still there. I didn't know at the time that she was being shifted from one foster home to another.

Mother told her I had a good job at Douglas Aircraft, and she started asking me about my work. I told her what I did and what airplanes I had worked on. I told her I danced at the Palladium in Hollywood and Casino Gardens, and she asked me to take her dancing. Well, she was thirteen, and I was twenty-one. I could just hear the guys down at the casino if they saw me with this beautiful young girl. I was known by this time as a kind of ladies' man, and I felt like an old roué.

But I thought, what the hell? It would please her.

Away we went. Luckily, none of my old bunch was around that Sunday afternoon. We danced without interruption. I taught her all the simple steps, and in no time, she was doing quite well. We had a great afternoon. It wasn't easy to control myself because she had a full-blown body for a thirteen year old woman/child.

She was real San Quentin jailbait. Wow! I took her home, she thanked me, and I took off. God, she was beautiful!

I was dating a lovely girl named Jean Reid, and I told her all about my "date" with thirteen year old Norma Jean. She got a kick out of it. I added, "For God's sakes, don't tell the guys about it," and she didn't. Jeanie was an amazing girl and a marvelous dancer.

We dated for about a year or so, and I still talk to her once in a while. She was a cousin of Deanna Durbin and mentioned Deanna's elbow had been broken and was crooked like mine and how she handled it on the screen. We went to see her films, and you couldn't tell that her arm was crooked. She was a lovely singer and actress.

Thank you, Deanna, if you ever read this. I learned a lot from you and always enjoyed your performances. You were special in your films, and I hope your life is still full and happy.

★ ★ ★

For three months, I studied music with George Walker. He had an incredible pianist who tried teaching me music. They never charged me anything, but it was way over my head, and I didn't respond. I learned a lot, but Mr. Walker was very austere. He'd been a great bass, was very proud of his work, and couldn't understand a young man who didn't have any professional goals.

One day, he told me I wasn't serious enough to be a singer and that he was wasting his time with me. I agreed with him and apologized.

He said, "You have a fine voice, and one day, you will be called upon to do something. It will test your courage. When it does, go to a quiet corner and talk to yourself. Just repeat to yourself you are a fine singer and you can do it. Think positive."

I thanked him for all his help and left. I wasn't very proud of myself for walking out.

A month or so later, I found out that a man named Ralph Blohm held singing classes on Wednesday and Friday nights at Los Angeles High School. I found more than fifteen singers there, each taking their turn singing. He had a pianist who could play anything. Blohm, a very understanding and talented man, loved working with young singers. Even if they didn't sing very well, he always offered positive criticism—never smug and above it all.

The first time I stood to sing in front of all these youngsters, my heart pounded so hard that you could hear it in my voice. Soon the good singers helped me and taught me a lot.

One night after the first few weeks, Mr. Blohm said, "I want to talk to you after class."

I waited for him, and he told me about a group called the American Music Theater. They worked in an auditorium doing the opera, *Mignon*, in English. "I talked to them about you, and they would like to hear you tonight."

I said, "Now?"

He said, "Yes."

That night, Mr. Blohm introduced me to George Houston and Dr. Hans Lert. I sang my favorite art song, "Myself When Young" by Tolstoy. They were very complimentary, although they had nothing for me at that time. I was asked if I'd like to come in and watch them rehearse. They rehearsed from 10:00 A.M. to 5:00 P.M. and then seven to ten every evening until performance day. Since I worked midnight to seven-thirty in the morning, I could watch as much as I wanted. From then on, I didn't miss a rehearsal.

In addition to the brilliant George Houston being a fine singer, actor, and director, he spoke five or six languages and translated all the operas into English.

In World War I, long before the Americans entered the war, he'd been a male nurse overseas. He was captured by the enemy, lined up against a wall, and almost shot as a spy. Afterward, he was awarded the Croix de Guerre for bravery.

Dr. Hans Lert, conductor of the Pasadena Symphony, had a great sense of humor and handled the singers with warmth and understanding.

One day, I was invited to Dr. Lert's home in the Riviera section of West Los Angeles. I found his beautiful home, rang the doorbell, and was invited into a huge living room with a full Steinway piano. Mr. Houston and Dr. Lert got right to the purpose of my visit. It seemed a young bass, who had been scheduled to sing an aria in the third act of the *Aritorio*, "Saul and David," skipped out on them with the performance two days away. They would have eliminated the aria, but it was too important to the story.

They played the aria for me. It was so beautiful, I was stunned at the thought of singing it. They played it for me again, then asked me to sing it. I did, and with my quick ear, after a couple of times, I seemed to get through it fairly well. I tried it a second time through, and the words flowed more easily.

They conferred for a second, then Dr. Lert said, "We think you can do it. Would you like to?"

I thought here were two great artists asking me, a complete amateur, if I would do it. I must have been out of my mind, but I figured I could and said yes!

This was Friday, and the *Aritorio* was to be performed Sunday evening. I worked with a talented female pianist, Shibley Boyce, on Saturday and rehearsed Sunday after-noon with a 110-piece symphony orchestra. Dr. Lert told the musicians that this was my indoctrination to serious music and to give me their complete attention. They took me through it twice. What a thrilling experi-ence to stand in front of a great orchestra and sing.

Shibley told me where to rent my white tails. Come Sunday night, my mother, Art Shields, Walt Young, and a lot of my friends were there. The symphony auditori-um was packed with three thousand patrons and a cho-rus of one hundred singers and soloists like Harold Peterson, Nan Merriman, Joe Sullivan, and George London. Backstage I waited through the first two acts. After each one, Harold Peterson, one of the soloists, would check on me and offer encouragement.

The whole thing was going well, but I was getting worked up. I'd never worn tails before, and the collar seemed to be getting tighter and tighter. The second act ended, and I had about five minutes to get myself ready to go.

For some reason, I remembered what George Walker told me. I found a quiet corner and talked to myself. Hell, I'm the best bass in the world. I know this little aria, and I can sing it better than any bass in the world. Chaliapin, Plancon, even Pinza. I'll show them how to sing this aria. I kept talking to myself, telling myself how great I was. When it came time to go onstage, I walked out, sat down, mentally peed all over the front row and thought, "Are you ready audience? Well I am!"

I stood tall and sang that little aria to a fair-thee-well. The song poured out of me like rich red wine. I received a great hand from the audience and a big wink from Dr. Lert. It was one of the greatest thrills of my life.

Afterward, George Houston approached me and said, "I can't talk to you now. I'm too worked up, but I want to see you tomorrow morning at my place, twelve noon."

I said, "Yes, sir!"

I think I earned $100 for the evening.

Boy, what a night. My mother came backstage and gave me a big hug. She showed me the program where they had mistakenly printed my name as Harold not Harry.

"Well," I said. "Harold sounds a little more dignified than Harry. I guess I'll have to use Harold as my professional name from now on."

Maybe they thought Harry was a nickname for Harold. Who knows? But for years, until a famous Hollywood gossip columnist entered my life, I would be known professionally as Harold Keel.

8

War and Marriage. Will They Last?

★ ★ ★ ★ ★

The next day, I was at George Houston's door at twelve sharp.

He greeted me with, "You were wonderful last night. You did us proud, lad. Now I want you to understand something. I want you to work with me. I never want anything from you monetarily or physically. I just want the pleasure of trying to help you. You have a great voice and natural talent. You can do wonderful things, and I want to help you and guide you."

What a privilege for a young man of twenty-two to become George Houston's protégé. Singing lessons included working with Shibley on French, German, and Italian repertoire.

One day, I sang a beautiful French song and put my soul into a lovely phrase. She stopped playing, a cigarette dangling from her blood-red lips. She said, "What the fuck are you doing?"

I said, "Singing this beautiful phrase."

She replied, "Look, the phrase IS beautiful. Don't try to make it MORE beautiful."

I never forgot that advice. In a very short time, this great teacher and brilliant accompanist taught me so much.

★ ★ ★

That was early in the fall of 1941, and I worked and learned my music under George's tutelage. Then wham! December 7, the Japanese attacked Pearl Harbor, and we were at war. In one instant, the whole country was in an uproar. The hatred for the Japanese was intense and unanimous. All the aircraft factories were camouflaged for safety, and Douglas went on a seven-day week, twenty-four-hours-a-day schedule building airplanes.

I wanted to fly in the worst way as did Clay Millar, a friend of mine. We went to the recruitment office together. They took one look at our qualifications and said, "Get out. You are too valuable doing what you're doing."

I returned to Douglas and finished the SBD dive bomber. They transferred me into production control to break down a new dive bomber, the SB2D.

I continued working with George Houston as much as I could, but he was doing a series called *The Red Rider*. Once in a while, I'd join him at Griffith Park and ride horses with him. He was an excellent horseman. I had no way of knowing how much that would help me later in my motion picture career.

When I wasn't working with George, I played badminton with Clay Millar and Jack Elson. One day Jack said, "I want you to meet my girlfriend, Andree's sister."

I said, "Who's she?"

Jack said, "She's in *Ken Murray's Blackouts of 1942*."

"A show girl? No way!" I said.

"You're crazy, man. She's beautiful, and she's nice."

"You sure?" I asked.

"Hey, I'm your buddy, man."

Reluctantly I agreed, after all I had a brand new 1941 Oldsmobile convertible to show off. One night Jack, Andree, and I went to the El Capitan Theater where *The Blackouts* was playing and waited. Andree went backstage and returned with the most beautiful auburn-haired girl I'd ever seen.

Now Ole Hairbreadth Harry knew all about show girls and what gold diggers they were. Andree introduced me to Rosemary Cooper (her stage name was Rosemary Randall), and I said, "I only have a couple of bucks. You want to go somewhere and have a drink?"

"Sure," Rosemary said.

We drove to a nightclub on Beverly and Fairfax, then Jack and Andree split, leaving us alone. At first, I thought I was in over my head with Rosemary, but she was nice and seemed down to earth. I slowly left my suspicious shell, and we talked for the longest time.

She invited me to see the show and arranged a seat for me the next night. Warmth and humor exuded from Ken Murray, and the riotous Marie Wilson added glamour. Rosemary's stunning long hair and show girl body had me panting. Whew!

After the show, she recommended a place on Sunset near Highland. She knew the owners. They had good food and a great pianist.

After we got there, for some reason, I opened my big mouth and blurted out, "I can sing, you know."

"You can?"

And I, of course, said, "Sure. I'm not a pop singer. I

have an operatic voice. I'm a bass, and I'm studying opera."

"Well, sing something for us, please."

The pianist and I worked out a key, and I sang "Without a Song." What a square, I thought. But they applauded and made me sing again. This time I sang "Old Man River." I surprised the hell out of Rosemary. Her friends paid for the drinks, and we had a grand time. I appreciated her sense of humor.

Her father, Andrew, joined us on our next date. He and I hit it off immediately. He was a sensitive man, and when I sang, I scored a lot of points with him. I needed a father figure, and he fit the bill. We had terrific times together.

★ ★ ★

In early 1943, about the time I finished breaking down the new SB2D, Douglas was slow getting production started. I got bored doing nothing. I decided to look outside manufacturing and found they needed a man with experience at Murray Body Works in Detroit, as a representative for Douglas. This included a substantial raise in pay, and I agreed to take it. They wanted me in Detroit in a few days. I called Rosemary. "I've got to talk to you."

After I picked her up, we drove around a while, then parked. I told her about the job and that I had to leave right away. She started to cry. I'd never seen her cry before, and I asked her what she was crying about.

She said, "I just found you, and now you're leaving me."

Ole Hairbreadth Harry immediately popped up with "Do you want to get married?"

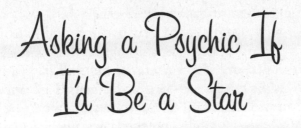

Asking a Psychic If I'd Be a Star

★ ★ ★ ★ ★

"Yes!" she said. I couldn't believe it. In an instant, our lives had changed.

Mother and I shared an apartment near Melrose and Vine. First, I had to break the news to her. My mother liked Rosemary very much and was happy about the whole thing, but I felt obligated to help her find another place to live. I sold my Olds and gave most of the money to mother.

Rosemary and I were married on St. Patrick's Day, March 17, 1943, and the next day we left by train for Detroit. We stayed through the summer, then Douglas transferred me to San Francisco to take charge of things at Hammond Aircraft. I didn't sing much in Detroit and even less in San Francisco.

We lived in San Mateo, south of San Francisco. One night, we saw a sign in the foyer of a theater that read, "Write a question, put it in the bowl, and get your answer from the mind reader during intermission."

I wrote, "Will I have a future as a singer and when will it start?" I signed it H.K.

During the intermission, the psychic answered a few questions, then he called out "H.K."

We were sitting in the first balcony, and I answered, "Yes."

He called out, "You asked if you will have a future career as a singer and when will it start? The answer is yes. You will meet with some success in late 1944. Then it will slow for a while and then pick up again in 1945, and you'll go right to the top."

What a crock, I thought. Rosemary and I had a great laugh over that.

★ ★ ★

In the spring of 1944, we were transferred to East Moline, Illinois. My boss, Curt Walker, put me in charge of the empennage department at the John Deere Works near Rock Island. During the fall, I read in the papers that Ezio Pinza, the great bass at the Metropolitan Opera House in New York, would be appearing in a concert in Davenport, Iowa, just across the Mississippi River. I called the concert agency and was told that the tickets were all sold out.

I begged the ticket lady, "I'm a young bass, and I'd love to see him in concert. Do you have standing room? My wife and I are even willing to stand just to see him."

She said, "Look, you two come over, and we'll work something out."

Mrs. Otillie Isles, a lovely lady, had selected two seats for us in the sixth row. We thanked her profusely.

While Pinza's voice was beautiful, I found him cold as a performer. Rosemary thought he was kind of grumpy.

Afterward, we spoke with Mrs. Isles and thanked her again. She said she and a Mrs. Waterman, a singing teacher, would like to hear me sing. We set up a date, and I worked with a young girl pianist, Doris Gray, who was bright as hell and a fine accompanist. We worked well together, and Mrs. Isles and Mrs. Waterman were very impressed.

Mrs. Isles said she would sponsor me if I worked up a concert.

I worked with Mrs. Waterman, an understanding teacher and a lovely lady who didn't suggest any drastic changes. She listened to me and said, "Just continue with your thoughts and sing."

I loved girls and later transferred my love to women. It'd be natural that my very first concert would be in a girl school's auditorium. My performance went very well, and the audience was very appreciative, particularly Mr. and Mrs. Curt Walker, my boss and his wife. Mrs. Isles and Mrs. Waterman were thrilled with their new discovery and organized two additional concerts for me: one in Muscatine, Iowa, and one in Rockford, Illinois.

I entered the East Moline Valley summer festival. Accompanied by the local symphony, I sang *"O Isis unt Osiris"* and *"The Song of the Flea"* and won the contest.

The guest artist that night was Lawrence Tibbett, one of my favorite singers. He was not only a great opera singer, but a prominent concert singer. In 1939, I had heard him at the Hollywood Bowl. He was magnificent standing on that stage with only an accompanist and no microphone. Those are magical nights you don't quickly forget.

Tibbett walked onstage, but he seemed a bit off-center, not at all the same singer I'd heard at the Bowl in 1939. But when he sang "Who Is Sylvia?" and "The Glory Road," it was the old Tibbett. He reentered to sing an encore, and he said, "Ladies and gentlemen, I was going to sing 'The Song of the Flea' as an encore, but the young man before me sang it so well, I don't think we need hear it again tonight. I'll do the aria from *Pagliacci*."

I couldn't believe my ears. To have such a compliment from Tibbett was like a marvelous dream. I met him at the party after the show and told him that I was a protégé of George Houston. He said that he and George were great friends and that George had been with him the night of his greatest success at the Met. Tibbett gave me great professional encouragement.

The East Moline Festival was a subsidiary of the Chicago Land Music Festival, and I won that, too. That night we sang at Soldiers Field with a crowd of 100,000 with a national radio hookup. The cast of *Oklahoma* starring John Raitt, who was playing Curly, appeared and sang, too.

I first met John when George Houston lived on Franklin Avenue near Sunset in Hollywood. George said, "I want you to meet someone. John, stick your head out here."

And John said, "How are you?" There was John Raitt polishing George's shoe for him.

The first time I heard John sing, he blew me away. I had parked my car on Sunset Boulevard when I heard this voice a short distance away. I walked about a block and a half until I found him.

★ ★ ★

I returned to Moline and prepared a concert for another girl school's auditorium in Rockford. At each event, my voice became richer and stronger. I wore white tie and tails. As I exited the stage after the last song, I felt something under my feet. I stood proud during my first encore, walked offstage, and still felt something under my feet. But I was so enamored with my reception, I ignored it. I walked out, and again I felt it, but I bowed and bowed, then walked off with that feeling of greatness and invincibility.

I brought out my lovely young accompanist for a bow. She said out of the corner of her mouth, "Your sock's garter strap has fallen down."

I bowed again, and my triumphant smile turned into an embarrassed half-smile as I walked off with as much aplomb as I could muster. Only a flapping garter strap can bring you down like that … but I sang well … You… Little Ego Benders.

I sent my reviews to George, and he wrote back saying he was ecstatic and couldn't wait for Rosemary and me to get home. The following day, I received a call from my mother telling me that George had died. I was devastated. He'd been working on the series *The Red Rider* during the days and at night at the American Music Theater. He'd gone home after a full day on the series, tossed back a couple of Scotches, took a stroll by himself, and suffered a serious heart attack.

The police who found him thought he was drunk and threw him in the tank where he died. I cried for two days. Rosemary tried to console me, but I had lost a man who was like a father to me. I was a walking zombie.

A short while later, when I received a notice to

61

appear for a physical for the draft, I was ready. I took a train to Chicago. They took one look at my left arm and put me in 2b again. That left arm probably saved my life.

I received a call about performing Handel's "The Messiah" at Christmas. I met with a professor of music at Rock Island College, worked with him about a month, and learned the bass role, which is a mouthful. He paid me $150 for the performance and charged $150 to teach me the piece, but it was worth it.

★ ★ ★

In 1945, I transferred to Los Angeles and worked for outside manufacturers, chasing around Southern California, pushing subcontractors.

About the first of May, I sang for N.C.A.C. (National Concerts and Artists Corporation), a large opera concert management group. A famous Austrian soprano, Lotte Lehman, approached me after I completed my song. She said, "He's a young Pinza."

The first thing they asked me to do was to go to 20th Century Fox and sing for Oscar Hammerstein. He and Richard Rodgers were writing *State Fair*. I was taken to where Mr. Hammerstein was on the lot and ushered in to meet this tall man. He put me completely at ease as I sang an aria from "Simon Boccanegra" for him.

Mr. Hammerstein asked me, "Do you know 'Beautiful Morning' from *Oklahoma*?"

Yes, Mr. Hammerstein, I Know the Words to Oklahoma

★ ★ ★ ★ ★

After I sang it, Mr. Hammerstein asked if I could come to the Beverly Hills Hotel Sunday and read for him.

I didn't have a car, so I hitched a ride to Sunset and walked the rest of the way. I read a few scenes with him, and he said, "I want you to sing and read for the Theater Guild in a couple of weeks."

I sang and read, as did Kathryn Grayson's brother, Michael. The guild offered us work in New York. I was asked if I wanted to fly or go by train. I thought flying must be awfully expensive, so I selected the train. And for the four-day trip, I sweated it out thinking it was a hell of a chance I was taking, but I had to risk it.

Douglas had offered me a general supervisor's job in Oklahoma, but I turned it down for a chance to sing the Broadway musical *Oklahoma*. What a coincidence!

★ ★ ★

They put me up at the Algonquin Hotel in New York and gave me third-row center seats to see *Carousel*. I thought I would see *Oklahoma*.

John Raitt, as Billy Bigelow, sang like a god, and Jan Clayton was incredible as Carrie. After the show, I went backstage to see John and met Andy Anderson, the stage manager.

Andy said, "You want the sides for *Carousel*?"

I said, "The what?"

He repeated, "The sides, the sides."

And, having no idea what "sides" were, I said, "Just give me everything. I'll need it!"

After a discussion regarding the rehearsal time, we agreed on 9:30 A.M. The next morning, I joined the director, John Fernley, and Iva Withers, an understudy. We started on the bench scene. After fifteen minutes of working on it, I had a funny feeling. It was like someone touched me on the shoulder and said, "Howard, you can do it. This is what you want to do in life. You've got it!"

I wondered what the hell is IT? I must have found IT because I learned the part in just three days. They lowered the score for me, and I auditioned for the Theater Guild and Rodgers and Hammerstein. They signed me to a three-year contract.

I called Rosemary, and she watched my first performance, a matinee. Just before they called, "Places everyone," John Raitt said, "Do this one for George."

"Will do. Thanks, John."

★ ★ ★

I really killed them. It was one of the finest moments in my whole career. I walked onto the stage that night with great confidence because I'd done three concerts and the "Messiah," and that's a tough sing. Even though I'd never done a stage performance, when I walked on that stage, everybody was on my side. They said I was a genius at learning the role so fast.

The producers always measured the night's success by how long the audience stood and applauded. The response was tremendous, especially after the "Soliloquy," which is one of the great songs of all time.

And I not only sang beautifully, I gave much more of an acting performance than John Raitt did. Actually, I never thought about the acting part of the role. I just became Billy Bigelow. I played it the way I thought Billy would have lived it. I discovered that I'm an interpretative actor/singer.

I found IT in that role. The cast was flawless, and that enriched my presentation. It was my finest performance ever. You just know it. And the next time you do it, you never quite make it. But I never gave up and always tried to reach that pinnacle every time I was onstage.

After the performance, they asked me if I'd like to stay in for the rest of the week. John Raitt had another half-week added onto his vacation. What a great time. What a thrill, for a coal miner's son from Gillespie, Illinois, to play Billy Bigelow in a great show on Broadway with the original cast. I walked on air for three of the most exciting weeks of my life.

Reggie Hammerstein, Oscar's brother, cast me in the part of Curly, and I learned *Oklahoma* in a week, then played Curly with another terrific cast. After playing a part like Billy Bigelow, playing Curly, was kind of a comedown.

Reggie was a nice guy, but he simply told me where

to stand and when to say my lines. I received no direction beyond that. After a couple months, I was a little bored.

One afternoon, we had kind of a quiet audience, and I decided to just walk through the role. The minute I started, I felt so lousy for what I was doing, I said to myself, I'll never do this again to an audience, and I never have.

I kept wondering with all the great talent in New York, why they picked me. I decided to listen in on the Thursday morning auditions. I went every Thursday for about three months. In all that time, I only saw a couple of people that I thought had any talent, and I began to realize that I did have IT.

One night, not long after that, the Theater Guild people and Rouben Mamoulian were in the audience. Mamoulian called for a rehearsal, and the following day, we started at the top and ran through the entire show. He gave me a couple of pointers here and there, and I took off like a shot. Boy, what a difference when a professional teaches you direction, emoting, and staging. What a complete revelation even humor is, especially in the Smoke House scene.

Over the following three years, although I was tired sometimes, I never got bored doing *Oklahoma* again.

About three months into the role, I sat in my dressing room getting ready for a performance. Dick Rober, who shared the dressing room with me, was reading his newspaper.

I started to comb my hair and stopped dead in my tracks. "Holy God! The guy was right!"

Dick Rober said, "What are you mumbling about now?"

I told him the prediction the psychic made about my career at the movie house in San Mateo, California. "He said my career would start in 1944, with some success, then dwindle out. But in 1945, it would start up again, and I would go right to the top. Here I am on Broadway in the fall of 1945, playing *Oklahoma*. Holy shit, wait till I tell Rosemary!!! Wow!"

★ ★ ★

When called upon, I still covered John Raitt in *Carousel*. *Oklahoma* played in the St. James Theater; *Carousel* played in the Majestic. They were directly across the street from each other.

I remember one night I stood in the wings in cowboy costume and makeup ready to go on in *Oklahoma* when they rushed in and said I had to go on for John. Flooding prevented him from getting into New York for his performance. I ran, changed into my costume for *Carousel*, and went on. The *Carousel* scene went fine, and I made my entrance into the bench scene. My first line of dialogue was "Shut up. What's going on, spitting and sputtering like three lumps of corn popping on a shovel?"

Jan Clayton, Jean Darling, and the carnival lady began to giggle and could barely get out their dialogue.

After the scene was over and we were offstage, I asked Jan Clayton, "What's going on?"

Jan replied, "Your Okie accent was sticking out, and it broke us up."

During the year, Raitt contracted hepatitis, and I went on for him an additional six weeks. The doctor didn't want him to do his matinees the first week he returned to work. I did Billy Bigelow in the matinee of *Carousel* and then played Curly in the evening performance of *Oklahoma*, a carney during the day and a cowboy at night.

In the two years I played on Broadway, Rosemary and I moved eight times. The war had ended, but we still couldn't find a decent place to live. We found a dumpy one-room and kitchenette in the Beaux Arts building on the East Side. Rosemary was a terrific cook and a great seamstress, too.

Early in 1947, the Theater Guild asked if I'd like to go to England. I was the last one they asked because Jerry White, who was going to direct the show in England, and I had a big argument about Mamoulian's great direction.

I told them I'd go, but wanted a raise. I was making $300 a week and asked for $500.

When White exploded and called me a few choice names. I proclaimed, "That's it."

I'd seen a few Curlys by this time and thought I was the best one. They paid me. Rosemary and I decided I'd go first because they wouldn't pay for her passage. She returned to the West Coast, and I went to England.

There was one thing I felt I had to do, and that was to get a permanent so I would have curly hair.

It always embarrassed me to say the line, "Curly headed, ain't I?" Then I'd take my hat off and didn't have one curl. They snuck me into a hair salon. In those days, no man would have a permanent, much less enter a woman's salon. They hung shields around me, so no one could see me. Christ, it was embarrassing. The perm took about three hours.

I headed to the St. James Theater to see the cast

and say goodbye, wearing my hat to cover up the new hairdo. Frankly, I didn't like the look, but I was stuck with it. Dick Rober, our New York "Jud," said, "Let's see the new hairdo." He grabbed my hat and took it off, then fell apart laughing. He thought I looked darling. The bastard! I said my goodbyes and left.

I departed for London the following morning, and even though I would brush it to keep it clean, I didn't wash my hair for about four weeks.

Will British Audiences Like Me?

★ ★ ★ ★ ★

They had cast the show in New York. Some of us flew to England, and the rest would arrive by boat. A few worked well with each other. Others didn't. That would prove both troublesome and exciting. The entire chorus, including singers and dancers, was very good, but most of them weren't seasoned performers. With directors Gemze de Lappe and Erik Kristen at the helm, they quickly blended into one excellent company.

We were scheduled to open in Manchester, England, at the Opera House and play for two weeks, then move to London's Royal Drury Lane Theater, one of the most beautiful theaters in the world.

The cast had rehearsed in New York, and we planned to rehearse again a couple of days before opening. A few important characters were to arrive by boat. A huge storm struck the English coastline, and by the time we were due to open, the boat hadn't docked. The producers and the director were in a panic and immediately began rehearsing with understudies. We worked each day until we dropped.

They had a room for me at the Midland Hotel. One night, I returned there exhausted. I had just turned out the lights and put my head on the pillow when the phone rang. A young lady's voice said, "Mr. Keel?"

"Yes."

She said, "What time would you like to be knocked up?"

I said, "I beg your pardon?"

And she repeated it.

I said, "Well, at your convenience, I suppose!"

She giggled and explained, "What I mean is, what time would you like to be called in the morning?"

I replied sorrowfully, "Oh, I'm sleeping in, in the morning."

That was the beginning of a whole new glossary of words and sayings I was to learn whilst being in England. It was quite illuminating and great fun speaking English in England.

The next night, the producers decided they'd delay the critics' attendance for opening night. About 6:00 P.M., the "Boat People," as we called them, arrived, and we opened that night with them. Boy, the critics were peed off then.

But they watched the next night and gave us rave reviews, and that included Leonard Mosley of the *London Daily Express*, who wrote, "*Oklahoma* is a gem. It's one of those musical plays that I believe will carve a niche in the memories of all who see and hear its songs."

The audiences went wild. It was a very exciting time for the birth of a new musical.

Backstage deportment was different in England than in New York. One big distinction was "Call Boys" who would cue all the principals on their scenes and entrances. We never had anything like that in New York.

But what the hell, when in Rome. It seemed theatrical and cool. After the Smoke House scene, I would go to my dressing room, comb my hair, then saunter to stage right for my entrance at the start of the ballet. Erik Kristen danced Curly in the ballet, and Gemze de Lappe danced Laurey. I had plenty of time, and I used to watch Erik warm up. We'd chat and be early for our entrance.

At the beginning of the ballet, Laurey finishes the song "Out of My Dreams" and stands. I would take two steps on stage right and look at her, then Gemze would enter stage left and stand by Laurey. Erik entered stage right and stood beside me. Then Laurey and Curly would back off, and the ballet would begin.

One night in Manchester where we were breaking in the show, I went stage right to start the ballet, and Erik wasn't there. I thought nothing of it. I made my entrance, and Gemze made hers, but Erik didn't make his. For two years, I'd been doing this show, and I always watched the start of the ballet and then made my change for the end of the ballet.

When Erik didn't show up, I looked at Gemze and asked out of the side of my mouth, "Where's Erik?"

Gemze shook her head. Laurey and I backed off and still no Erik. I said to myself, "What the hell? I'll start it."

I dropped my gun belt and walked out. There was no describing the look on Gemze's face. We walked toward each other in character. I kissed her lightly on the lips. We did the first lift. She ran stage left, and I went down stage right to try the next step where she jumps and I catch her in my arms. The minute I reached that point to catch her, a voice said, "Get your ass offstage."

I waved good-bye and backed off. All the time this was going on, it didn't bother me a bit. But the minute I got off the stage, I shook all over. Poor Gemze was out there for thirty or forty bars of music dancing and trying to make up a ballet by herself. Erik eventually appeared, but the ballet was a little strange that evening.

We banished the "Call Boys" from the theater. They'd forgotten to alert Erik about his entrance, and he was beside himself.

★ ★ ★

By the end of our two-week stay, we were in great shape and ready to go. We traveled to London's Drury Lane and did a brush up, because the stage had quite a rake, a slant from the rear down to the footlights. This was more of a chore for the dancers in the ballet number.

I was escorted to my dressing room. I walked across a huge stage and into a room framed with floor-to-ceiling mirrors and dance bars. I passed through that room into a long narrow room with clothes hangers. My escorters opened another door into a large room with a sofa, tables, and several chairs. The last room was round and contained a fantastic dressing table and mirrors. I couldn't get over it. New York theaters had small, dumpy dressing rooms.

I didn't know what to say. Mr. Pope, the curator of Drury Lane, said, "Every great star that played Drury Lane always had this dressing room."

I was walking on hallowed ground. This would be

my very first official opening anywhere, and my courage was being seriously tested. I needed to find a nice dark corner and start Mr. Walker's exercise.

I dressed and had put on my makeup when Jerry White walked in. He gave me a big hug and said, "You're going to be great tonight. Can I do anything for you?"

I told him, "Yes. I don't want to see anybody when I walk out of this dressing room to my place for my first entrance."

He said, "You got it."

***

I'll always remember going to my place for my first entrance. I stood alone in the wings, listened to the overture, and waited for my cue. I'd been doing Curly for nearly two years, but that night was different. That was my first opening night in the Big Time, and I was ready.

On cue, I entered singing a cappella "There's a bright golden haze on the meadow. There's a bright golden haze on the meadow. The corn is as high as an elephant's eye," and I walked across the stage on that cue. At that moment, the audience began to clap wildly, something that I'd never experienced before. I held character and sang right through it.

Oh, what a hand they gave me when I finished "Beautiful Morning."

The burst of applause broke out again and again. I didn't know what to make of it. I stood there looking at Mary Marlo, who played Aunt Eller, and she winked at me. We were off and running.

The British audience's reaction to the show was incredible. When the curtain came down after the ballet ended the first act, the applause and bravos went on and on. We started the second act with the number "The Farmer and the Cowman Should Be Friends," and that stopped the show again.

Finally Aunt Eller took a gun out of a holster collected from the men and fired it. That settled the audience down long enough to get the show going again. Now it was time for the big number, "Oklahoma."

We had planned on at least one encore, but we wound up doing fourteen. After the curtain came down so many times that night, they left it up. Walter Donahue, who played Will Parker, made a wonderful speech, and the audience went crazy again.

We invited the audience to join us on the stage, and we all drank Champagne and talked for forty-five minutes. It was one incredible night in my life and in the theater. I never did less than six encores for *Oklahoma* after that.

Gemze de Lappe was my date for the night. We went by horse and carriage to John Gielgud's house where we celebrated until the wee hours. Such an unbelievable night. The audience needed us, and we needed them. This was a most unusual occurrence. Nothing like this had ever happened to anyone in that cast before, and we knew it. We were over the moon.

12

I Meet the King and Queen of England and Lt. Douglas Bader

★ ★ ★ ★ ★

Queen Mary attended a performance and loved the show. A few days later, I was to be presented to King George and the Queen Mum, along with Princesses Margaret and Elizabeth, and Elizabeth's fiancé, Philip, the duke of Edinburgh. During the interval, they told me to put my chaps back on.

I said, "Meet the king and queen in a pair of cowboy chaps, for Christ's sake?" Oh well.

After a few minutes of speaking with the king, although he stuttered quite badly, I discovered he had a wonderful, warm sense of humor. He was quite cordial and nice to me. He asked what I did to keep my voice in shape. And after about a minute or so, he put me completely at ease. I shared backstage humor with him, and his hearty laugh spoke volumes about his wholesomeness. Meeting England's royalty for the first time became a highlight in my memory book.

★ ★ ★

Some time later, I found a half-decent place for food called the Belfry. It had been an old church. Even though we were postwar, food rationing remained a problem. Sometimes the Belfry staff would sneak us a steak or fresh eggs.

On Saturday nights, I'd get bombed because I did nine shows a week. I remember sitting there alone one night having a drink when in strolls a guy who's walking kind of different, throwing his legs first one way and another across the floor toward his table. He was with a couple of guys and gals, and they were raising hell.

He recognized me as Curly in *Oklahoma* and asked me to join them. His name was Lt. Douglas Bader. We had a rocking good time that evening. He regaled us with his awesome war stories. He'd been a World War I pilot who lost both legs when his plane crashed.

He simply flew the Bulldog too low. The left wing struck the ground, the plane cartwheeled, and rolled into a ball of wreckage. His legs were crushed beyond surgical repair. He was twenty-one, but his ardor for conflict had just begun.

After a long painful recovery, he met Marcel Dessoutter, an aircraft designer who'd also lost a leg in an airplane crash. Dessoutter owned a company that made artificial legs using light metal alloys. Douglas Bader became its first customer.

In 1939, at the onset of World War II, Bader, despite his handicap, applied to the RAF for flight duty. At age twenty-nine, he joined a squadron, and in February 1940, during a Spitfire flight, he crashed again, uninjured but for the bent alloy legs and a bruised ego. He admitted his flight mistake and moved on. As flight commander, he downed the first of many enemy planes in the mid-1940s.

During a mission over France in 1941, he suffered a midair collision with a Messerschmitt Me-110 during a dogfight. He bailed out, but one aluminum leg caught on the Spitfire, and he hung suspended there as the plane plummeted toward the ground. The leg broke free, and he parachuted right into German hands. Out of respect for Lieutenant Bader, the Germans notified the RAF, and they allowed a British fighter to parachute a new leg to him.

Within forty-eight hours of receiving his new leg, Bader escaped from the prison hospital by tying sheets together and rappelling to the ground.

Coincidentally, London had a warrant out for his arrest on speeding charges.

He was recaptured and sent back to POW camps from which he escaped several times throughout the war. The frustrated Germans locked him in Colditz prison, a 200-year-old castle surrounded by 70-foot walls, at the top of a sheer 100-foot cliff for the remainder of the war.

★ ★ ★

Later, I heard the following story, and I swear it's true because I knew the two brilliantly charming men involved: King George and Lt. Douglas Bader.

The story goes that despite the war-torn state of the country, the king scheduled a grand celebration (that the British called "the lot") to award Lieutenant Bader the Distinguished Cross at Westminster Abbey. As he arrived, large crowds greeted him. When he entered the abbey, military bands played as he walked, throwing first one leg, then the other, clop, clop, clop, down the red-carpeted aisle toward the altar and the king.

Lieutenant Bader wore his full uniform and a heavy cape and sweated profusely as he knelt before the king and bowed his head.

The king, draped in rich velvet robes and his bejeweled crown, stuttered, "L-L-Lieutenant Douglas Bader having shot down th-th-thirteen Fo-Fo-Folke-Wolfs, I award you the D-D-Distinguished C-C-Cross."

Very few people knew that when Bader was really nervous, he stuttered. Lieutenant Bader looked up at the king and said, "B-b-beg your pardon, your h-h-highness, it wasn't th-th-thirteen Fo-Fo-Folke-Wolfs, it was th-th-thirty-three Fo-Fo-Folke-Wolfs."

The king thought the mickey was being taken out of him and replied, "Well Lieutenant Bader, th-th-thirteen Fo-Fo-Folke-Wolfs or th-th-thirty-three Fo-Fo-Folke-Wolfs, you're only going to get one f-f-fucking cross."

I Meet a Great Wit and Almost Get Kissed

★ ★ ★ ★ ★

You know being in show business, I worked around a lot of people with a different sexual orientation than mine. We had lots of male dancers and singers, and they were a lovely talented group of people. No one ever made a pass at me except one memorable occasion when I was introduced to Noel Coward, and he tried.

By that time, I stood 6 feet 4 inches and weighed 180 pounds. This charming and delicate Englishman escorted a beautiful South African woman backstage after one of my performances and complimented my work. Then he gushed, "You must see my play."

I politely told him, "I'd love to some time."

Later, I saw his play and then went backstage to congratulate him on his brilliant writing. He became so excited, I narrowly missed his kissing me on the lips by ducking just a bit.

★ ★ ★

There's a funny story about Noel Coward meeting Chuck Connors, who starred in the "Rifleman" television series. Noel was in Vegas doing a show. Chuck went backstage and said, "Mr. Coward, I'm Chuck Connors."

"Of course, you are my dear boy."

14

We Love England, and They Love Us

A fter two weeks in Manchester and two weeks in London without washing my hair, my head began to itch. So one morning before a matinee, I washed it. Great, now I looked like I'd been electrocuted. The hair no longer lay in gentle waves. It stood on end in tiny pigtail curls all around my head. I couldn't believe my eyes. What the hell was I going to do? I couldn't go on stage like that.

I lived in some digs off Piccadilly, and a few girls from the cast lived in an apartment down the hall. I knocked on their door to see if they could help me. They flew into hysterics the moment they opened the door.

They recommended that I set my hair, and I said, "Well shit, how do I do that?"

"Look, come inside, and we'll try to help you."

They worked on it for quite a while, and I admit it looked a little better. But I looked a lot more like Goldilocks than Curly McLain. Thank God my hair grew fast.

* * *

Everyone at the theater couldn't do enough for us. We had a great stage manager named Peter Sontar, who was only twenty-five or twenty-six years old. A lady named Elsie Beyers, with H. M. Tennent, co-producers with the Theater Guild, came backstage every night to check on us and see if she could help us. If we had any problems, she solved them herself or had them taken care of. We called her the Lighthouse.

Food was very difficult to find after theater hours, and every night that first week, she took us to a Soho restaurant called the Moulin D'Or. A little old lady and her two sons, Albert and John, ran this after-hours restaurant. What the food lacked in taste and variety, they made up for by making us feel at home. No matter where you went at that time of the night, you could only have one of each of these: bread, potatoes, or dessert.

All of England maintained strict rationing. The food was either turbot fish or chicken and always Brussels sprouts. I never wanted to see another Brussels sprout again as long as I lived! The dessert was generally cheese and wine.

The Moulin D'Or, while very expensive, was frequented by people of the stage, ballet, and movies. The lovely ballet dancer, Margot Fonteyn, and my favorite actor, Robert Donat, were among its frequent patrons.

The night that Robert Donat dined with a lovely actress named Catherine Deneuve. I told Albert, the eldest son, that I was a great fan of Mr. Donat and could I meet him after he ate.

He relayed the message, and Mr. Donat invited Gemze and me to his table. He and Catherine were great fun and put us completely at ease. We drank a lot of wine and had a wonderful time. When we left, it was quite foggy out, and Donat's little car didn't want to start. We shoved it down the street until it kicked off, and away they went into the London fog.

The following week, I returned to the Moulin D'Or, and Albert asked, "Where were you last night?"

I said, "What do you mean?"

Albert said, "Mr. Donat was here to have dinner with you."

"Oh my God, my sotted mind didn't remember."

"Well, he left his number and said to give him a call."

When I called him the next day to apologize, he said, "That's all right, old boy. Let's have dinner tonight. Are you free?"

We had a lovely dinner. He was starring in a play titled *The Sleeping Clergyman* and asked me to attend a matinee.

We did nine shows a week, but I'd take a matinee off once in a while to give me a breather, and I agreed. That wonderful voice of his, his stage presence, he was incredible. I'm very proud of our friendship.

In spite of all the great things that had been happening to his career, the Oscar for *Goodbye, Mr. Chips* and all, when World War II began, he dropped everything and returned to Great Britain to help his country, as did a lot of English actors.

★ ★ ★

One of my favorite Laureys, Betty Jane Watson, who had a voice like a gun, flew with us to England. Unfortunately, when they asked her to come, she was about four months pregnant. After a couple of months, her body revealed its secret. Well, naturally the gossip-mongers spread it around that I had knocked up *Oklahoma*'s leading lady.

The Theater Guild took her out of the show and replaced her with a lovely girl, Isabel Bigley. Her mother stuck to her like glue and saw to it that I never got close to her.

I missed Betty Jane. We had worked together for more than a year and had a lot of good times together. Her performance was as solid as a rock.

We had 2:30 matinees and 7:00 evening performances and very little time between shows to eat. We ate what we could find, and that often wasn't very good. I always tried to eat at least two or three hours before a show in New York, but in London between shows, no chance!

One memorable evening performance with Betty occurred during the second and third verses of "Surrey With the Fringe on Top." Laurey became upset with Curly and rushed at him with a carpet beater. Curly avoided her and jumped a fence. It was a good run, and the jump wasn't that high, but I had to clear the fence.

Sometimes when I jumped the fence, it would jostle my stomach, and I would burp. No problem, I would burp and continue with the song. But one night, the burp wouldn't come up all the way and caught in my throat. I tried to clear it, but it wouldn't clear.

I started to sing the last verse, and Laurey went downstage to sit on the churn. "I can see the stars gettin' blurry, when we ride back home in the surrey, ridin' slowly home in the surrey with the fringe on top."

By this time, the tears were in my eyes. I went

downstage, put my hands on Laurey's shoulders, and sang, "I can see the day gettin' older, feel a sleepy head near my shoulder, noddin', droopin' close to my shoulder, till it falls kerPLOOOOOOP . . ."

That old burp comes out LOUD and CLEAR. The audience gasped, and Betty Jane went bananas. Even Aunt Eller broke down. I managed to finish the song, but no one applauded. It was one of the most embarrassing moments of my singing career.

15

My Marriage Goes Kerplop

★ ★ ★ ★ ★

During this period, Rosemary and I realized that our marriage had been a mistake. Time and distance does that to show-business marriages. It wasn't going to work out for us, and I felt very sad. Here I was the toast of the West End in London and faced the guilt of a failed marriage and losing Rosemary. It wasn't her fault, mostly mine.

I'd become emotionally involved with a cute girl playing Laurey with me in New York. Mary Hatcher was the best Laurey of them all. We never became involved sexually. I was plain nuts about her. She had a father who was a real Pop Carnes. He watched us like a hawk, and we never had a chance to see each other alone. I suffered tremendous guilt about that little piece of nonsense.

About three months after opening, Walter Donahue, who played Will Parker, told me he knew a nice young lady who would like to meet me. The next night after the show, he brought her to my dressing room and introduced us. This beautiful young woman had a serene elegance about her. We enjoyed a quiet dinner and wound up at my place near Covent Garden where we made love for three beautiful hours. I hadn't been with a woman sexually for sometime, and she was also love starved. Her friend was away in Europe for quite a while. I tried to take her home, but she wouldn't let me. She said her friend was of European royal blood, and she had to be very careful. She wouldn't even give me her phone number, saying she'd let me know when we could meet again.

Two weeks later, she called. Only this time we didn't waste time with dinner. This arrangement continued for about three months, then it ended. The affair was divine while it lasted. I learned a lot from her—like her name. She was Lillian Craig Bertil. She later married Prince Bertil von Schweden whose father was King Carl Gustav of Sweden. I had slept with a princess.

Isabel Bigley was a lovely young lady who looked a lot like Jennifer Jones. One night, she bragged about all the young men she'd met and dated. I wondered how experienced she was with young men. I thought, tonight I'll find out. In the second act, I ask her to marry me, and we kiss. I French-kissed her. She went limp and didn't finish the duet with me. She just looked at me, her mouth agape.

When the curtain came down, I said, "You really don't know too much about kissing boys, do you?"

Mortified, she ran off to her dressing room tittering a little like a Giggling Gerty. What a cute girl. Completely unspoiled. She later returned to New York and played Sarah in *Guys and Dolls* and became the toast of New York.

London wined and dined us at every opportunity. One day before a matinee, I was invited to a luncheon. Since I didn't have breakfast, I figured that I'd enjoy a nice meal.

I didn't drink much at that time. They served me a couple of Champagne cocktails that I thought were just Champagne. Time flew by. I looked at my watch, and it was nearly 1:45 P.M. The curtain call was 2:30 P.M. I hated being late and flew out of that luncheon without eating, crossed town to the theater, and was in makeup and costume in a half-hour. I felt no pain, but warmed up the voice and stood in the wings stage left waiting for my cue.

Offstage I sing a cappella, "There's a bright golden haze on the meadow, there's a bright golden haze on the meadow, the corn is as high as an elephant's eye," and entered on, "and it looks like it's climbing clear up to the sky."

As soon as the spots hit me, so did the Champagne cocktails. My tongue got so thick, I couldn't pronounce the words. I sounded like a drunken cowboy, and when I reached Aunt Eller, she told me so out of the side of her mouth. She'd been playing Aunt Eller for five years, and you didn't play tricks on Mary Marlo or you'd catch hell.

I worked through the performance, thank God, and I never drank any alcoholic beverage and walked on the stage of any performance anywhere ever again. It was an accidental lesson, but a good one.

* * *

One weekend, the king and queen of theater, Sir Laurence Olivier and Vivien Leigh, invited Gemze, Max Coker, and me to their new home, Notley Abbey.

It was a one-and-a-half-hour train ride from London, followed by a twenty-minute car ride. The train left at 8:30 A.M. On Sundays, work was done on the trainways, and there were always delays. I had a date the previous night and didn't get home until about five in the morning. I slept until 7:30 A.M., raised up from the pillow with a major hangover, and just caught the train as it left the station. Gemze and Max Coker, a friend of ours who, it seemed, knew everybody in London, poured me on the train, and I slept until we arrived at the station around eleven o'clock.

A driver in a Rolls-Royce picked us up for the ride to Notley Abbey. When we reached the grounds, we drove down a long lane and pulled up in front of the abbey. What a magnificent estate. The abbey's stone exterior stood quite desolate on the vast acreage.

We exited the Rolls, looked up, and there stood Sir Laurence Olivier and Vivien Leigh. All I could say was "My God." I stood there awestruck, stunned into silence, and stared at those two beautiful people.

They greeted us on the steps and ushered us into a beautiful drawing room. The first thing the servants served us was a Gin Fizz. I managed to get one down and began to come around.

Sir Laurence asked me if I would like another.

And Ole Hairbreadth Harry said, "Yes, please."

Vivien Leigh handed the drink to me, and I immediately spilled it all over my front and down both my trouser legs. I jumped up, dropped the glass, stepped on it, and tried to apologize for being so clumsy, but they would have none of it.

They took me to the nearest bathroom to clean me

up. There I stood, Sir Laurence Olivier on his knees washing off one leg, and Vivien Leigh on her knees scrubbing off the other. I looked down to see the king and queen of theater kneeling before ME, and I began to giggle.

Larry, as we called him by this time, looked up at me and said, "What the fuck are you giggling at, Harry?"

And I said, "If the old gang could only see me now. Wow!"

They fell apart laughing, and that cemented our friendship.

★ ★ ★

I moved into the Atheneum Court on Piccadilly. Winter neared, and I had to live in a place with central heating. The Atheneum had very small, expensive suites, but I needed to keep my voice in good condition, and dodging the cold English weather was imperative.

By this time, Rosemary and I decided on reconciliation. I sincerely missed her and bought her a nice ring to surprise her. She wanted to make the trip across the ocean by boat.

The six-month anniversary of the show approached as did the high English taxes for those who stayed past that time limit. Many original cast members opted to return to New York, but the producers asked me to stay. I tried to get them to set money aside for me to offset taxes, but they couldn't.

I sat down and logically thought through the whole damn mess. I knew if I stayed with the show, the taxes would kill me, and I'd probably wind up broke. The situation could only get worse if I stayed.

On the home front, I was down in the dumps and had been a horse's ass as far as Rosemary was concerned. If I let her down again, that'd be unforgivable.

Regarding my obligation in England, if I didn't stay, I'd let down a large number of cast members and friends I'd made during that period. Every audience had been tremendous and always left the theater smiling and humming our songs.

After much rationalization, I sent a cable: *Don't come. Letter following.*

You think show business is an easy life. BULLSHIT! It can really rip out your guts.

I believed I did Rosemary a big favor. I still love her understanding and kindness to me and will never forget that. Never!

★ ★ ★

I had another reason to stay, a beautiful blonde dancer, who had performed with Balanchine, named Helen Anderson. Her irresistible smile, fantastic body, and great legs made a captivating package. Our six-month affair in England ended when her contract was up and she returned to New York.

The situation worsened. I stayed and, after English taxes, returned home with a mere $2,000.

Oklahoma in England

★ ★ ★ ★ ★

Dick Rober, who played Jud with me on Broadway, had a great sense of humor, always had a bag of tricks up his sleeve, and was a damned fine actor as well.

Whenever I begged him, "Please Dick, I have friends in the audience tonight," he'd pull another trick from his repertoire. There was no way to get angry with him because he was so funny. It took three months into the Broadway run before I learned all his tricks, and by then, he couldn't break my character no matter what he did. I loved the old bastard. We were great friends.

Lap dissolve. (Means "change in scene.")

Henry Clark, who played our London Jud, left at the six-month period and returned to America. Another American actor, Earle MacVeigh, replaced Henry. After a few weeks, Earle tried to break me up.

I told him my Dick Rober story. "Look, I was broken in by Dick Rober who played Jud in New York, and you haven't a chance. No way! This is my favorite scene in this little opera, and I don't like it being screwed up. So lay off."

Audiences loved *Oklahoma*, and so did I.

One evening performance, my stomach had been giving me hell, and I had no time to take any medicine. I was in serious pain, but managed through "Beautiful Morning," "Surrey," and "People Will Say We're in Love." I still hadn't passed wind and felt my stomach was going to blow up.

After "People Will Say We're in Love," they moved the Smoke House down into position, and the scene began.

As Curly, I entered and started agitating Jud. I picked up a rope with a loop in it, spun it like a cowboy would, and said, "Nice rope, Jud." I looped it over a hook on a rafter and slowly pulled it up, like a hangman's noose.

"You know, Jud, you could hang yourself on that."

Jud said, "What?"

"Hang yourself! Why it'd be as easy as fallin' off a log." I'd tell him how wonderful it'd be for him to have folks gather around him at his funeral and say nice things about him. The preacher would make a nice sermon and say good things about him, and they'd all sing sad songs.

By this time, Jud took the bait and watched everything Curly did as I sang, "Poor Jud is dead, poor Jud Fry is dead, all gather round his coffin now and cry."

Suddenly my poor stomach rolled around, and I let go with a silent fart that lasted for at least fifteen seconds. Jud walked over and stood by me and aped everything that I did. I continued singing through this. "He had a heart of gold, and he wasn't very old. Oh, why did such a feller have to die? Poor Jud is dead. Poor Jud Fry is dead. He's lookin' oh so peaceful and serene. He's all laid out to rest with his hands across his chest," then both Curly and Jud cross their hands across their chests.

I looked down at the coffin, glanced toward the sky, and sang, "His fingernails have never been so clean."

Jud looked down at the coffin, looked up, then put his nose in the air and sniffed a couple of times, and I went ballistic. The timing was incredible. I tried to finish the song, but he kept looking at me and sniffing, with this questioning look on his face, and I kept singing and laughing.

Blissfully, we finished the scene and came off the stage. Earle said, "What the hell is wrong with you?"

I told him about the fart, and we laughed like hell. For the next two weeks, we couldn't look at each other in that scene. It's torturous, yet funny times like that one that makes the theater rich and memorable.

17

I'm Ready for My Closeup, Mr. Warner

★   ★   ★   ★   ★

In January of 1948, I flew to Los Angeles to test for Warner Brothers. At the time, I asked myself why? They had Gordon MacRae, Merv Griffin, and Dennis Morgan, all terrific singers. But I had a vacation coming, and Rosemary and I needed to talk about our impending divorce.

In spite of all the wonderful things that happened to me in England, I wasn't happy. I felt lonely and guilty about our failed marriage. I'd been so driven with acting and singing and making enough money to support the family that my marriage died a natural death.

Also, after two-and-a-half years of singing with a light adjustment of my voice, I was experiencing vocal trouble. I felt that I had either sinus trouble or the voice was just worn out and needed a rest. Maybe a good teacher like Papa Rossi in New York, who had helped me before, could do so again.

With all this on my mind, I didn't have the courage and confidence to make a test I needed to take. A very nice lady at Warner Brothers named Rosensweig helped me with a singing test, which I didn't think was too good. I simply wasn't in good voice. Overall, I don't think Warner was very impressed either, because they said nothing to me.

I met with Rosemary, and we agreed to call it quits. I visited my mother and my longtime buddies, Art Shields and Walt Young. We enjoyed a steak dinner, but I ignored the only vegetable on the plate, Brussels sprouts, which I had a belly full of in England.

I flew to New York for a couple of days, saw Papa Rossi, Rheba Jury, and Papa's boys, then returned to England. On the plane, I met Howard Crane, a very distinguished-looking man, who was an architect and president of the American Club in London. We played gin, he cleaned my plow, and we became instant friends.

Later, he helped me locate a nice apartment on Belgrave Square, and every Sunday, I'd have brunch with him and his wife. The Sunday gin game cost me about twenty pounds, but it was worth it because his wife was a great cook!

In May 1948, an English agent named Kenneth Carten arranged a test for me in a picture called *The Small Voice*. The producer would be Anthony Havelock-Allan, who also produced *Great Expectations*. His wife, Valerie Hobson, would star with James Donald and Michael Balfour as her costars. I won the part, but still had to take a leave from *Oklahoma* to do the movie.

I negotiated with the Theater Guild, and agreed that after the picture was completed, I'd do an additional six months of either *Oklahoma* or *Carousel* if I was needed. I loved both shows.

We started blocking scenes on the picture when the agent, who had arranged the test at Warner Brothers, flew to London, called me, and said, "What are you doing?"

I told him, "I'm making a picture."

He had tickets that evening at the Palladium to see Sophie Tucker and invited me to attend. At the Dorchester Hotel, he introduced me to one of his clients, Allan Jones. I told Allan I thought he was a fantastic Gaylord Ravenal in *Show Boat*.

During the show, the agent casually said, "By the way, I called Anthony Havelock-Allan and negotiated a raise on your contract." It was the same money that Kenneth Carten and I had agreed to. I guess he thought I was stupid.

About three weeks later, I received a strange phone call. A voice said, "They want you at MGM to do *Annie Get Your Gun* with Judy Garland." I hung up. Somebody was playing a cruel joke on me. After a few minutes, the phone rang again, and the voice said, "Don't hang up. It's me, your agent in Hollywood, and it's true, they want you for *Annie Get Your Gun* with Judy Garland."

"I'm making a picture here and won't be through for a while."

He said, "That's all right. They won't start the picture until the fall."

"I have two more pictures to do for Anthony Havelock-Allan."

"Have you signed a contract yet?"

"No. But we have an agreement."

He said, "If you haven't signed the contract, walk away."

"Look, I gave my word that I would do the extra pictures for them. I can't just walk away!"

"Don't be an idiot. That agreement doesn't mean a thing if you haven't signed that contract."

"Hey, I have to shave my face every morning, not yours. You're fired! I want nothing more to do with you."

I hung up and stood there dumbfounded. "What the fuck have I done? Well, Ole Hairbreadth Harry, you've just turned down MGM, *Annie Get Your Gun,* and Judy Garland. That's what the fuck you've done."

I walked to the mirror and said, "Let's go get drunk."

Okay, So I Blew Off MGM and Judy Garland

★ ★ ★ ★ ★

Tony Allan and Valerie Hobson were very understanding and agreed to find me good scripts.

We completed the picture, and they drove me to Southampton where they said a bon voyage as I boarded the *Queen Mary*. The first night, I sat at the captain's table and dined on elegant food.

A cute little girl and her mother joined us. They were taking a young Italian boy of about thirteen to New York to have him fitted for new arms. He had lost his during the war.

The mother and daughter mentioned they were experiencing a problem with the boy, who refused to bathe and was getting gamey. I told them that he was becoming a young man, and he'd be embarrassed to have females bathe him. I volunteered to help. He was a great little guy. Although it took a lot of negotiating and gesturing, I won out and we became good friends.

For entertainment, they had boxing matches on board, and he loved it. I'd put him on my shoulders above the crowd, and he would punch and jab just like a boxer with his injured arms.

★ ★ ★

When we docked to New York, I was met by Rheba Jury, who took me to John Fernley's apartment. John, who directed me in *Carousel*, said I could stay at his place. He was working for Rodgers and Hammerstein on *South Pacific* with Mary Martin and Ezio Pinza.

I contacted an agent at NCAC who booked concerts. He referred me to the William Morris Agency. The first question I was asked was what I'd been doing.

I said, "I just finished a picture in London and also *Oklahoma.*"

"What else?"

"I had to turn down *Annie Get Your Gun* with Judy Garland."

He said, "You did what?" and I told him the story.

After placing a call to Abe Lastfogel with William Morris's Hollywood office, this agent said they'd call me. Sure, I thought.

But the next day, I received a call from someone in the agency who assured me that if anyone in Hollywood could work it out, it'd be Abe Lastfogel, and two days later, he did.

This was 1948. I signed a seven-year contract with MGM starting at $850 a week for forty weeks. Anthony Havelock-Allan agreed to drop one picture, and if MGM decided to keep me after *Annie Get Your Gun*, they'd pay Anthony $40,000. Wow!

I told John Fernley my fantastic news, and he said, "That's great. Now I've some other news for you. Dick and Oscar want you to play Lieutenant Cable in *South Pacific*."

This was too much. I'd always wanted to do something new with Dick Rodgers and Oscar Hammerstein, and now I had to turn it down. Holy mackerel. I'm either the luckiest guy in the world or the unluckiest. That's show business. Shit!

The next day while they rehearsed at the Majestic Theater, I met with John Fernley and Dick and Oscar and told them my dilemma. They said they understood and wished me well. To turn down a chance to do something with these two men was one of the hardest things I've ever had to do in my entire career.

That night, John brought home a record. He said, "Sit down. I want you to hear this. It's Pinza's first song in *South Pacific*."

The song, "Some Enchanted Evening," stunned me. Little did I know that I'd do many performances of *South Pacific* singing that magnificent song a few years down the road.

The following day, I was about to cross Fifth Avenue at Fifty-third Street when a tow truck with a beautiful red Cadillac convertible jacked up behind it stopped for a light. A young guy in the Cadillac yelled at me. "Hey, Harry Keel, I'm George Englund, Pat Englund's brother."

"You're kidding."

He said, "No, hop in. I'm going over to a shop and get this jalopy fixed."

Pat Englund played Ado Annie with me the last six months in England. She was the best Ado Annie I ever heard. I never saw the original cast production, so I never saw Celeste Holm.

There we were being towed across New York City in a beautiful Cadillac swapping stories. I found out he was leaving for California that day to deliver the car to Patty Andrews of the Andrews Sisters.

He invited me to go with him.

I told him I'd go as far as Chicago. I wanted to see my girlfriend, Helen Anderson, who was dancing there in the *Oklahoma* touring company.

We left New York around two in the afternoon and arrived in Chicago by eight the following morning. We broke that Cadillac in for Patty. How we never got a ticket, I'll never know.

I stayed with Helen for a few days, then flew to California. I checked into the Beverly Hills Hotel and called George Englund. He invited me to stay with him and his mother, Mabel, who lived in a palatial home in Benedict Canyon. She was a charming lady and a fine actress.

The following day, George dropped me off at William Morris for my appointment with Abe Lastfogel. I was ushered into Sammy Wisebord's office, who was Mr. Lastfogel's secretary, and there sat Norma Jean Baker.

It had been about eight years since I'd seen her, and I couldn't believe my eyes. She was breathtaking. Our eyes met, and I was speechless. She told me she had a new name, Marilyn Monroe.

A buzzer startled us, and I was ushered into Abe Lastfogel's office. Mr. Lastfogel, a short, chubby little man with a great personality, told me MGM wanted me for the part of Bosiney in an English classic, *The Forsyte Saga* with Greer Garson and the next day I should go to MGM and meet the casting director, Billy Grady.

What else could a coal miner's son from Gillespie, Illinois, want? On contract to MGM and Marilyn Monroe sat in the lobby waiting for me. Don't ask me. I don't have a clue what she wore that day. She exuded an innocent sensuality that drew me into her web, and I knew I was a goner.

"God," I told Marilyn, "you're even more beautiful than when I saw you when you were thirteen."

She said, "Why don't we have dinner?"

I said, "That's great."

She offered to pick me up.

We dined at a quiet little restaurant and shared stories of our loves and losses. She'd been married and divorced, and I'd been married and was in the process of divorce. We quietly talked, held hands, and all too quickly, dinner ended.

I told her I needed to call a cab. She offered me a ride in her little Ford convertible. What's a fellow to do? She didn't have much money and shared a room at the Studio Club with other starlets. Therefore, we couldn't go there.

On the way through Benedict Canyon to Mabel Englund's house, we shared more of our lives. The more we talked, the more we understood each other. Ole Omar the Tentmaker stirred. I thought, Jesus, I was getting divorced and wide open. No problem. I was supposed to be getting married, but what the hell? I invited her inside to meet Mabel.

Lucky for me, no one was home. There was a

romantic study off the living room with a fireplace. I lowered the lights, tossed a few sofa pillows on the carpeted floor, and kissed her. She dropped her dress off her shoulders and let it fall to the floor. I remember it was a nice, but not a sexy or low-cut dress. She stood before me, breathtaking in her nakedness. She didn't wear undergarments. She didn't need them. She had a magnificent body. And, although I didn't get all my clothes off . . . *c'est la vie. C'est la vie.* What a magical romantic evening in her arms.

She wasn't an experienced lover, but not exactly naive either. She appeared both vulnerable and voluptuous and certainly was an eager student under my direction.

We heard a car enter the driveway and scrambled for our clothes. We left out a side door. I drove her home to the Studio Club and took a taxi back to the Englunds. The next morning, I went down for coffee, and Mabel met me in the kitchen with, "Did you have a nice time last night?"

I told Mabel my history with Marilyn and how I met her when she was thirteen, then didn't see her until she was a starlet, several years later.

"She's a very attractive young woman," Mabel said, "and you're not the most unattractive young man, either. Just be careful."

By that time in her career, Marilyn had posed nude in a picture. A fellow named Johnny Hyde acted as her William Morris agent. He believed she had talent in her wide-open, very sweet innocent woman/child way. I got to thinking we had to be very careful about our affair.

An amazing singer named Charles Fredericks, who

was the best Gaylord Ravenal, simply disappeared off the MGM screen after he slept with the wrong gal. His producer found out about his affair, and he was gone. The last thing I saw him in was *My Fair Lady*.

The following night, Marilyn and I had dinner and agreed to just one more fling before going our separate ways. Marilyn was a sweet and lovely girl, and I could have gone for her in a big way, but the timing was all wrong.

Only one more fling? Who were we kidding? Marilyn and I had brief trysts throughout the years. *Asphalt Jungle* made her a huge movie star. Later we worried a lot about getting caught because we were both quite well-known by then.

Think of the synchronicity here. Marilyn had a car, but no money. I had no car, but had some spending money. We met too young in our lives, then again at the William Morris Agency during the early part of our careers, when the time was perfect. Kismet.

19

But Annie Get Your Gun Waited for Me Anyway

★ ★ ★ ★ ★

On November 10, 1948, I received a letter from MGM Vice President Louis Sidney setting forth the contract terms that included reimbursing me $198.61 for my trip from New York to Hollywood for the screen test. The terms included $25 a day for living expenses during my stay in Hollywood from October 24 to November 7, 1948. Big money.

The next day, I went to MGM and met the casting director, Billy Grady. What a terrific guy.

He said, "I saw your test, and you're going to be great. Come on, I want you to meet the show's producer and songwriter, Arthur Freed."

I was wondering how they found me, when on the way to Freed's office, Bill told me the story. "That little rat agent didn't have a thing to do with you getting this job. The casting director at Warner Brothers called Al Trescony, a talent scout for MGM, and he said 'There's a guy Warner turned down, and I think you ought to take a look at him.' Al Trescony looked at your test, brought it to me, and I called Arthur Freed. Arthur told me you're the guy that he wants for Frank Butler in *Annie Get Your Gun*."

That's how it happened.

★ ★ ★

During the film's casting, Billy Grady and I were in his office. He said, "Excuse me, kid, I gotta make some phone calls." He made a call, then slammed down the phone, and said, "Dammit, I just lost this actor I was trying to get to play an Indian for *Annie Get Your Gun*."

I popped up with, "How about J. Carrol Naish?"

Arthur said, "Hey, kid, that's a hell of an idea."

He called Naish's agent, Carrol was available, and that's how they cast the part for Sitting Bull. Arthur said, "I got him. That's great, kid. Have you got anything more?"

"What are you going to pay me?"

He chuckled and said, "Don't call me, I'll call you."

★ ★ ★

I left his office and walked toward the East Gate when I heard a voice, "Hey, Harry, where you going?"

There stood Mario Lanza with a beautiful redhead on his arm.

I said, "Hey, Tenori, how the hell are ya?" I had met Mario in New York near Carnegie Hall just before I left for England, and here he was at MGM. We gave each other a great big hug, and he introduced me to his lovely lady, saying, "I'm gonna eat her in about five minutes. This is Amanda Blake."

She giggled, and I blushed. That was Mario.

Amanda Blake went on to play Miss Kitty on the for-ever-running TV show, "Gunsmoke."

★ ★ ★

Most of my money was tied up in English banks. I explained my predicament to Mr. Lastfogel, and he called MGM and arranged for me to stand in for a few tests with other actors to earn extra money until *Annie* started.

I tested for the role of Philip Bosinney in *That Forsyte Woman*, and it was awful. The clothes made me look fat, and Benny Thau, an MGM executive, insisted that I go to a gym and get in shape. I weighed 180 pounds. They pulled my wisdom teeth, and a few pounds dropped off. That saved me. I never weighed more than 190 pounds until I quit smoking during the filming of *Seven Brides* in 1953.

Howard Strickling, the head of publicity at MGM, arranged for me to escort Ava Gardner to an opening. She quietly dated Howard Duff at the time, and he wasn't happy about this arrangement. But all the contract studios scheduled "dates" for their stars during that period. They also arranged a "date" for me with a young woman named Ann. Secretly, she was Mickey Rooney's girlfriend. Even though it made me feel like a gigolo, it was my job, and I did as I was told just like every contract star. They were nice girls and all, but that was all. I wanted to be married, and I missed Helen.

Publicity also decided to change my name. They thought of a few humdingers that included John Smith and John Henry. My birth certificate says Harry Clifford Keel. When I sang in the Pasadena Symphony, they misprinted my name as Harold. I stayed Harold Keel all through Broadway and in England.

Hedda Hopper solved the name problem when she mentioned in her column that Ava Gardner's new chaperone was MGM's newest singer, Howard Keel.

I talked to Howard Strickling. He thought it was better than Harold, and I agreed. That's how I became known as Howard Keel.

20

Can MGM Do That?

Rosemary went to Las Vegas for a quickie divorce, and Helen and I decided to get married after the first of the year.

Mother and I had an apartment in Beverly Hills on Peck Drive and Olympic Boulevard. Mario Lanza lived nearby, and we would get together and sing.

Mario's beautiful, powerful voice would make your hair stand on end. He'd been a piano mover in Philadelphia, and his 230 pounds were pure muscle. As a mercurial character, when sober, he was a doll, but after drinking, he could be rough and foul mouthed. I felt I understood him. Maybe it was shades of my father. I only saw one incident of his bizarre behavior after a Warner Brothers showing of *Serenade*.

Terry Robinson, an extraordinary trainer who could handle anyone himself, was always with Mario. Terry had a good sense of humor and patience. When Mario died, Terry raised Mario's children.

★ ★ ★

When my divorce from Rosemary became final, Helen and I married. On January 3, 1949, Art and Janis Shields stood up for us as we exchanged our vows in the chapel at the Riverside Inn. MGM arranged for us to honeymoon at the La Quinta Hotel in a remote area near Palm Springs.

Los Angeles was wet and cold, and we hoped it'd be beautiful and warm in La Quinta. After all, that was the desert. We left the Riverside Inn around eight o'clock. The further we drove, the colder it became. Flaps on the Ford convertible kept coming loose, spraying us with chilled air. Trying to find La Quinta in a windstorm on an absolutely black night was becoming a serious problem. Parts of the road were paved. Parts weren't. There weren't any road signs, and I'd never been to the Coachella Valley before.

People gave me more bad directions than you could ever imagine, but we eventually located the valley. It nestled in a secluded cove against the Santa Rosa Mountains. It was about 2:00 A.M. A beautiful suite, a roaring fireplace, and loads of Champagne awaited us.

In the morning, we wanted to swim, but the water was frozen solid. We dove back into bed.

We rode across the desolate sand dunes on horseback. While the dunes were all covered with snow, the weather was great for a honeymoon. The chill kept driving us to the toasty suite for Champagne, a warm fire, and our eager arms.

After the honeymoon, we settled into a little house off Sunset Boulevard and Thirteenth.

In late January, filming began on *Annie Get Your Gun*. I rehearsed first with Roger Edens, then Bobby Tucker. One day after I had finished shooting, I was on my way to the commissary when I heard a voice call out,

"Harold! Harold!"

I turned around, and there stood all 5 foot 1 inch of Judy Garland. In her twenties, she was cute as a button and awesome to work with as I later would learn. Also, she was a huge star.

She said, "I just saw your test, and I think you are going to be wonderful as Frank Butler."

That stunned me. After an awkward silence I said, "Thank you. I know you're going to be a great Annie."

That's how we met.

That afternoon we worked on "Anything You Can Do, I Can Do Better" and "Falling in Love Is Wonderful." Working with Judy *was* wonderful. She was so warm, giving, and easy to be with. I never saw her in a temperamental mood.

A couple of days into rehearsal in a hall that they now call the Judy Garland Rehearsal Hall, MGM producer Arthur Freed walked in with Irving Berlin. Arthur asked us to do the two songs for Mr. Berlin. And we did.

Mr. Berlin said, "Very nice and nice to meet you," and they walked out.

Judy and I stood there with our mouths wide open. We had given it our best, we worked well together, but we felt let down. Mr. Berlin gave us no encouragement whatsoever.

A few days later, Judy and I began recording the sound track.

Before I started on *Annie*, I still wasn't happy with my voice and told Lillian Burns, who was a very powerful acting coach at MGM. I told her Papa Rossi in New York had been my voice teacher.

She referred me to L. K. Sidney, her father-in-law, and L.K. sent for Papa Rossi. We had two weeks during the recording sessions, and that helped me.

The first song I recorded was "The Girl That I Marry." An incredibly talented sixty-piece orchestra, using Connie Salinger's orchestrations with Adolph Deutsch conducting, brought one big lump in my throat, and I could hardly breathe, much less sing. I apologized and asked that we start at the top once more.

At that moment, in walked Arthur Freed with three of the most beautiful young starlets you could imagine. They stood in front of the podium where Adolph and I were and asked if I'd sing one time before recording it.

I looked at Adolph, who winked at me, gave the downbeat, and we did it. Freed was ecstatic and said, "Now we'll get out of your hair, and you can go to work."

I thought to myself, as I etched the pictures of those girls in my mind forever, I repeated, I'll never have a "to do" with those girls. No way, José!!! Did I have an affair with one of them? Well, there was one little jaunt. A beautiful face . . . no names, please.

Then Judy Garland and I sang "Falling in Love Is Wonderful." Louie B. Mayer walked in and said, "I hear it really is wonderful. I'd like to hear it."

Judy's nerves caused her to shake, so I put my arm around her for support. At the time, I thought, that's strange. I should be the one that's nervous, and she should be the one holding me up. When we finished, Mayer gave us both a big hug.

He said, "You kids are great!"

My big number was "My Defenses Are Down," and Papa Rossi told me not to worry about the F-sharp I had at the end of the number. He said, "It's in your voice, just do it." When I nailed it, he jumped up and down like a little kid. What a divine man.

Working with Frank Morgan and Keenan Wynn was a hoot. They were special, particularly Keenan. He helped me enormously, always a pat on the back for encouragement, and we became great friends.

When we completed the studio recording, the shooting began with Busby Berkeley directing. The train arriving at the station had been the first shot, and that took all of one day. The following day, we shot inside at the hotel. MGM built a huge stage showing the entrance of the hotel where they filmed horses and wagons coming in and going out. I sat around all day because they had to get all those shots out of the way before they could shoot my scene. I didn't mind. I was fascinated by it all.

Around 5:30 P.M., they called for me to mount up. I had to enter the scene from the opposite direction, starting behind a backdrop from about twenty feet and at a full gallop, make a sharp turn into the entrance and stop in front of the hotel. I was to dismount, do a scene with Keenan Wynn and a couple of the girls, and exit through the hotel.

I sat a pretty good saddle, and the scene didn't seem that difficult. Blackie appeared to be a good strong horse, and we rehearsed the run six times. No problems.

Harry Stradling, the cinematographer, told Berkeley he'd gotten the shot, but Buz insisted on one more take. I remounted Blackie and at a full gallop, started the quick turn once more for Buz.

Blackie lost footing on his back legs, and down he went with me still in the saddle. It happened so fast, I didn't have a chance to react. I think they forgot to rake the dirt and tamp it down. When the horse's hooves hit

115

the slick floor, down he went. It wasn't the horse's fault. It was Berkeley's.

I felt like a fool with this big horse sitting on me. I never felt any pain until they pulled Blackie off and I tried to stand. It hit me like a kick in the stomach. My steel stirrup had caught in the trim that held the dirt in, and my right ankle was bent double. By this time, the intense pain made me sick to my stomach, and I threw up.

The medical crew came to haul me off to the studio doctor, but each time they moved me, I stopped them. The spasms were that bad. I guess the nurse didn't hear me because when she jerked the ankle, I kicked at her and followed up with pretty foul words.

The following morning, Billy Grady heard about it and had me moved to a hospital where they operated and set the ankle. The doctor did an expert job, and after a couple of days, they put me in a walking cast and sent me home.

Poor Helen, I put her in a spot. My Ole Hairbreadth Harry flared up again. It sure as hell looked like I was doomed not to do this picture.

After a couple of days, I went to MGM. Judy was out on Lot 3. I sat around and tried to figure out a way to do something to relieve her. She'd filmed two musicals back-to-back, *For Me and My Gal* and *Girl Crazy*, and was physically and mentally exhausted when she jumped into the role of Annie. MGM pressed her for the contract commitment. She knew it was a huge part, but she needed energy. The studio talk was that she was on one pill to make her sleep and another to give her energy. They called them uppers and downers. Every day I would go to the set and watch. They filmed a couple of closeups with me, but it was futile to try long shots.

The day before Arthur Freed fired Judy, I was on the set, and they were shooting "I'm an Indian Too." She looked like a wild woman. I knew this was a wild song, but Judy didn't look well.

She'd begun to lose her hair. They said she was pulling it out. I'm no doctor, but she looked physically drained and acted strangely. She wasn't the same Judy I started the picture with.

When I heard they fired her, I couldn't believe it. Her condition was brought on by four things. (1) She'd filmed two musicals, then jumped into another musical role as tough as Annie. (2) My accident caused her to have no time off at all. (3) A quack doctor loaded her up with pills that had made her wacky. (4) The studio had a complete lack of understanding about the amount of the energy it took for a woman to make a physical musical.

Women had to be in the studio at the latest three-thirty to four in the morning and, if we were lucky, stopped shooting at seven at night.

Do that for four or five months, and see how you feel! The only tacky thing I ever saw MGM do was firing Judy. She would have been a great Annie if they'd helped and understood her more. Although she was a great artist, one of the greatest in pictures and in the world, she always tried to give back the gift she had. Unfortunately, nobody knew how to help her and be honest with her. I loved the few moments we had together. God bless you, Judy Garland.

Know who wrote the brilliant *Annie Get Your Gun*? A fine man who would become a lifelong friend. He went on to become one of the world's most famous authors. Maybe you've heard of him: Sidney Sheldon.

21

Talk About a Difficult Annie!

After the studio fired Judy, they removed Berkeley, and George Sidney took charge. As L. K. Sidney's son, he'd been born to show business. He was a gifted director and a nice man, too.

George loved to shoot skeet and traps at the Santa Monica Gun Club, south of the Santa Monica and Douglas Airport.

One day, he invited me to go with him and learn to shoot skeet. He felt it'd help me get used to handling a gun. He introduced me to Jake Harrison, an expert shooter who taught aerial gunners during World War II. Jake taught me so well that in three months, I won my class in the Western Championships.

There I also met actor Robert Stack, a great shot, who'd appeared in the U.S. Olympics several times.

★ ★ ★

The crew learned that Betty Hutton had been cast for the part of Annie. I wore a walking cast for about two months, then the doctors removed it, and in another month, I was walking well. In the meantime, Frank Morgan died, and they cast Louis Calhern in the role of Buffalo Bill.

We recorded what had to be done and started shooting with Betty. She was sweet, had a good sense of humor, and we got along fine. But the rest of the cast wasn't happy with her. Betty upstaged everyone in every scene, and actors don't like that. She was effervescent and full of energy. While George held her down as much as he could, she was a fistful.

Louis Calhern and I became good friends, and I would catch a ride home with him when possible as we lived close by. He stood about 6 feet 2 inches tall, a rough character, and a real brawler. The story goes that he and another guy fought in a New York bar, and they destroyed the entire pub.

Louis had such a big honker on him, he should have played Cyrano de Bergerac. He was a fantastic actor. Later he'd play Lear, then Oliver Wendell Holmes. If Calhern liked you, he'd give you a moniker. He called me Puny. One night on the way home, he said, "Puny, what are you going to do about Hutton?"

I said, "What do you mean?"

He said, "She's upstaging the hell out of you."

"I know, but I'm a new face, and I have plenty of room to show what I can do. If I've got it, they'll see it. If I don't, they won't. Let her go. The camera will have to come around on me once in a while."

He agreed.

One day late in the picture, Betty and I had a scene on a staircase where I could upstage her, and she couldn't do anything about it. She kept stopping the scene. Finally George Sidney said, "What's the matter, Betty?"

"I'm being upstaged," she said. She moved me up and down the stairs, and I played it big and dumb. After thirty-five takes, George said, "That's a wrap."

Thirty-five takes!

Now Calhern, Keenan Wynn, J. Carrol Naish, and Edward Arnold were all watching this. As I joined them, they all said, "You big son of a bitch, if you had backed off one inch, we'd killed ya!"

We had a great laugh.

I'd like to believe Betty was unsure of herself in the part and grabbed every scene that she could. In hindsight, after working with Doris Day, I thought Doris would have been a much better Annie, but she was under contract to Warner Brothers and not available. Betty was loose from Paramount and dying for the role, so that was that.

They blocked my number, "My Defenses Are Down," late one afternoon on Lot 3, and we shot it the following morning. I didn't know at the time, but it was scheduled to be taken out of the picture. The original lyrics had censorship problems. When the studio had the first sneak preview, that number received the biggest hand, and they left the song in, but the lyrics were changed.

I think it's the single number that made me an MGM star.

★ ★ ★

During the filming of *Annie*, I had these lines, "I like to know where I stand with others. They have a right to know the same from me. You've got one life. Why waste any of it on phonies?" I didn't realize the importance of these lines until later in my life.

I'd Need More Than Three Balls for This Movie, Too

★   ★   ★   ★   ★

My next picture was to be *Pagan Love Song* with the beautiful Esther Williams. She was five minutes pregnant and not feeling too well. But she was a 5-foot-8-inch beauty and very easy to work with.

Arthur Freed and Harry Warren wrote the words and music. When I heard the score, I wasn't too happy. It just didn't appeal to my tastes at all. I couldn't say anything because Freed stood by me through the Annie debacle.

Stanley Donen was set to direct. Esther and I tried to get into the script, but it was a piece of shit. I talked to the writer about his interpretation for the role. "Who is this guy you write about?"

He told me he had Cary Grant in mind and for me to play him.

While Cary was one of my favorite actors, I couldn't imitate him. I wish I could, but I didn't have his style. This would be only my third picture, and I didn't have any acting depth yet. Lillian Burns could break down a script better than anyone I knew, but I still had a difficult time trying to find this guy. I'd never studied acting and didn't have a clue how to go about finding my character.

By this time, rumors flew around the set that Esther wasn't happy about Stanley Donen. I don't know the whole story, but Esther had been the biggest money-maker MGM ever had, and they would do anything to keep her happy, pregnant or not.

Stanley Donen was out, and they assigned us Bob Alton who, at that time, was basically a choreographer and had never done a picture at MGM. I asked Lillian Burns if her husband, George Sidney, would direct us. He wouldn't touch the script.

We tried recording, but some of the songs just didn't sing. There were a couple I could have sung better, but they never blocked one song before I recorded it. In all the singing I did in pictures, the only songs that were blocked were "I Can Do Anything Better Than You" from *Annie Get Your Gun* and "Gesticulate" from *Kismet*. All the other songs were simply recorded, and you were stuck with them. This made it very difficult to get a performance on the recording.

Bob Alton suggested that the character I played might be a teacher. Where did this teacher come from? Why would he come to Tahiti? Vacation to chase pretty Tahitian maids? Paint them in the nude? I thought I might wear glasses, but Charles Rosher, the cinematographer argued against it.

Few people knew that without her glasses, Esther was as blind as a bat. A lot of people thought she was stuffy and snobbish, but she just couldn't see. I thought the two of us wearing glasses would be a good link between us, but it was a NO! NO!

When I worked with George Sidney in *Annie*, before every scene, he'd say, "Three balls." Every day on Kauai, I received a card on which was written, "Three balls." That was the only piece of acting direction I received the entire shoot in Hawaii.

How the hell do you ever discover any sensitivity in a character with the direction "Three balls"? The frustration at this point in my career caused me great stress. I'd never studied acting or anything, and while I'm a fast study, I needed lessons. They weren't available.

When I returned to MGM, I thanked George Sidney every time I saw him on the lot. I guess I should have read Stanaslovsky. Hell! I can't even spell it.

★ ★ ★

The studio booked a cabin on a commercial ship for Helen and me for the four- to five-day voyage to Kauai. At the last minute, Arthur Freed decided he'd go by boat, too. He was furious that Stanley Donen had been removed as director.

The first night out, Helen and I and Arthur Freed had dinner together. He was in a black mood, and I tried to talk about everything he liked. All I received in return were grunts for answers. After a while, Ole Hairbreadth Harry took charge. My stomach was boiling so much that I became seasick. I excused myself, went to our stateroom, and rode it out. Helen returned to our cabin, and I apologized to her for losing my temper.

Here was the man who put me in *Annie Get Your Gun* and stood with me through the whole disaster, then put me in my second musical with a big star and a score I didn't like or understand. I didn't feel qualified to express my thoughts.

Arthur and I stayed away from each other the balance of the cruise. It was tough on Helen, but she'd worked with Balanchine in ballet in New York, so she'd seen a few tantrums. She handled it better than I ever could.

When we arrived in Honolulu, Helen and I stayed at the fabulous Royal Hawaiian Hotel. Esther, her husband, and children stayed in a beautiful private home.

★ ★ ★

In the scene where I rode a bike near the ocean's edge in the "Singing in the Sun" number, notice a towel covering my left arm throughout that song and the following scene where I'm in the water. They wanted to protect my bum arm.

More Balls in More Ways Than You Know

It was 1950 when I took up golf. I'd quickly learned the trombone as a child; football, shooting pool, dancing, and fighting in my youth; skin fitting, horseback riding, developing memorization skills, and gun handling as an adult. How hard could golf be?

Ben Gage, Esther WIlliams' husband arranged a game of golf one day at the Waikele Golf Club. My shots were a little wild, but Ben was a good ball striker and very patient with me.

The production moved to Kauai, and they housed us in the Lehui Inn in Lehui for two months doing the location shots.

Kauai had a nice nine-hole golf course with two sets of tees, and I played whenever I could grab a little time off. The pro, a Japanese named Toyo Shirai, had been the first Japanese golf pro born and raised on Oahu to qualify for the U.S. Open.

One day, they assigned me a rather small Portuguese caddie. He knew I worked on the picture and showed up the next morning on location. Although he was about twelve years old, he became an assistant, running errands, and caring for my script, etc. He was there every day, and I began to wonder where he'd come from and why he wasn't in school. I learned he was playing hooky to be with me, located his school, and talked to his teacher.

She said he wasn't a good student and despite his age, was only in about the third or fourth grade. He was a cute kid, and it broke my heart, but I refused to let him on the set from then on.

However, the teacher, who looked like a young Tallulah Bankhead, held great appeal to me. I naturally followed my hormones, and we had a lovely relationship throughout the shooting of the movie. She was an unusual and lovely young lady.

★ ★ ★

Another Portuguese kid, Abraham Lincoln Lopez, became my second caddie. He was as bright as a tack, and I asked him what he wanted to be when he grew up.

He said, "I want to be a doctor and come back here for my people."

I thought to myself, how in the hell can he accomplish that?

Years later at the Bel-Air Country Club in Los Angeles where I was a member, I went out to play golf one morning, shoed up, and walked toward the putting green. There stood a caddie I hadn't seen before at the club. He was a dark, curly-haired young man, and he handed me my putter.

I said, "Do I know you?"

"You met me once."

I asked him where, and he replied, "Kauai."

Although absolutely stunned, I recalled his name. "Abraham Lincoln Lopez, you're the young man who said he wanted to be a doctor."

"That's me. I'm in premed school at UCLA. I found out you're a member here, and I wanted to come and see you and tell you how I'm doing."

He packed me that day, hit a few good shots, and told me Toyo Shirai taught him.

We had a great day together, and I tipped him real good and sent him on his way. I found out later from the dean at UCLA, who was a member at Bel-Air, that Abraham was on a scholarship and head of his class. A remarkable young man.

★ ★ ★

A tall, well-built character who appeared in the picture as a Tahitian prince, Charlie Mauu, was indeed a Tahitian prince and one of the sweetest men I've ever known.

He loved Tahitian music and kept telling me about a song that would be good in the picture. One day he made me sit down as he strummed the ukulele and sang one of the great Tahitian songs, "Beyond the Reef."

Timing! Timing! Timing! I couldn't sing that song because Freed and Warren didn't write it, and the song didn't fit in the movie. Andy Williams made a smash hit of it later.

★ ★ ★

Rita Moreno, who was sixteen or so and really cute, also appeared in the picture. She hung out with Leslie

Stephenson, the picture's dialogue director. I had no scenes with her and didn't get to know her, but she certainly carved a solid niche for herself in the business over the years.

The island natives were sweet and friendly, especially Nawiliwilwi, my taxi driver. He was a happy, rotund guy and like many of the natives, would play the ukulele and sing at the slightest provocation. *South Pacific* later made that gorgeous location famous. Boy, would I have loved to have done that one.

We filmed the movie in two months, and that helped me get to know Esther better. She was a bright and very beautiful lady, and we developed a good friendship. The chemistry between us was like a sparring match. She always tried to find out what made me tick, and I brushed her off. Hell, I wasn't sure myself.

I dreamed of becoming a serious concert singer, and movies drove me away from that.

* * *

In 1951, *Three Guys Named Mike* came about when Wild Bill Wellman, an old friend of mine, met a charming airline stewardess named Pug Wells on an American Airlines flight. She charmed him with stories about her shortcomings as a new stewardess. Wild Bill told Dore Schary the story, who told Sidney Sheldon, who then wrote the screenplay. Pug became the picture's advisor.

I liked my part, which included my first fight in a picture. Barry Sullivan and I brawled, and we mistimed a swing. I caught Barry on his eye with the knuckle of my little finger. He had three days off with a little cut. I worked with a sore knuckle. Watch yourself in a mock fight with a new actor.

Jane Wyman was great to work with, and I learned a lot, but I lost the girl at the end. I guess she thought airline pilots were a wayward lot.

American Airlines made me an admiral in their Admiral's Club. I later met C. R. Smith, president of American Airlines, who used to fly himself, checking up on his aircraft and staff. Apparently, he was a great president because everyone on the airlines loved him.

I still see Pug Wells once in a while. She's a wonderful lady, married and living in Pasadena the last time I saw her.

People in Gillespie wished me luck during the filming. They mailed me a message on a three-by-five-foot postcard.

★ ★ ★

Helen enjoyed the Kauai trip, too. Our lovely daughter, Kaija, had been born January 14, 1950. The April trip helped Helen through the baby blues and gave my mother a chance to play grandmother.

We had rented a little prefab house on Barrington between San Vincente and Sunset in Los Angeles. A friend from Douglas El Segundo, Jack Quick, lived a few blocks away and could look in on my mother while we were away. Jack stood head to head with me, and many people thought we looked like brothers.

Jack and another great guy, Art Spees, and I often played the Baldwin Hills Golf Course. We discovered the Fox Hills Golf Course near Baldwin was a little too tough for hackers like us. Golf is a left-handed game, and with my bum left arm, the sport was doubly difficult.

Being a pure masochist, the game fit me perfectly. I had no patience with myself, and a hot temper waited in the wings to explode. I was really a horse's ass for a while.

★ ★ ★

In 1951, I was asked to narrate *Across the Wide Missouri*, a film starring Clark Gable, and in October, one of my Illinois cousins, Beulah Jones, visited us. Later, she told the Gillespie newspaper that she had visited with me, Helen, and eighteen month old Kaija Liane in our Hollywood home. They quoted her, "The most interesting article of furniture in Howard's home is the bed he had specially built, six-and-a-half-by-seven feet. He is 6 feet 4 inches tall, you know." My family got a kick out of that article.

Why Did I Love You?

★ ★ ★ ★ ★

I heard they wanted me to play Gaylord Ravenal in *Show Boat*. I didn't particularly want to do that show. I'd seen the 1946 version in New York where Charles Fredericks, a fine baritone, played Ravenal. He was also a good actor, but they made Ravenal such a weak character, I wanted no part of it. Moreover, I'm a bass baritone, and the part had usually been played by a tenor.

Then I read the new script by John Lee Mahin and agreed. Kathryn Grayson and I hadn't met. She was filming *The Toast of New Orleans* with Mario Lanza at Stage 15. It was such a huge sound stage that it contained a large marina and a small-gauge railroad.

Mario had been working out using props. The set's railroad ran on a small-gauge axle with two wheels attached at opposite ends and weighed in the neighborhood of 400 pounds. He had just pressed it as I walked on.

He put it down when he saw me. "Hey, paisan. What are you doing here?"

"I'm here to see Kathryn Grayson, not you, you ugly spaghetti gargler."

He laughed like hell. "I just recorded 'Granada.' It's in my dressing room."

I listened to the song, and it was gorgeous. When I met Kathryn, she appeared open and charming. I introduced myself, expressed my concern about the keys, and she assured me the problem would be resolved.

Mario was bench-pressing the wheels again as I left. I called over, "Hey, Mario, la voce kaput!" I left for home. Later, they told me he dropped the wheels with a loud bang, walked off the set, and didn't return for the rest of the afternoon.

Three weeks later at the MGM golf tournament at Fox Hills, Mario walked across two fairways to find me. "What do you mean my voice stinks?"

"Hey, I was just putting you on. The recording was beautiful. I'm sorry if I upset you. I was just being a smart ass."

"You son of a bitch. I love ya," Mario said.

I never tried putting him on again.

★ ★ ★

Bobby Tucker was working with Kathryn and me on the keys when Johnny Johnston, her estranged husband, walked in. I lightened my voice to make it sound as romantic as possible, and we recorded our first song.

The moment we sang, the chemistry between Kathryn and me was more than I could control. She was so beautiful, she took my breath away. I knew I was a goner. When we were in the same room, the romance and atmosphere became electrified. Sparks flew.

During our first duet, "Make Believe," I tried to be

professional and walk away from her. But some force wouldn't let me go.

Howard Hughes was crazy about her, and one of his guys tailed her home every night. Even that didn't deter my pursuit.

Helen and I lived in the Palisades above the fifth hole at the Riviera Country Club. Katie lived above the Riviera's thirteenth hole.

One night, Katie and I drove toward Malibu and stopped along the beach. I told her, "I'm sorry, Katie, I have to tell you that I'm in love with you. I've tried not to, and I feel very guilty. I promise you that I won't do anything foolish or hurt you. You have enough on your mind, but if there's anything I can do for you, I'm here."

It turned out she felt the same about me. What a mess we were in, and it hurt, I mean HURT. She was going through a divorce, and I was married with one child and another on the way.

Through our friendship on the set with Ava Gardner, we learned she and Frank had been going through the same thing, only they had been more open and vulnerable.

I don't think many people on the set were fooled, either. They watched us like hawks, particularly in the love scenes. The kisses had to be very formal, but we fooled them once in a while.

Even Hedda Hopper called me and said, "I hear things are going on between you and Kathryn."

"*Show Boat* is a love story, Hedda, and nothing more. The whole cast is in love with each other, and I think when you see the picture, you will recognize it. Love permeates the screen."

133

I don't think she believed me. Love flowed over our set, from Captain Andy on down, George Sidney, Charles Rosher, Adolph Deutsch, Connie Salinger, and John Lee Mahin. Ava Gardner's Julie was brilliant, and as far as I'm concerned—she was Julie. No one sang "Old Man River" like William Warfield, who was a sensational Joe. Marge and Gower Champion, Joe E. Brown, Agnes Moorehead, Robert Sterling, and Owen McGiveney were all magnificent cast members who told a love story for all generations.

The audiences loved us, too. *Show Boat* became a huge box-office hit and proved again that Arthur Freed was a great producer.

Variety reported, "Kathryn Grayson and Howard Keel have voices with a show-tune ableness. Their singing captures the ears and tear at the emotions."

★ ★ ★

Around 1951, when I was filming *Show Boat*, Grandmother Osterkamp became very ill. She'd been in the hospital before and had rallied. This time was more serious. She declined traditional medicine because it was against her religion. Her doctors called me about giving her a blood transfusion. They told me she was so weak that she wouldn't make it through the night without the blood. I told them it was against her religion, but I gave them permission to do the procedure anyway.

The following morning, I visited her and said, "How are you, Mama?"

She looked at me with those icy blue eyes and said, "HARRY, they gave me BLOOD last night. Why'd they do that?"

"Well, Mama, I haven't had much time to spend with you. I'm always going away some place. I never got to know you except when things were negative. I wanted to have you see me prove myself a little bit. I wanted to spend more time with you. If I didn't give them permission to give you blood, you might not be here."

She said simply, "You know there's just one trouble with this life, Harry. You've got to live a life to learn how to live it."

She forgave me for going against her beliefs.

★ ★ ★

Freed had wanted to use the Mississippi River as the film's location, but the cost was prohibitive. The studio decided to use the Tarzan Jungle Lake located on MGM's back lot. They drained the lake and for five weeks built the *Cotton Blossom* paddle-wheeler. The construction costs on the boat ran $126,468.

An oil-injection tank on the boat caught fire during the filming and nearly destroyed the *Cotton Blossom*. It took $67,000 more dollars to repair and repaint it.

We used the vessel again when I appeared in *Desperate Search*. Except for that, what was probably the most expensive prop in MGM history at that time was left to rot on the lake.

The only thing about *Show Boat* that irked me was a scene where Ravenal, who was down on his luck and had hocked things to get by, argued with Nolie. Gay grabbed Nolie and said, "Nolie get a hold of yourself, things will get better."

Nolie said, "Gay, take your hands off me before I hate you."

135

That stunned Gay, and his next line is, "Well, we'll have to do something about this." And Gay leaves Nolie a note.

Katie didn't want to say the line " . . . before I hate you."

I told her, "Katie, you have to. Gay would not be stunned by 'Take your hands off me.'"

She acquiesced and said the line.

When they held the big premiere at the Egyptian Theater, the scene came on the screen, and she said, "Take your hands off me," then cut to me saying, "Well, we'll have to do something about this."

I groaned, "OH! NO!" and walked out of the premiere. I couldn't believe it. She and the editor cut the words, thus making Ravenal appear pretty weak.

I still love Katie, but I never forgave her or the cutter.

***

In a lovely boudoir scene in *Show Boat*, Katie and I sang the first verse and chorus of "Why Do I Love You?" then we were to waltz into the bedroom during the musical interlude and finish the song. We had never blocked the scene. George Sidney simply laid it out for us.

This would be a very sexy and beautiful moment. We sang, then began to waltz. Katie, this beautiful little creature, not only moved like a Mack truck, she tried to lead.

I didn't know until 1998 that Katie didn't like being held close because of her large breasts.

Well, the scene was disaster. George Sidney said, "All right, cut the lights. Howard can't dance."

Stunned into silence, I stood there and looked at him. When I found my voice, he said, "Get Bob Alton down here, and let's rehearse Howard."

Alton said under his breath, "Having a little trouble, Twinkle Toes?"

"No. Katie moves like a goddamn truck and wants to lead as well."

Katie, in her heels, stands 5 feet 2 inches to my 6 feet 4 inches, and that added to the problem. Bob and I danced, and I cussed under my breath while Katie sat on her sweet little ass eating chocolates. That didn't help matters. After rehearsing, Katie joined us and still moved like a truck and tried to lead. There was no way that her tiny little legs could keep up with my long ones. They cut that scene from the picture.

They never said a word to Katie nor did Bob Alton dance with her, but I got even with her in *Kiss Me Kate*. You couldn't help but love Katie, but she could be a caution at times.

25

Because You're Lovely to Look At

★ ★ ★ ★ ★

Bob Sterling and I became golfing buddies. He'd invited me to play at Bel-Air, and I'd reciprocate at the Riviera where I was a member. At that time, Bob was a plus-two golfer and helped me with my game. One day, he invited me to join the Bel-Air. He and Bill Grady placed my name for membership, and I was voted in.

During the filming of "Dallas," I would become known as the Simon Legree of the Greens Committee. The golfers ignored club rules with respect to their golf carts and were well on their way to destroying the course. I had a white-line painted along the fairway boundary. I made every golfer who drove his cart beyond that white line—walk.

It was truly a magical period in our lives, and I loved it. The Bel-Air pro was Joe Novak, the first president of the PGA, whose golf accomplishments are many.

Golf became my stress reliever. Or was it my stressor?

My next picture was *Texas Carnival*. I played a good ole boy, and Esther Williams, Red Skelton, Ann Miller, and Keenan Wynn rounded out our hoot of a cast.

Red was something else, always painting or playing the jester. When he turned on that enormous talent, he was unequaled. There was one scene that turned him on, and when he was on, you just stood back and let him go.

I had the morning off, arrived at noon, and checked in with the first assistant director.

He told me, "We haven't got a shot yet."

"You're putting me on."

"No, Red is so funny in the scene that no one can keep from breaking up, and I mean no one."

"I've got to see this."

The scene was between Red and Keenan at a bar. They rolled the camera. Keenan was seated at the bar. Red, who's supposed to be a drunken cowboy, entered, took about four steps, and the first thing he sees is the enormous head of a moose on the wall behind the bar. He ad-libs, "I wonder how fast that moose was going when he came in."

I fell on the floor roaring with laughter and ruined the scene. They kicked me and everyone else off the set.

It took all day to film what was to be a one-half minute on the screen. Red's timing was fantastic, and poor Keenan damn near bit his forefinger off to keep in character. You can see it on screen.

* * *

Callaway Went Thataway, what great fun, with Fred MacMurray, Dorothy McGuire, Jesse White, and Stan

Freberg. Norman Panama and Melvin Frank produced and directed. During the sneak previews, the audiences loved it, but on broad release in the theaters, the movie bombed.

I also got even with Fred MacMurray. They had a little start party when everyone could meet. They introduced me to Fred, and I said, "I already know you, Fred. I'm that skinny kid that used to park your car in front of Paramount. I used to keep it all nice and clean, and you never tipped me one dime. Maybe you can make up for it by helping me with my acting now that we're better acquainted."

Dorothy McGuire was an amazing actress. I was a great fan and thrilled to work with her. Yet, she was a little strange. She'd walk on the set in the morning, looking beautiful. When she was through shooting for the day, she'd go to her dressing room, remove her makeup, and come out looking like another person entirely. Apparently she didn't like all the froufrou and cosmetics. She painted a self-portrait for me, and it's very unusual.

I had lunch one day with John Wayne and Boo Roos, our business manager, and Wayne said, "Kid, it won't work today. You can't kid in Westerns and cowboys."

He was right. You can't make fun of Westerns. They're real stories. Maybe that's what happened to *Callaway*. Funny Westerns aren't funny.

★ ★ ★

I hit my first of four hole-in-ones at the Bel-Air Country Club in 1952. Later, I'd hit a fifth at The Lakes in Palm Desert, California.

I knew Clark Gable only slightly when we played golf

together one day. We were never very close because one of the things that I couldn't stand was the minute *Annie Get Your Gun* premiered, the press dubbed me a "singing Clark Gable."

★ ★ ★

Then MGM sent Kathryn Grayson and I on a tour of the Caribbean and South America to plug *Show Boat*.

MGM flew us in DC-6s on a three-week publicity junket to Cuba, Peru, Chile, and Brazil. Kathryn was a huge star in those countries, and they sent me along to introduce me. Braniff Airways and the State Department also sponsored the trip, and we were treated royally in Havana, Lima, Valparaiso, Rio de Janeiro, São Paulo, and everywhere. We flew through Argentina, but relations weren't good with the U.S. at that time. We merely landed and refueled in Buenos Aires.

After each theater opened with *Show Boat*, Katie and I would sing a few numbers from the picture and finish with "Là cidarem la mano" from *Don Giovanni*. The audiences loved us.

It was torture for Katie and me to pretend to be just good friends when our love for each other grew and grew. We were carefully watched by a snitch from MGM's publicity department wherever we went.

In Brazil, we stayed in a beautiful hotel overlooking the Rio de Janeiro Bay. A huge banquet had been planned. Before the event, they took us down to a ballroom and sat us in large thronelike chairs. Rio's elite marched in a long receiving line and stared at us. And, as though we were statues, they examined our eyes and face so close it embarrassed us. Katie became restless. I took her hand and tried to calm her down with ESP.

Half an hour later, a limousine drove us to the theater. We entered a square two blocks by one block near the theater where a monstrous, screaming crowd blocked our entrance.

People climbed onto the limo's hood to get a closer look at us. All the car windows filled with people screaming our names. The limo rocked to and forth. The frantic scene frightened Katie. I held her hand and said, "Just smile and say hello."

Eventually the police and a truck carrying two long benches arrived, and the officers beat the people back. They weren't gentle, and it was difficult to watch. I thought Katie would get sick. I held her face to my chest, and they quickly cleared the way.

When we arrived at the hotel, Katie slipped me the key to her suite and said, "Give me half an hour to get rid of people, and come up."

I changed out of my tux and put on a sport shirt and slacks. Waiting for her would be one of the longest half-hours of my life. When she opened the door, she stood there in a beautiful negligee. God, she was so gorgeous. I couldn't believe this moment in my life. It was like our bedroom scene in *Show Boat* during, "Why Do I Love You?"

I pulled her into my arms and held her for the longest time. This was the first time in a year that we could hold each other and not hide our feelings. I was so in love with her, there's no way to explain my emotions. I was really nervous as we kissed the first time without cameras running, but my nervousness soon faded, and we made up for all the lost time. We melted into each other for it was our night. A night of two people consuming each other with love. And it was to be our one and only night together, ever.

We completed the publicity tour in São Paulo, then flew to Hollywood, and went right into rehearsal for Cecil B. DeMille's radio presentation of *Show Boat*.

We managed to escape the fans waiting outside the theater and went to lunch at the Brown Derby. When we returned, they caught us outside the theater for autographs. We were exhausted and grumpy a bit, but when a little voice said, "Please Miss Grayson and Mr. Keel, could you please smile?"

We looked at each other and began to laugh and cry at the same time. We were just exhausted. How we had the energy to do the tour, the signing and smiling, and the radio show, I don't know. But we did, and we sang well. We had one week off, then started rehearsals of *Lovely to Look At.*

* * *

Lovely to Look At, and it was lovely to look at with Kathryn Grayson, Ann Miller, Marge Champion, and all those lovely models. Wow! Red Skelton, Gower Champion, and I had a ball. I wasn't too happy with my part because, although Tony was a likable horse's ass, he was also conceited. I went to Mervyn LeRoy, our director, and he assured me they'd fix it on the set.

Mervyn wound up day after day saying things like, "Let's have a nice little scene. Action. Cut." He never talked to me about the part or expressed any concern. By this time, I had learned directors didn't discuss things with actors. The actors were pretty much on their own. I improvised and made the part of Tony as charming as

143

I could.

Kathryn and I were mad about each other, and there was no way to stop it. I tried to make the most of my day in our scenes and then went home and tossed back a few martinis to forget. It was a very unhappy time for both of us. I'm amazed we didn't say to hell with it and go some place alone together, but that would have hurt too many people.

This was Zsa Zsa Gabor's first picture, and her first scene was with me. She had a case of nerves, and Red Skelton took her into her dressing room and gave her vodka. I told her, "We all love you, and you're going to be wonderful. Just be your wonderfully, charming, giggly self."

She did, and to this day when I see her, she always thanks me for being so nice to her. She's a hell of a nice gal, and I love her. I also loved working with Carmen Dragon, who was the picture's conductor. Kurt Kasznar was a hoot, and I was fascinated watching him play way out and then come back. Marge and Gower danced as one beautiful team. Marge was sexy and cute, and Gower handled her with cool precision. Red was Red, and his piano scene with Gower was hysterical. I learned to tune off Mervyn.

★ ★ ★

June 21, 1952, was special to me. My beautiful daughter, Kirstine, was born.

26

I'm a Cowboy for a While

★ ★ ★ ★ ★

A period of "B" pictures: *Desperate Search* and *Fast Company*, followed the musicals.

In *Desperate Search*, it was a stretch for me to play a recovering drunk who was a bush pilot in Canada, but we had a terrific cast that included Jane Greer; Patricia Medina; my old buddy, Keenan Wynn; a good director, Joe Lewis; and a fair script.

Two beautiful women costarred: Jane Greer, who had a good sense of humor, and Pat Medina, who was very bright. I wish we had a better story, but the studio put no real money behind it.

In *Fast Company*, I had the opportunity to meet a very funny man and exceptional painter, Sig Arno. Polly Bergen tried very hard in her role and later proved herself show-business worthy. But I seriously dug Nina Foch, a highly intelligent and sexy lady. Now, I'm a leg man, and she had a beautiful set of pins.

The two B pictures didn't do much for MGM, so arrivederci!

★ ★ ★

MGM lent me to Warner Brothers for *Calamity Jane* with their top star and beauty, Doris Day. She married Marty Melcher, a real Svengali, who did everything for her and, at the end of their marriage, took all her money, too. She studied Christian Science and stayed to herself a lot. Every time she had a chance, she joined her practitioner coach in her dressing room away from the set.

This top-notch cast included Allyn McLerie, Phil Carey, and Dick Wesson. With David Butler, a nice man and a strong director, and a charming score by Sammy Fain and Paul Francis Webster, we had a hit on our hands.

Although I didn't care much for my song, "My Heart Is Higher Than a Hawk," and I still don't.

The part of Wild Bill Hickock was written so colorlessly that the only way I could play him was to underplay against Calamity. I took the role apart, and I think I did a damn good job.

Doris's professionalism and innocent charm made her perfect for the part. I often wondered why she didn't do concerts and let people see and hear her in person. They showcased her singing with a slew of good songs, one of which, "Secret Love," won the Academy Award that year. Strangely enough, I sang it for the Academy Award show.

The song "I Can Do without You" was a hoot to do, and Jack Donohue did a great job choreographing the number. It was so physical that we decided to record it on the set with a piano and add the orchestra later. That was the only time I ever did a song that way, but it certainly worked. In two or three shots, we had the number pat. I wished we had done it that way more often at MGM.

Ride, Vaquero!, another so-so western, had a fabulous cast that included Robert Taylor, Ava Gardner, Anthony Quinn, and me. John Farrow directed.

I was told John was charming, but not to turn my back on him. He was one sadistic son of a bitch and started on me first. I wasn't going to take shit from him and let him know right away.

We shot this movie in three weeks on location in Kanab, Utah, a remote little town with a magnificent panorama.

Ava had a beautiful stand-in who I stole away from Farrow, and he didn't take too kindly to that. She was gorgeous and . . . no names, please.

I hated my part, but as they say, "It pays the bills."

Bob Taylor, who was a quiet loner, would shoot his scenes, lay down, and take a nap. He was from another film era entirely. Such a handsome fellow, nice, but not friendly, you know. The only happy people seemed to be two wild stunt men, Frank McGrath and Terry Wilson, my stand-in.

Ava invited me to her house for dinner one night, and there stood Frank Sinatra. He was in a great mood and told me he'd gotten the part of Maggio in *From Here to Eternity*.

Frank's career was in its infancy. I told him, "Goddammit, that's the part. Frank, that's it, kid. You're going to be great. You're on your way." I didn't know how far. He hung around the set for a few days, then took off. They were truly in love those two, but their love was star-crossed, too. Nobody could hold on to

Ava, and nobody could hold on to Frank. (In one of those strange twists in life, Frank would later marry John Farrow's daughter, Mia.) Katie and I had the same problem, but we couldn't show our love for different reasons.

In one bar scene with Anthony Quinn, he had to out-draw me and shoot my legs out from under me. Sounded like a simple setup. During the shootout, I out-drew Tony. I'd been practicing. We both laughed, and Farrow blew up.

Farrow said, "Look, Keel. You draw slower."

To which I replied, "Fuck you. You are the great director. You fix it. I'm supposed to be an ex-Union army officer and certainly able to handle a gun. The better I look, the better Tony looks."

He shot the scene every way he could, and the editor showed him how to cut it. Tony and I were good friends from then on.

Later, I heard Farrow had himself circumcised and had one hell of a time healing. At least now he's not as big a prick as he used to be.

27

Kiss Me Kate

While I rode horses and shot guns across the West Coast, MGM tried to decide who'd play Freddy Graham in *Kiss Me Kate*. They attempted to get Laurence Olivier to dub his voice. They thought about Danny Kaye, too.

I'd made an awful test of "Where's the Life That Late I Led?" Katie and George Sidney told MGM if they didn't use me, they wouldn't do the movie. That was one of the lowest points of my lifetime. I thought my MGM career had ended.

I'd done two pictures with producer Jack Cummings, and even he didn't want me. I was the last choice for the part and would have never gotten it without George and Katie's insistence.

I thought maybe I should try to get *Oklahoma*, but I knew Gordon MacRae had the inside track. I knew Dick Rodgers didn't like to lower the score, and Gordon had the perfect voice for Dick.

I went to see Louis Calhern, with whom I'd developed a father-son relationship, and asked him, "Lou, what's the secret of Shakespeare?"

"Puny, there's no secret. It's just the Bible for actors. You have to study it and attack it. There's a rhythm to it, but you're a singer and have great rhythm. Just work on it. You can do it. Look."

He stood and recited a few lines from *King Lear* that he'd been working on. I began to feel the rhythm and repeated some of the lines to him.

"That's it, Puny. You can do it."

★ ★ ★

The following day, my agent called to tell me I'd gotten the part, but now Jack Cummings wanted off the picture. Jack and I had a good relationship, and I went to see him. He honestly didn't think I could do it and told me, "Kid, this part will ruin your career."

I said, "CAREER? What career?"

He said, "Look, I got another part for you that you're going to be great for."

That pissed me off. I told him, "Jack, you're looking for someone who can sing like Lanza and act like Olivier, and there isn't anyone around the industry like that. But I'm a pretty good singer and a pretty good actor, and I'm going to work and show you, dammit."

I walked out mad as hell.

MGM had the greatest makeup and costume departments in the world. Their artisans could create anything. I went to see Bill Tuttle, head of MGM's makeup department. I told him I wanted to look like Petruchio. I had seen a picture of Pinza as Don Giovanni, and I wanted a black wig and beard and a gold earring in my right ear.

Tuttle was an amazing sketch artist. He called me a couple of days later and showed me his sketch. I loved it.

I'd been working on my voice with Maestro Cehparo, a studio coach. Bobby Tucker and I worked on the score. It's a fabulous piece of music and lyrics by Cole Porter.

MGM never took the time to block a song. You just learned the words and music and walked in and recorded. Ballads and love songs are one thing, but production numbers are another. They needed time. It was such a pleasure to work with Andre Previn during the recordings.

My biggest number, "Where's the Life That Late I Led?" needed blocking to find nuances and tempos. No! MGM rushed ahead and recorded, and you were stuck with it.

Hermes Pan, the award-winning choreographer, was so busy with dance numbers, I asked him to lend me his assistant, Alex Romero, to work on my numbers.

The studio couldn't decide whether to do *Kiss Me Kate* in 3-D or CinemaScope, so they made a few tests. When I finished "I've Come to Wive It Wealthily," I slipped into that extraordinary costume and makeup, and the ham in me came out. We had worked with a cape and all, and the powerful scene knocked them out.

Jack Cummings called me into his office and said, "Kid, I just saw the rushes. I was wrong. You are going to be great. Anything I can do to help you, just call."

We had an awesome cast with Katie, Ann Miller, Tommy Rall, James Whitmore, Keenan Wynn, Bob Fosse, Kurt Kasznar, Willard Parker, and Ron Randell. Saul Chaplin also worked hard for me.

Katie and I started the blocking of "Wunderbar." After a couple of hours, Katie complained she was dizzy. I suggested, "Katie, why don't you go home, and Carol Haney and I'll work it out?"

I told Carol not to help me, just hang on, and I'd physically carry her around. Carol was a very talented dancer and later performed an incredible number with Bob Fosse.

When we began filming, many of my makeup call times were 4:30 A.M. for a 7:00 A.M. ready. I pulled a Laurence Olivier and had a piece added to my nose to give me a more Shakespearean appearance. I had no time to block and work on "Where's the Life That Late I Led?" We'd shoot sometimes until 7:00 P.M., take a sandwich break, then work with Alex Romero until 10:00 P.M., be home by eleven, and up at 3:30 A.M. for the 4:30 A.M. makeup call. Many times, I'd stay in my dressing room and not go home.

Kiss Me Kate would become the only musical ever shot using the 3-D process. We would shoot in 3-D first and relight for a wide screen. The 3-D would take three times the light for the filters, and it'd get very hot on the set. When Ann Miller danced the number "Too Darned Hot" on a table on one of the first sets we worked on, it was 130 degrees on the set. Once you were under the lights, you stayed there because out of the lights it was only 85 degrees. They took shammy skins, dipped them in eau de cologne, and whirled them around until they cooled, then patted your face down to help you keep as cool as possible. It was a long, tough film.

Katie and Ann Miller were beautiful and brilliant. Keenan Wynn and James Whitmore made "Brush Up Your Shakespeare" a classic. You couldn't find better suitors than Tommy Ralls, Bobby Van, and Bob Fosse. "From This Moment On," danced by Ann Miller, Tommy Ralls, Jeanne Coyne, Bobby Van, Carol Haney, and Bob Fosse became another memorable musical number. And Kurt Kasznar and Willard Parker completed the perfect cast.

When we shot "Wunderbar," George Sidney wanted to expand the dance from Lilli's dressing room into Fred's dressing room, out into the hall, through Lilli's dressing room again, and finish the song, all in one shot. It sounded great except that Katie didn't know one step. They set up the shot, and we walked through the set hand in hand.

I suggested that George give all the directions to shoot, but not to roll the camera as it'd be a waste of film. He did, and the first attempt was just like the scene in *Show Boat*'s "Why Do I Love You?" What a mess with Katie leading and moving like a Mack truck.

We stopped, and I said, "Katie, I'm not going to be 'a good ole tangle foot' like in *Show Boat*. Now in this next take, don't do a damn thing. Just hang on, and we'll get through it. Trust me, 'cause I know how we can do it."

She got hot and said, "Well, you certainly aren't like you were on *Show Boat*," went into her dressing room, and slammed the door. That was perfect for the scene.

I told George to roll them the next time, and I picked her up and bounced her all around the set. Katie relaxed, and it worked out well. We did one take for 3-D and one for a wide screen. Katie and I recovered from our little spat and fell in love all over again. God, she was beautiful.

Later in the courtyard scene, when Petruchio tried to tame Kate, she had to slap me in the face, but she held back. I told her, "Katie, you have to slap me hard. Hold your hand limp and let go."

She said, "Howard, I can hit pretty hard. I had two big brothers, and they didn't tangle with me."

I assured her I didn't care and she'd have to hit me hard for the scene to work. I want to tell you I saw stars! From then on I ducked. God, could she hit—all 5 feet of her.

* * *

The lack of blocking before recording haunted me while filming "Where's the Life That Late I Led?" I was stuck with those tempos and couldn't do what I wanted to do. I did save them a lot of production time, though. We shot the long shot, medium shot, and closeup for both 3-D and wide screens in six takes. The song itself takes almost six minutes, and I did each take one time. I wasn't pleased with my performance, but I was stuck with it.

During the filming of *Kiss Me Kate*, I read the script for *Rose Marie* and decided not to play the Mounty. I also decided not to tell anyone my decision until we wrapped *Kiss Me Kate*. I was working too hard and carrying too much pressure.

I had met Cole Porter, and all he said was, "Glad to meet you." He didn't have one encouraging word.

During "Where's the Life That Late I Led?" a man and a little girl stood behind the camera right in my eye line. I heard him say to the little girl, "That's the man who's going to play the Mounty in my film."

I complained to George, who had him removed from the set. The man happened to be Larry Weingarten, *Rose Marie*'s producer.

***

I learned to use the bullwhip and could make it crack and wrap around a waist or an arm and not harm anyone. I used it on Katie in one scene, and she didn't blink an eye. She was one brave lady. I was amazed when I saw rushes how loud the crack of the whip was. I think overall, except for "Where's the Life That Late I Led?," I did a damn good job.

Katie and I remained completely wacked out about each other. We had a small last-take party in Katie's dressing room. *Kiss Me Kate* would be Katie's final picture at MGM, and several people dropped in from the cast. I said my good-byes and left as Joan Crawford arrived. I went to my dressing room to clean up. When I walked downstairs, I bumped into Joan Crawford, who said, "Why in the hell don't you marry Kathryn? She's mad about you."

I said, "I'm sorry, Joan, I can't. Too many people would be hurt, and I think the press would destroy us both. I have a wife and family, and I can't do that to them. And I can't do that to Kathryn. I love them all too much."

The critics realized the depth of our feelings, too. Bosley Crowther of the *New York Times* said, "*Kiss Me Kate* was beautifully staged, adroitly acted and really superbly sung. Miss Grayson's and Mr. Keel's voices and acting were juicy and uninhibited."

My MCA agent called that night to tell me they needed me in wardrobe for fittings for *Rose Marie* the following day.

Don't I get a day off between movies?

The Script Stinks

★　　★　　★　　★　　★

I told my agent, "I'm not doing *Rose Marie*. I read the script, and the Mounty part is a jerk."

"Howard, you can't do that. They'll put you on suspension."

"I don't give a damn. The Jeanette MacDonald-Nelson Eddy version is Academy Award material compared to this script."

The shit hit the fan.

They wanted to know why I didn't tell them sooner. I told them I carried too much pressure on *Kiss Me Kate*. I knew they weren't happy, but I was worn out and didn't care.

"You're my agent. You fix it," I told him.

Jack Cummings called and wanted to know why I was being so difficult. I suggested he read the script.

I called Lew Wasserman, head of MCA. I'd never met the man, but I thought, what the hell, go to the top.

Lew's response was, "Then don't do it."

I told him I'd been summoned to Dore Schary's office the next morning and would anybody from MCA go with me, but he declined.

Jack Cummings called after reading the script and agreed the part was lousy. Jack joined me along with Larry Weingarten; Mervyn LeRoy; MGM head of talent, Benny Thau; and Dore Schary. I told them what I thought about the Mounty character, Sgt. Mike Malone. Then added, that having Ann Blyth look into a mirror and see a vision of the murderer, as far as I was concerned, was an insult to the Royal Canadian Mounted Police. I wanted no part of the dumbness.

Larry Weingarten walked off as producer, and another writer was assigned to fix the problems. Mervyn LeRoy wound up as producer and director. I liked the changes that were suggested. We recorded the songs and started shooting. The film would be the first film musical to be made in CinemaScope.

MGM selected the beautiful mountains of Mammoth, California, as our location shoot. One morning, it took three hours to set the complicated scene for the Mounty's song. About fifty extras in full-dress Mounty uniforms sat on horseback two abreast and entered the scene from about two hundred yards down the road. They were all set to go. Mervyn, the camera, and the lights were situated on a huge overhead boom, and he was anxious to film the shot.

All was ready to call "Action" when a Mounty entered the shot about a hundred and fifty yards away and ambled at an easy gait toward the camera. No hurry. Just enjoying the scenery.

I thought Mervyn was going to do his drawers. He yelled to get that stupid Mounty out of the shot. Where the hell was Howard Koch, his first assistant? He kept cussing the Mounty, and Koch appeared, jumped on a nearby horse, and rode to the Mounty. After exchanging a few words, the Mounty nodded and saluted him, but kept loping toward the camera. Minutes dragged by.

Frustration escalated. They lowered the crane. Mervyn jumped off still cussing, and then pacing, and kicking dirt in frustration. The Mounty, by this time, had gotten closer when Mervyn angrily stomped toward him and screamed. Then Mervyn stopped dead in his tracks and fell apart laughing.

The Mounty was Jack Benny!

When Mervyn laughed, Jack, in his usual deadpan manner said, "WELL! I thought I'd never get here!"

We should have left that in the picture.

Jack had been working in Reno, and he and Howard Koch set up the whole thing. It cost MGM thousands of dollars, but it was worth it. From that time on, the atmosphere on location was a merry one.

I didn't sing with Ann Blyth, but she was a delightful cutie and sang beautifully. Fernando Lamas was Fernando, and he sang very well. Bert Lahr was Bert Lahr, and he and Marjorie Main were hilarious together. I watched their number, and he was very funny. Bert couldn't stand her. While Marjorie Main was a talented lady, there was something very strange about her, and that drove Bert up the wall.

Helen and I had moved into a beautiful Paul Williams home on Coldwater Canyon and Heather Road by this time. It happened to be a home that Bert

Lahr originally built. Bert wanted to have a look at it. I told him that the grass was lovely around all the avocado trees. He said he never had grass like we had.

I jokingly said, "Well, we do, and you can't see it."

* * *

The motion picture magazines were always after me to take pictures of my family, and I always turned them down.

My brother, Bill, spent half his life in prison for passing bad checks. He committed crimes against not only our mother, but other innocent people, as well. After I became a movie star, I gave him a truck and told him to go to work. He took off across country and wrote bad checks all the way. We'd been estranged for a long time when he died. I didn't want to have pictures of my family in any movie magazines.

I told Howard Strickling about it, and he protected me. He never explained the real reason to the magazines. He simply told them, "We're going in a different direction with Howard's publicity."

It was remarkable to have a man like that you could trust. He was one of the most respected and loved men in the motion picture industry and a great friend.

29

Sobbin' Women and Quittin' Smokin'

Louis Calhern was on the set of *Asphalt Jungle* doing a scene with Marilyn Monroe one afternoon when I stopped by to visit. She rushed to me and gave me a big kiss. Calhern said, "She never kissed me like that in my scenes with her."

"Eat your heart out, Big Nose. We're OLD friends from way back."

Marilyn and I agreed to meet at her place after shooting where we resumed our passionate affair then and for quite a while thereafter. She was so lovely, and we couldn't stop. I knew we had to someday, but God, what a beautiful woman. . . .

★ ★ ★

Jack Cummings was right about *Sobbin' Women*, later called *Seven Brides for Seven Brothers*. With a great score by Gene de Paul, those special lyrics of Johnny Mercer, and a great script by Albert Hackett and Frances Goodrich, how could we miss? Unfortunately, the studio disagreed. Someone decided to make *Brigadoon* a dance picture and put all the big money into it, which, at one time, Kathryn Grayson and I were to have.

It just so happened that our movie had one of the greatest choreographers, Michael Kidd. We did *Seven Brides* on the cheap, Stanley Donen directed, and George Folsey, an old golfing partner of mine, became the cinematographer. He made the Ansco film look like a Grandma Moses painting. We filmed the movie in thirty-four days.

The cast was magnificent, and the chemistry irresistible. Jack Cummings had his stamp on the whole picture. Jane Powell, as Milly, was perfect, and I loved working with her. She was cute and persnickety and a multitalented pro. As I said in my concerts, "That's like finding an Oreo cookie in your lunch box."

Jeff Richards, played the big, tough, good-looking, second brother. The other brothers, Marc Platt, Matt Mattox, Tommy Rall, Jacques d'Amboise, and Russ Tamblyn, all had individual personalities and were exceptional actors and singers. For one thing, they were all straight. Where do you find premiere dancers like that who can dance, sing, and act?

The girls, Julie Newmar, Ruta Lee, Virginia Gibson, Nancy Kilgas, Norma Doggett, and Betty Carr, were beautiful and talented.

It truly was one big happy family. By this time in my career, if I didn't like something, I spoke out. There were two things I didn't like. One, I didn't want to reprise, "When You're in Love" after Milly sang it. I thought it'd be wrong for Adam to sing it then. I didn't think Adam knew what love was all about. He was just a horny young man. I also didn't want to sing a soliloquy up in the winter cabin. It was too much like the soliloquy from *Carousel*.

Hackett and Goodrich walked off the picture, and Dorothy Kingsley took charge. I'm sorry about the original script writers walking away, but I think I was right, and Jack Cummings agreed with me. I guess people thought I was still an inexperienced singer-actor when I entered that picture, and maybe my head was getting a little big. But when I entered this business, I wasn't stupid, I was just inexperienced. I learned my craft quickly, and from then on, I'd speak up if I had something to say.

Dorothy Kingsley wrote a nice scene for Gideon and Adam. I think it fit the picture like a glove. The big brother helping the little brother. I didn't know Milly was going to sneak in on the scene and get hurt. I never recorded the soliloquy. I hated losing it because I liked it, but it just didn't fit.

I walked in one day on the barn set, and Michael Kidd said, "Hey! You want to see 'Sobbin' Women'?"

He called all the brothers together, and he sang my part. It was a fabulous number. I said, "Don't change a damn thing. It's great." All the work Michael did in the picture was incredible.

We worked and rehearsed with Saul Chaplin. The night before we recorded "When You're in Love," Saul was driving home and listening to his car radio when he heard another song that started off with the same four notes as "When You're in Love." He called Jack Cummings about it, and Jack called Johnny Mercer and Gene de Paul. They were concerned about plagiarism and changed the notes.

I felt the other four notes were more romantic and sang wonderfully, but we had to change them. I said to Jack one day during the filming, "Jack, if this picture isn't a big hit, I give up. It's such fun to do."

By gum, we were right. The *New York Times* called it one of the top ten best films of 1954.

Stanley Donen did a good job directing *Seven Brides*, but the real hero and brains behind it was Jack Cummings. I wrote three letters to the Academy and asked them to consider the work Jack had done throughout the years, but I never heard from them. Jack was L. B. Mayer's nephew, and I guess he couldn't live it down. I still think he deserved a Lifetime Achievement Award. Jack was a wonderful friend.

Jane Powell was going through a bad time over her romance with Gene Nelson, who was filming at Warner Brothers. We were rehearsing with Saul Chaplin on "When You're in Love" when Jane started crying. We stopped and had her lay down. I knelt down beside her. Saul excused himself, and I said, "I know what you are going through, Jane, and it will get better. You're home now at MGM, and we are all on your side. It's a hard business, and we all understand. If you need help, just holler. You have a rest, and go home. We'll be here tomorrow, and it's a new day, and we all love you."

Russ Tamblyn as Gideon was undeniably the most effective Pontipee. Wherever he was, you couldn't take your eyes off him. His dancing and acting was electrifying. The old saying, "Stay away from kids and animals" was true.

He was the runt of a bunch of rough and tough characters, but you couldn't deny him. I loved working with him. He was young, fearless, and inquisitive. Those characteristics bit him right on the nose.

We had a group of stunt men who were fearless and full of the Old Nick. One of them, Charlie Horvath, who had a head like a lion, was big and tough at around 6 feet 2 inches and 240 pounds.

We had set up a little stunt for Rusty, that's what we called Tamblyn. We sat Charlie in a canvas chair, his feet propped up on a box, his hat pulled down over his eyes, and pretending to be asleep.

I told Rusty, "If you want to see a funny dance, give Charlie a hotfoot. He does the craziest dance you'll ever see."

I gave him a box of matches, and Rusty took the bait. He waited a couple of minutes, then put a couple of matches in the sole of Charlie's shoe, and lit the match to the shoe.

Charlie pushed his hat back and said, "You little son of a bitch, you're trying to give me a hotfoot." He flew out of that chair like a wild buffalo.

Rusty took off with Charlie right after him. Charlie had been a fullback for Brown University and could run like a deer. He chased Rusty all around the set until Rusty hit an exit door and escaped. We, of course, roared with laughter and cheered for Rusty. They didn't find him for an hour. He was scared shitless and avoided Charlie, who for days would simply leer at Rusty, and he'd take off.

The brothers performed all their own stunts and fight sequences in the barn-dance and barn-raising scenes. The stunt men were on the alert for any punches that were misdirected. Working with actors who'd never done a fight sequence before could be dangerous, as I had proved in *Three Guys Named Mike.*

We all hated to see the picture come to an end. My salary for the thirty-four days on the picture was $8,500, and this was charging double on the books. However, when the picture premiered, it was a sensational hit. They raised my salary and signed me to another seven-year contract.

30

On Tour in Vegas and England

★ ★ ★ ★ ★

Paul Small, my new agent and Dore Schary's brother-in-law, was a big braggadocio with a warm sense of humor and good connections. I felt he was on my side. He arranged a nice raise for me and my first shot at nightclubs, the first of which was for the "Boys" at the Last Frontier in Las Vegas while I finished *Seven Brides*.

I smoked heavily at that time and thought about my stint in Vegas: two shows a night, three shows on Saturday and Sunday. My voice got husky toward the end of each day. "I can't do Vegas and smoke," I thought.

One night after dinner, I quit cold turkey. I went to bed, awoke the following morning and ate breakfast, drove to the studio, and worked on *Seven Brides* all day without a cigarette. I was a little snappy and wacky, but I made it through the first twenty-four hours. Oh sure, I'd chew gum until it fell apart in my mouth, and I sat in makeup for about an hour and a half for the beard and everything, but I did it.

After I quit smoking, I sneezed for a year, except on stage. I never sneezed onstage. I'd come off and made a sneezing sound. A true actor—never messed up onstage. I didn't smoke again until three years later. When I became hooked that time, it was tougher.

We hired a writer named Herb Baker to create the act for me. Two weeks before opening, he gave it to me. I read it that night and called him. "Herbie, this isn't me. I think you're a good writer, but this isn't me." I paid him off and let him go. We parted good friends.

I contacted Alex Romero, who had worked with me on *Kiss Me Kate*, and he created an act around my body of work at MGM. The MGM staff built a special stool and a complete dressing table that I could roll onstage. I'd sit there and in front of the audience, turn myself into Petruchio and sing "Where's the Life That Late I Led?"

I hired a young singer, Angel Catalano, to sing duets with me.

Two days before the Vegas opening, we booked the Ciro Night Club on Sunset Boulevard for an afternoon run-through. Lou Calhern and his wife, Slats; Paul Small, who was nervous as a cat; Eddie Traubner, my CPA; Sammy Cahn; Herman Hover, who owned Ciro's; and his assistant and bouncer, George Slaughter attended and loved the act.

We opened in Vegas to good reviews. The only problem I had resulted from my not smoking. The desert wind, sand, and dust made me sneeze constantly. I guess my clean sinuses couldn't take the pollution.

★ ★ ★

In late October 1954, Grade Agency sent me to England to tour in *Variety* for six weeks with that show. We opened in Glasgow at the Empire Theater. I had grown up with a lot of Scottish people in Illinois and decided to close the show with "Annie Laurie." I knew the first chorus and hurriedly learned the second and third.

On opening night in Glasgow, the show went fine, and when I returned to the stage for "Annie Laurie," I sang the first chorus. No problem. I almost missed the words for the second chorus, but remembered them just in time. Came time for the third chorus, no words appeared in my memory bank. I said, "I'm sorry, ladies and gentlemen, I've forgotten the words."

The whole audience stood, gave me a lead in, and sang with me to the end. What a thrill! I was scared to death it might happen to me again, but it never did.

If you were a success in Glasgow, the audience would go out in the street and stop all traffic until you stood at a window on the third floor backstage and sang to them. They told me I'd have to do it. I stuck my head out that window and couldn't believe the size of the crowd. Streetcar bells clanged, and automobile horns honked. Finally they quieted down and a voice yelled, "Sing 'The Black Hills of Dakota,' Howard."

I hadn't sung that song since I did it with Doris in *Calamity Jane*. But the words stayed, and I sang it. What a night.

We played Liverpool, Manchester, Birmingham, Edinburgh, and Newcastle. They invited me to do a Royal Command at the Palladium in London. I hopped a sleeper train to London, packed in at the Savoy Hotel, and at about 2:00 A.M., woke up with a high fever, aching all over. I called Pearl, my publicist, and she called a doctor who diagnosed me with a flu bug. He gave me several shots, but I couldn't hold anything in my stomach. I drank tea and held it as long as I could and then upchucked.

I told Pearl, "There's no way I can do the Royal Command tonight."

She told me I had to do seven minutes. We arrived at the Palladium with her tea. Gratefully, they excused me from rehearsal, but I couldn't hold anything down. When my time came, I carried my cup of tea in one hand and my bucket for upchucking in the other and followed Norman Wisdom, a tiny little guy that you could not deny. He is the nicest, funniest, cutest little man I have ever known and the most incredible comedian.

He stood in the wings, and I walked up near him. He couldn't see me for the lights. He took out a jar of Vaseline and opened it, put his finger in the jar and put a glob of Vaseline in his mouth and rubbed into his gums and teeth, like he was brushing them. Well, I threw up in the bucket and wiped my face and said, "Norman, what the hell are you doing?"

He said, "Well, old boy, I put this on my teeth because my mouth gets so dry when I'm nervous that my lips get stuck on my teeth when I smile and won't let go. Then I have to walk around looking like a bloody idiot. I put Vaseline on my gums, and it gets my saliva running, and I'm all right. I later told Judy Garland about it, and she spread the good word. It really works."

I did my seven minutes, left the stage, and upchucked. Then I stood in line deathly ill for thirty minutes to meet the royal family. The Queen Mum didn't speak. We knew the protocol and followed them to a "T."

Afterward, I took off for the Savoy with Pearl, the upchuck bucket, and tea for two.

Its Kismet

★   ★   ★   ★   ★

In late November 1954, I flew to New York to meet Helen at the Sherry Netherlands Hotel. We shopped for Christmas and returned to California. She told me I was to be a father again.

On June 3, 1955, Helen blessed me with a son. I was so thrilled. On the spot, I named him Gunnar Louis Keel, after my lifelong friend, Louis Calhern.

* * *

I saw *Kismet* opening night in Los Angeles, starring Alfred Drake. I had followed him in *Oklahoma* on the stage and *Kiss Me Kate* on screen, but had never seen him perform and wasn't disappointed. The show was a bit rough, but showed great promise.

After six months on the road, it opened on Broadway at the Ziegfeld Theater, and while the critics weren't too kind, fortunately, there was a newspaper strike, and no one read the notices. The actors publicized the show on television, and the show became a huge box-office hit.

MGM had the rights to film *Kismet*. Arthur Freed decided I should go to New York and see it. I loved it the second time, too. The cast came together with marvelous singing and acting.

Doretta Morrow's voice had a beautiful rich quality, and she was stunning in the part. Joan Diener! What can I say about this blonde bombshell? She had a wild, exciting voice and was all-out sexy in the part. One of the Ababoos lost her bra during a dance scene, and that spiced the show up a bit, too.

I went backstage and up three floors to see Alfred Drake. His dresser invited me into the dressing room and asked me to wait.

Alfred said, "Harry, my boy, have you been watching?"

"Yes I have! And what's good, I'll take with me and what's not I'll leave with you." We became very good friends and through the years have shared many laughs.

★ ★ ★

Upon my return to MGM, Andre Previn conducted, and we rehearsed with Bobby Tucker and Jeff Alexander. Our first recording was "Olive Tree" that, onstage, was sung to Omar the Poet, and later changed in the film and sung to Marsinah, my daughter.

Andre was extremely professional, and after our first take, Vincente Minnelli, the film's director, said ecstatically, "Great Howard, just GREAT!"

I was naturally pleased at his reaction and thought it'd be exciting working with Vincente. All my early training had been in serious music. I'd never ever thought of doing musicals. Here was *Kismet* with gorgeous music by Aleksandr Borodin and the brilliant lyrics by Bob Wright and Chet Forrest. I absolutely fell in love with it.

Ann Blyth, who was amazing as Marsinah, sang the score beautifully with great feeling. Dolores Gray sang and performed Lalume with that wonderfully lush voice rich with sex appeal. Vic Damone sang with great delicacy, but needed help with his acting.

The Caliph is not the easiest part in the world. The story of *Kismet* is farcical and I believed, in many places, should be played that way. I worked on "Gesticulate" four hours a day for two weeks with Jack Cole and Jeff Alexander and a drummer. It's the hardest performance song I ever attempted. When Jack Cole did it for me the first time, I fell apart. He was hilariously funny, sexy, and dirty. The tempos and the Asian's gestures were right down his alley. In two or three days of working on "Gesticulate," there wasn't a bone or muscle in my body that didn't ache. The coordination of singing and doing the gesticulation took complete concentration.

After two weeks of rehearsal, I said, "Jack, I'm having difficulty in two places getting my breath, and if I can take out two gesticulations, it'll help me to breathe."

He said, "Let me see it."

I showed it to him. He said, "FINE" and walked off and never spoke to me again. When we recorded the number, he just sat in a corner sulking, offering not one word of advice.

By this time in my career, I had a hide like a rhinoceros, so he didn't bother me at all.

To show the difference in artists, Andre and I were having problems with tempos. After three attempts, I went to him and said, "Andre, I'm getting tired vocally. Jeff and I have been on this number for two weeks, and he knows me like a book. Would you mind giving Jeff the baton on this next take and see if we can get one?"

He said, "Hell no. Why didn't I think about that myself?" He talked to the orchestra, gave the baton to Jeff, and we got it the next take. It was still too fast, but I was so worked up with adrenaline, I did not notice it until I started working to the recording.

I didn't get to know Minnelli until we started working on the set. I heard that we had lost Cyd Charisse and then Robert Morley, and he was upset. Still, I didn't expect what happened next. Right off the bat, he cut dialogue that I thought was humorous, and when I approached him about it, he just threw up his hands and said, "There's no humor here, and it's out."

I said, "Vincente, there is humor, and I'd like a chance to find it. So please help me."

He sat and pouted. I wanted to play Haji as the bad poet who doesn't know it, playing it overly sensitive and fey. But that idea went right out the window. We fought about dialogue constantly, especially the scene on the mosque steps in the beginning of the picture.

While this little tirade was going on, I looked down at one of the beggars during rehearsal and saw these great big eyes looking up at me, and I said, "You are the most beautiful-looking beggar that I've ever seen."

He said, "Thank you, but Mr. Minnelli doesn't think so and is on my ass on everything I do. Would you please help me?"

I told him, "Just ignore the son of a bitch, and do what you think best. He has it in for this picture."

The beggar was Aaron Spelling, during his early acting days in films. Aaron is one of the most successful producers in television today. One of the camel boys, Ross Bagdasarian, would become a great songwriter, composing "Come On a My House," among others. Jamie Farr, later famous in "M*A*S*H," played the fruit merchant I tried to strangle with my foot. What a bevy of undiscovered talent.

Poor Vic Damone received most of the brunt of Minnelli's wrath. Vincente was terrible to Vic. Instead of trying to help him, Minnelli berated him at every opportunity and in front of everyone. I went to Vic and said, "Vic, you don't have to take this shit from him. The next time he does it, just say Mr. Minnelli, don't talk to me like that. Just tell me what you want me to do, and I'll try to do it. But don't talk to me like that."

Vic wouldn't do it.

One day, they were filming "Stranger in Paradise" on this enormous ornate set, which was MGM's largest set at that time. Vic was singing the song beautifully. As he strolled by the bushes in the garden, something caught Minnelli's eye.

Minnelli, sitting on a boom high above the stage, pursed his lips, and hollered, "GODDAMMIT! What's going on back there? Who the hell is back there? Where's the peacock?"

Now, this guy in charge of the tethered peacock was a bit of a drinker and always about half in the bag. He popped up from behind the bushes and responded, "I'm sorry, Mr. Minnelli. I missed. I missed. I'll try again."

I went around the back side of the set and asked, "What the hell's going on?"

He said, "Well, you know, we got this peacock. And I've got this long stick, and I gotta go through these bushes, and when I goose the peacock, he goes, 'blah-h-h' and spreads his feathers."

You had to hit the peacock right in the center of the butt, and the stick was so long, about six feet, that you couldn't weave it through the bushes and hit the spot every time. This also assumed that the peacock would stand still, and no one could guarantee that, either. Now a peacock will only fan its feathers when it wants to or when it's goosed—in the right spot. Not surprisingly, it was many takes later before the peacock cooperated.

If you look at that scene very closely, when the peacock jumps a bit and fans his feathers, the trainer is hiding in the nearby bushes, and the bushes move. I'm never able to see the NBC peacock logo without thinking of that story.

Where they found Sebastian Cabot, I don't know, but he was all wrong, didn't have a clue how to play the part, and Minnelli didn't help him or anyone. Cabot looked the part, but played him like a pompous bore. The only thing that interested him was, "When's my next closeup?"

I invited him to my home for lunch one Sunday. He and his wife came, and Helen fixed a lovely luncheon with nice wine. He sat down, heaped his plate like it was his last supper, then asked, "Is that all there is?"

I jokingly replied, "For your share, yes."

In his corpulent way, he said, "Well I never. It's not enough."

In my Ole Hairbreadth Harry way, I said, "Sebastian,

175

there's a drive-in restaurant three blocks west of Beverly Drive on Wilshire Boulevard in Beverly Hills. Luncheon for you here is over, as far as you are concerned, and you'll not be asked back. I suggest that you get your ass out of here and dine elsewhere. Now piss off!"

After that incident, his scenes with me were practically through except for his drowning in the pool, and that would be more than pleasurable acting for me.

★ ★ ★

Shortly before the drowning scene started, Minnelli sat reviewing scenes for another film, *Lust for Life,* and I said to myself that enough was enough and went upstairs.

I told Arthur Freed, "If Minnelli is on the set tomorrow morning, I'm not on it. So pull whatever strings you have, and get someone else. I am not finishing this picture with Vincente."

Mervyn LeRoy completed the picture, not Stanley Donen as was publicized. *Kismet* was doomed from the start. Nothing planned fell into place.

During the days when you were under contract to a studio, you were never in on all the politics and manipulations before a picture starts. You were cast in a picture, and you did what you were told to do. But with a script and score like *Kismet*, you chomped at the bit to get started. I know I was eager, but the excitement didn't last long, and it became drudgery to play it.

I had one great line, "I'm a collector of women." Following that, Dolores Gray sang "I Envy a Life Totally Without Monotony" as she seduces me on a love seat while I look for the Wazir over my shoulder and say something, "Bewildered, but not bored." That was great fun. The whole film could have been the same if they had cared.

I hate performers who quit performing and producers and directors who quit doing their job. The Play is the thing. And when you have the Play and the cast and chemistry isn't there, you're in deep shit trouble. That's what happened to *Kismet*.

I understood Minnelli didn't want to do the picture in the first place, and when he lost two important actors and couldn't replace them, he lost interest and threw *Kismet* away.

Ninety-nine percent of direction is casting. Most directors don't know how to talk or handle actors and don't want to. Minnelli certainly didn't. No care was taken to bring the scenes together with closeups, etc. He just shot it as fast as he could to get rid of it. Worse, it seemed the studio let it happen.

The characters in the script were obvious, and any actor worth his salt could play them. *Kismet* took imagination and little in life to draw upon. That's why it took six months on the road to bring the play together. We didn't have that time.

I also think *Kismet* is not a critic's play. It's an audience's play. I played that role many times in the round and proscenium, and found myself having a great time with it. It took me a while to find the character, but I did. Too bad I didn't find it when I filmed it. *C'est la vie*. That's *Kismet*.

No Vestal Virgins

* ★ ★ ★ *

When I signed with MGM, I was so in awe of the place that I didn't question what they had in store for me. In my mind, it was the most powerful studio in the world with an exciting roster of stars like no other. Every time I walked into the commissary for lunch, I was starstruck.

To catch a glimpse of Clark Gable, Walter Pidgeon, Lionel Barrymore, Greer Garson, Ann Miller, June Allyson, Kathryn Grayson, Jane Powell, Katharine Hepburn, Robert Taylor, Spencer Tracy, Esther Williams, Red Skelton, Van Johnson, Keenan Wynn, Gene Kelly, Fred Astaire, Cyd Charisse, Ann Sothern, Betty Garrett, Van Heflin, Leon Ames, Ricardo Montalban, Mario Lanza, George Murphy, Edward Arnold, Reginald Owen, Ginger Rogers, J. Carrol Naish, and many others who had created breathtaking moments in motion picture history was incredible.

★ ★ ★

Films don't do farce very well, and that's what *Jupiter's Darling*, my next MGM film with Esther Williams, was about. It was filmed on MGM's back lot and on Catalina Island. Marge and Gower Champion did a brilliant dance with elephants. George Sanders was perfectly cast. He had a great baritone voice. Unfortunately, his songs were left on the cutting-room floor. Bill Demarest was another bit of excellent casting along with Richard Haydn, who was a hoot as the philosopher. And, of course my old buddy, George Sidney, directed.

Based on a play titled *Road to Rome*, it sounded more like a picture for Crosby and Hope. I suggested *Hannibal's Darling*. They tossed around that title and *Jupiter's Darling* and they selected the latter.

Esther played a vestal virgin who must come from the gods. No matter the plot line, I think it was the best picture we did together. She was damned good in the part, and we had a ball. Her swimming scenes were beautiful and daring, and she looked terrific and sexy. I didn't feel like a brother in this film. She turned me on. She was one gorgeous lady. It was hard to resist a goddess like that.

Her husband, radio singer Ben Gage, and I were friends. I looked at myself in the mirror and said, "You may look, but do not touch."

We had one scene one hot, late afternoon when I showed her my elephants and reviewed my troops. I had Esther on one arm and a pet leopard, on a chain, on the other. We strolled along and met my master sergeant, Bill Demarest.

Esther and I stopped, and I introduced them. The leopard became bored and laid down. We lost the sun and the light, and the day's shooting ended.

The next morning, I waited to be called in to do the shot when I heard strange noises coming from the bushes near the scene and went to investigate. The leopard wasn't in a very good mood, and the trainer had tried to settle him down by punching him in the nose, saying, "Stay! Stay!"

When shooting began, Esther entered the scene, and we attempted to get the staying-pissed-off leopard to stand up and walk out of the scene. No matter how much I jerked or pulled, he wouldn't get up.

George suggested, "Why don't you pick him up and carry him out of the scene?"

I said, "You want me to pick up that angry carnivore and carry him out of the scene?"

George sat there with that innocent look on his face and nodded.

I said, "Look, get him settled down a little bit, and I'll give you one try."

The trainer petted him for a while, and the cat seemed in a little better mood. Esther entered the scene, and they rolled the cameras.

I reached down and picked up the pissed-off pussycat. He took a shot at me with one of his paws and bit into my shoulder. I threw him about thirty feet through the air, and he took off. That was the end of the pussycat and the end of the scene. Luckily, I had a suit of leather armor on, and he didn't get to the bones in my shoulder. Thank God for Walter Plunkett's costumes.

There was another terrific scene between me and George Sanders. As Hannibal, I sat atop an elephant as my army attacked Rome. The Romans faced a hopeless situation. George stood on a wall that surrounded the city and tried to persuade Hannibal not to raze Rome. George was surrounded by a bevy of vestal virgins that included the top virgin, Esther. As dictator of Rome, he's all dressed in his glorious wardrobe with a band of golden leaves and a crown around his head.

I stood on a ladder off-camera to do the scene with him. He said, "What do you want to spare Rome?"

I said, "I want that woman!" and pointed to Esther, who was his favorite vestal virgin.

He said, "But we have many other lovely women."

Well, that scene hit my funny bone, and I began to giggle. George climbed off the wall, walked around the cameras toward me, and said seriously, "What the fuck are you laughing at?"

I said, "In that getup, George, you look like an old whorehouse madam trying to sell her wares."

He exploded laughing, and I did, too. Well, when two actors get the giggles about something—good luck filming. He couldn't keep a straight face to save his ever-loving ass. They sent me home, and he spoke the lines without me. Every time we saw each other after that, we got the giggles. It was a funny scene, particularly the way he played it. George was a great character actor with true star status.

★ ★ ★

All in all, I think the part of Hannibal was my best performance at MGM. There was a story that I became seasick riding elephants. Not so. I almost broke my ass several times trying not to fall off. Old Babe was as gentle as a lamb, but she stood about 11 feet tall, and when you put a houdah (saddle) on her and on top of that a

181

throne, you're on a platform around 15 feet off the ground.

Then to stand on the throne and sing a song called "Hannibal Mighty Hannibal" with a straight face is hard enough, but to keep your balance and not fall on your ass is even harder. An elephant's pace is unlike that of a horse. When he or she is walking, there's no rhythm to which you can adjust. To sing, stand, and look heroic on top of that throne that's rocking around, and getting a good take is a miracle, particularly if you're prone to acrophobia.

Another little scene where I had to drive a four-up with a chariot (four horses bound side-by-side with harnesses) was a fistful, too.

There was a scene at night with Esther and me. Hannibal, by this time is madly in love with Amytis, and sings a lovely song to her called "Don't Let This Night Get Away." Romans discover us, Hannibal whistles for his horses. They come running in and stop. I throw Esther into the chariot, fight off the Romans, hop into the chariot, and drive away. The team worked well in rehearsal. They bring them in on fine steel wires that you cannot see, and a wrangler stops them when their heads are out of scene, and the scene continues. We film the take, and the horses come in. But they stop too soon, and the wrangler can't reach in and stop them because he'd be seen in the camera shot.

I toss Esther in the chariot and start to fight off the Romans when the horses start running. I yell, "Cut!"

I'm standing there watching the wranglers trying to stop the horses, my right leg goes up in the air, and I'm being dragged across the stage by the horses.

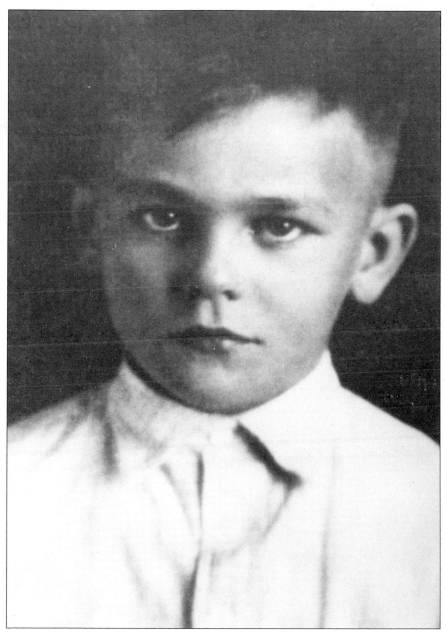

Howard in his youth.

Howard's first wife, Rosemary Randall.

With his second wife, Helen Anderson, and
their three children, Kirstine, Kaija, and
Gunnar.

Howard with his third wife, Judy
Magamoll, and their daughter, Leslie.

As Curly in *Oklahoma* with Betty Jane Watson as Laurie (1943).

As Frank Butler in Berlin's *Annie Get Your Gun* with Calhern and Hutton as Annie (1950).

(*L to R*): Betty Hutton, Howard, Louis Calhern, Benay Venuta, J. Carrol Naish, Keenan Wynn, and Edward Arnold in a company photograph.

With Ann Miller and
Kathryn Grayson in
Lovely to Look At by
Jerome Kern (1952).

With Esther Williams
in *Pagan Love Song*
(1950).

(*Right*) *Left to right:* Howard's mother, Grace Keel; Kathryn Grayson; Howard; and his grandmother, Mathilda Osterkamp on the set of *Show Boat*. (*Below*) Howard as Gaylord Ravenal with Ava Gardner as Julie in the vastly popular third film version of *Show Boat* (1951).

With Dorothy McGuire and Fred MacMurray in the western comedy
Callaway Went Thataway (1951).

With Doris Day in *Calamity Jane* (1953).

(*Right*) On the set: director George Sidney, Cole Porter, Kathryn Grayson, Ann Miller, and producer Jack Cummings surrounding Howard. (*Below*) Kathryn Grayson and Howard in the film version of Cole Porter's hit musical *Kiss Me Kate* (1953).

Howard with Jane Powell in *Seven Brides for Seven Brothers* (1954).

Howard as Roosevelt with Michelle Meyers as Eleanor in *Sunrise at Campobello*.

Howard as King Arthur in *Camelot*.

As Don Quixote in *The Man of La Mancha* with Louis Criscuolo as Sancho Panza.

At the annual dinner of the News Photographers Association at the White House. (*L to R*) Joe E. Brown, Ray Bolger, Howard, Connie Russell, President Eisenhower, Lena Horne, and Liberace (1955).

Between Dolores Gray and Ann Blyth in the musical film *Kismet* (1955).

Patron
HER MAJESTY THE QUEEN

We the undersigned,
tender our sincere congratulations to

Howard Keel

on being one of the Representative Artistes
selected to appear at the
Royal Command Variety Performance

held at the

LONDON PALLADIUM

on November 1st, 1954

The Performance being in aid of the
VARIETY ARTISTES' BENEVOLENT FUND and INSTITUTION
for INDIGENT VARIETY and CIRCUS ARTISTES

A certificate honoring Howard for his Royal Command performance.

Chatting with the Queen Mum in London. Ethel Merman is between them.

With his wife Judy Keel and Princess Margaret—Sylvia Budd can be seen in the background.

(*Above*) As Clayton Farlow in the eleven-year TV run of "Dallas." (*Right*) With Barbara Bel Geddes as Miss Ellie in "Dallas."

Eventually a wrangler made them stop and broke his leg doing it. I looked at my leg. One of the wires had twisted around my ankle and had just cut through the strap of my sandal with a slight cut into my ankle. If the wrangler hadn't stopped them, it would've cut my foot off.

A few underwater stunts off Catalina Island were also very dangerous. Fortunately for me, I played Hannibal, who couldn't swim.

Listen, I Know Airplanes, I Used to Build Them

★ ★ ★ ★ ★

In 1952, Walter Pidgeon and George Murphy had asked me if I'd run for the board of the Screen Actors Guild. I felt flattered that two men of such stature would ask, and I said I'd be honored to run. I was voted in. Once in a while when I thought other board members weren't making any sense, I made a couple of suggestions that they picked up on.

By 1955, the guild made me first vice president to Leon Ames. During 1956 and 1957, Leon wasn't in good health, and I became acting president. In 1958, I became president. During those last three years, I worked very closely with Jack Dales, a brilliant man and our executive secretary. All those years, we worked with all the guilds on the SAG-AFTRA (American Federation of Television and Radio Artists) merger, which I was against and still am. More importantly, we laid the groundwork for what is now our Pension and Health fund.

When the negotiations for the sale of the pictures

made previous to 1958 became the issue, I had to be in New York for a new musical, *Saratoga*, that appeared to be a big hit.

These negotiations were very important because the amount of money involved in the sale would be used as the economical basis for the SAG Producers Health and Welfare Plan. The members of the guild approached me. "Howard, you're going to be in New York during these negotiations, and we will need someone strong and informed to stand with us. Would you stand aside for Ronald Reagan to be president and sit in on the meetings here in Hollywood?"

I said, "Hell, yes."

He was the best president we ever had—in so many ways.

As it worked out, *Saratoga* flopped, and I returned as first vice president and sat in on the negotiations anyway. It was a tough battle, and we settled for what we thought was a good price. We received a lot of flak from actors, both established and newcomers, but there was simply no way to distribute the money to actors in the pictures.

Many actors had died, and their estates were tied up in courts. There were no computers back then to keep track of the productions. The accounting rules always favored the studio, not the talent, anyway. Like in *Seven Brides*, my salary looked like it was $8,500. Actually it was $4,250 because they added it twice to the salary line.

The capital that we received formed our Pension and Health Fund that's now the best in the world.

I loved being on the board of SAG, and I went a lot further than I expected. Then I resigned. I was having some family problems as I had a tête-à-tête with a woman high up in both Equity and AFTRA, and I didn't want that to get out and affect our decisions on the merger.

Charlton Heston sat on the board, and I thought he'd be a good man to take my place. I was right. He later became president and a damned good one.

★ ★ ★

I saved Jack Dales's (who invented the word "residuals") life for the guild and my own, as well. We were on-board an American Airlines 707 taxiing out for takeoff from what is now Kennedy Airport in New York. At that time, first class took up the front of the fuselage to the trailing edge of the wing, and I always tried to get a seat at the rear. It was a softer ride.

Jack and I sat in those seats with me at the window. I was watching them actuate the various flaps on the wings. It was very exciting in those days to fly by jet. I had worked at Douglas and North American Aviation for eight years and loved flying.

Suddenly, I realized liquid was leaking out of one of the actuating arms on one of the flaps. That was curious because I'd never seen that happen before on any of my flights. I watched it for a short time then called for the stewardess.

When I told her what I was seeing, she said, "Oh, that's just water from the air conditioning," and walked off.

Well that didn't sit very well with Ole Hairbreadth Harry, and I told Jack so, then punched the call button again.

Another stewardess walked down the aisle to my

seat. I said, "I'm not an alarmist or a nut. But if I don't get an answer about the liquid that's leaking out of the wing of this airplane, I'm getting off. I want an answer now!"

Jack thought I was crazy.

The stewardess walked toward the cockpit while we waited. A flight engineer peeked out the door at me, disappeared into the cockpit for a moment, then walked up to me, and said, "Mr. Keel, you're right. We've lost about half of our hydraulic fluid already. Thank you. We're turning around and going back to the gate."

Jack and I left the airplane, went up to the Admiral's Club, and had a few martinis. We might have taken off, but getting down would have been rude. I still fly American. It's a great airline.

It's Show Business When My Kids Get in the Act

★ ★ ★ ★ ★

In 1957, producers Ben Segal and Buster Bonoff asked me to do a week of *Carousel*. I would rehearse in Wallingford, Connecticut, and play a week in Warwick, Rhode Island, then repeat the performance at the New York City Center Light Opera. If I agreed to City Center, I'd have to do *Carousel* in Warwick at night and rehearse in New York for City Center during the day. I must have been out of my mind to try to do both.

They wanted Janet Blair to play Julie. I'd seen her do *South Pacific*, and I didn't like her version of Nellie Forbush. Since I had cast approval, I said, "No."

Jean Dalrymple had already cast her, so we locked horns. I said, "All right, get Janet here, and let's do the bench scene. Maybe I'm wrong."

About halfway through the scene, Janet said, "Am I being auditioned here for you?"

She became extremely upset when I replied in the affirmative. I told her MGM put me through many auditions, and I wanted to see what she would do with the part. I told her Jean cast her without asking me, and I wanted to see her do the bench scene.

I told her, "I must say after hearing you, I think you'll be wonderful."

She flew off the handle, told me she'd never been so insulted in her life, and walked out. I was surprised she did so well. I realized I blew it by being so honest with her. She managed to get in her licks with the press in New York, and Sid Skolsky called me and said, "What have you got to say, Howard?"

I said, "Nothing. I think she could have been wonderful in the part with John Fernley's direction. Julie is not an easy part, and I just wanted to see her do the bench scene. She was good. Jan Clayton was something special in the part, and Janet showed she had something special in it, too."

I was never angry or upset with Janet. Dalrymple was the one I battled with. It's too bad, but that's show business.

They cast Barbara Cook. She was lovely and sang it beautifully. The traipsing back and forth to Warwick, Rhode Island, bested me, and I caught a heavy cold that developed into bronchitis. I didn't have the voice I wanted to sing the role, and we closed the show.

* * *

The Theater Guild asked me to do *Sunrise at Campobello*. I had read an earlier version of it and told Dore Schary that it was a story about Louis Howe, the executive secretary to Roosevelt, not a story about Roosevelt. I asked him to let me have a script to read on my way home to California.

189

I boarded the plane, and it was packed. I was still sick with bronchitis and sat beside a chatty gentleman, so I didn't get a chance to read it. Thirteen hours later, we landed in Los Angeles, and I was ushered home to a big party that lasted until 3:00 A.M.

The next morning, I was so sick, they hauled me off to St. Johns Hospital with double pneumonia. I grabbed the script, but they put me in intensive care in an oxygen tent, and I couldn't read anything.

After a couple of days, they took the tent away, and I went through the script.

I called Dore immediately and said, "Dore, it's wonderful."

His reply was, "Howard, I'm sorry, but we're in negotiations with Ralph Bellamy."

"Well, what can I say, but the best of luck."

Show business, my ass. Timing! Timing! Timing!

That's the Fickle Finger of Fate. I often wondered why they never asked me about the national company of *Sunrise at Campobello*.

* * *

In 1959, *The Big Fisherman* came out of the blue. I had played golf with Frank Borzage, the man who would direct the picture. Buena Vista produced the movie, and they wanted John Wayne, but he was tied up. They called me in for a test. Producer Rowland Lee thought I'd be too sophisticated for the role.

I proved my versatility as an actor. I tested on a Wednesday, and we started shooting the following Monday in an area that's known as "the Cove" section of La Quinta, California. I hadn't been to the La Quinta

Resort and Hotel since my honeymoon in 1949, but things hadn't changed much. It was still a secluded area with a few adobe homes surrounded by a vast desert, beautiful mountain ranges, sagebrush, and date palm trees.

No expense was spared for the props. Magnificent Arabian sets rose from the Coachella Valley desert floor including tents, palaces for the Romans, a marketplace, hovels, and temples. Rare silks and brocades were flown to the site from Damascus. We had been filming there for about a week when a windstorm blew everything, the sets, everything to pieces.

The remainder of the film was shot at Rowland Lee's ranch in Simi Valley, California. It's the place where they made the first rockets.

My call in the studio was 3:30 A.M. for a normal shooting day. It was a tough picture. My makeup man was Lynn Reynolds, and he was a great one. Each day, it took three hours for the beard, wig, and nose piece. Lynn had a wild corny sense of humor, and we became good friends.

Howard Estabrook wrote the motion picture script, and they wanted it word perfect. Producer Rowland Lee used to direct his own pictures, and I was always between him and Frank Borzage. Lee never talked to me, but he was always on Borzage, who had the patience of Job. I loved Frank and went along with him. I think we were right. The picture had several distinguished actors, Susan Kohner, Herbert Lom, Alexander Scourby, Marian Seldes, Beulah Bondi, John Saxon, Martha Hyer, and Marianne Stewart.

But the script couldn't hold a candle to another religious epic. That year we were up against *Ben Hur*.

***

Floods of Fear became my first picture in England since *The Small Voice.* Sydney Box produced, and Charles Crichton wrote and directed. Anne Heywood, Cyril Cusack, Harry Corbett, and John Crawford were the principals. We filmed it in early spring of 1959.

All the flood scenes were filmed on one of the large stages at Pinewood Studios. The water had to be both dirty and cold, and it was. They couldn't heat it for fear it might get rancid. That was another tough picture. Anne Heywood never once protested about the water. Crichton, who had a great sense of humor, had directed some very funny pictures.

Cyril Cusack and I were good friends. We had a little contest over Anne. He was a real cutie, as well as a hell of an actor, but I won out.

One day, we finished shooting early, and Cyril and I went to the Irish Club for dinner. We sat at the bar having a drink when a man who was a member of Britain's Parliament walked in with a couple of other men. Their talk got under Cyril's skin. He started giving the member such a bad time that they asked us to leave the bar.

We left calmly, stopped by the dining room, and ordered dinner. By this time, we're feeling no pain. A couple of guys recognized me and wanted me to sing. Cyril was absolutely incensed and said, "How dare they ask you to sing?"

I agreed, and we got into a shouting match and were kicked out. How dare they?!

★ ★ ★

About halfway through the picture, I had to do a "Sunday Night at the Palladium." I tried to get out of it, but Lew and Leslie Grades were adamant that I perform.

They were very good British agents, and Lew later became a lord. I was very upset at the way I sang and told Leslie Grade. He assured me that I wasn't that bad and insisted that I listen to the tape. I did and couldn't believe it. He was right.

I'd been staying at the Dorchester when Buena Vista called me and said the Palladium was having a big opening in a couple of days and would I stay over and attend the opening. I asked them to pick up the cost of the suite and I'd do it. They declined, and I flew home. How could they be so cheap?

★ ★ ★

During our filming of *Floods of Fear*, *My Fair Lady* opened. It was the same night I opened in *Oklahoma* at the Royal Drury Lane ten years earlier. I arranged a seat. I finished shooting for the day and rushed to the Dorchester, cleaned up, and caught a cab. I rushed out of the cab and slid into my seat. A hand tapped me on the shoulder, and the usher said, "Mr. Keel, you forgot to pay your cab, and the man won't budge."

I apologized, gave the man twenty pounds, sat back, and enjoyed a great opening with the original cast. Although I guess I was the one responsible for the late curtain.

Drury Lane, one of the most beautiful theaters in the world, had been completely refurbished and stood in all its grandeur for the opening.

★ ★ ★

In 1960, I went to New York to start rehearsals for a summer stock company of *Sunrise at Campobello*. I had a fabulous cast. Michaele Myers played Eleanor, with Russell Collins as Howe; Nancy Cushman as Sarah Delano Roosevelt; Walter Peterson, an old friend from *Oklahoma* days; Vera Lockwood; and John Cecil Holm. Jean Barrere, one of the best directors I ever worked with, steered the cast and did a terrific job.

We opened in a tent in Latham, New York, and the show came together superbly. We played the Playhouse in the Park in Philadelphia in the round for two weeks. That season of *Sunrise* was pure joy.

I asked the publicist if Ernie Schier would come out, and he said, "Sure, but he'll probably stay for one act and cut out."

Ernie Schier was a Philadelphia critic who had ripped *Saratoga* apart. After a couple of weeks into *Saratoga*'s run in Philly, I was doing a publicity radio interview. The broadcaster asked me what I thought of Ernie Schier as a critic, and I said, "Not much."

The interviewer said, "He's a friend of mine."

To which I added, "Good luck." I then took off on Schier's reviews. I told him we needed constructive, not destructive, criticism. If he wanted to be a great, feared critic, he should move to New York.

I had to dress in the orchestra pit for the second act of *Sunrise*. When I came offstage at the end of the second act, the publicist told me, "Schier is still there, and he thinks you are wonderful."

In his July 12, 1960, review of *Sunrise*, Schier wrote, "Keel makes a superb F.D.R. Keel turns in a winning, modulated, and completely relaxed performance." He added, "It is an entertaining and moving evening." Schier also suggested we let bygones be bygones. I called and thanked him and told him I was pissed off about a lot of things that night on the radio, and he received the butt of it.

★ ★ ★

I packed up the family, and we toured New England for seven weeks, then went into rehearsals for *South Pacific* at Ben Segal's in Wallingford, Connecticut; Warwick, Rhode Island; and Framingham, Massachusetts. Gunnar played a great Jerome, and the beautiful Kaija played Liat. My kids were the best Tonkinese kids you ever saw. I later had to use Kirstine as another child to keep peace in the family.

The mosquitoes had a field day on Gunnar. On his exit in the second scene, he scratched his ass, and the audience went into hysterics. He never missed scratching his ass after that. Pure ham. He also discovered he could collect Coke bottles and get a dime for them. He made a couple of extra bucks each night.

The rest of the cast was great, too. Elizabeth Allan played Nellie to the hilt; Odette Myrtil was Bloody Mary; Cliff Norton played Billis; and Brandon Maggart was Stewpot.

Opening night, Ole Hairbreadth Harry had a go at the orchestra in Wallingford. We had to use union musicians from a little town called Medford, and they were the worst. I had experienced their performance once before doing one night of *Carousel*, and opening night was horrendous.

I made a little curtain speech. I thanked the audience

for their patience and then took off on the orchestra. I looked down at them and said. "Well, you haven't changed a bit. You are still the worst orchestra that I've ever worked with. How you can sit in the pit and stand to listen to each other? I don't know. As actors, if we were as bad as you are, we'd be booed off the stage. You evidently don't care or you would improve. Take your parts home with you tonight, and see if you can help yourself. Ladies and gentlemen of the audience, I apologize for this interruption, but it had to be done."

The entire audience stood and applauded.

I Direct a Second Unit and Almost Get a Guy Killed

★ ★ ★ ★ ★

I quit smoking again for about seven weeks. I went home and played golf for a while, then signed to do *Saratoga* in New York. I wasn't too happy with the score, but with Harold Arlen and Johnny Mercer, I felt things could be worked out during rehearsals. Boy was I in for a surprise. We went into rehearsals in New York, and *Saratoga* was put on its feet fast.

During rehearsals, I heard on the radio that Mario Lanza had died in Italy. I wasn't surprised. He had been under tremendous pressure. What he went through, no one could survive. I had many wonderful memories with Mario at MGM. To know him was to love him. But to watch what he went through to control his appetite and weight was both mind boggling and depressing.

Originally, the producers wanted Rock Hudson, but settled on me for a price. I also had cast approval for the starring role of Cleo who would play opposite me. I had seen Carol Lawrence opening night in *West Wide Story*, and she was amazing. We had a brief encounter. She would be my Cleo.

Opening night in Philadelphia was a dud. The critics ripped it to shreds, and we were left for two weeks with no one around. We didn't see Mort DeCosta, the show's director and producer, for weeks. Arlen became ill, and we never saw him again. Johnny Mercer wrote a couple of new songs and lyrics. We received the songs one afternoon, and Robert Fryer, the producer, wanted to try them out that night in the show. I said, "No. Give us a chance to learn them and then try them."

He called me unprofessional, blew his cork, and left. I never saw him again. That sat really well with me, but for once I held my temper, and we put the songs in the following night.

We opened on Broadway to lukewarm notices. The show ran for three months because of a large ticket pre-sellout, then closed. It was very depressing, and it took me a long while to get beyond that.

★ ★ ★

We filmed *Armored Command* in Munich during the winter of 1960. The cast consisted of Tina Louise, Earl Holliman, Burt Reynolds, Carleton Young, Warner Anderson, Marty Ingels, and Brandon Maggart. Byron Haskin directed, and Ron Alcorn wrote and produced.

We spent a couple of weeks in Munich, then moved up to a huge camp named Hohenfels near the Czechoslovakian border. Hohenfels had been a training ground for Hitler's tank corps. I stayed at the BOQ (Bachelor Officer Quarters) and met a lot of nice American officers in our tank corps. All the battle troops were Americans who simply changed uniforms to become German soldiers. We had perfect weather: cold and snowy. Even the big tanks experienced difficulty maneuvering the slick, treacherous roads.

I directed second units for two days and had a ball. This was my first time to direct in motion pictures. Until! I had a sergeant—I wish I could remember his name, a nice guy—and a bunch of GIs behind a stone wall with machine guns. I told the sergeant when I called "Action" to start firing at the street corner, and when the tank rounded the corner and advanced, for him to clear out. I told the tank commander to come barreling down the street and turn the corner and smash down the wall the machine-gunners stood behind.

Well, on "Action," the tank flew around that corner and threw mud and snow in all directions. The tank commander started for the wall, which was about fifteen yards away, smashed it down, and stopped. The sergeant on the machine gun froze and didn't get out as directed, and the right tread of the huge tank rolled down on top of him.

I yelled, "Cut" and ran to, but couldn't see the sergeant. I thought, "Holy God. I've killed a man."

We moved the tank away from the wall, and there was the sergeant on his back staring up at us in a state of shock. The Red Cross ambulance arrived, put the sergeant on a stretcher, and sped off for the hospital.

We realized there was nothing we could do to help him, so we shot around that scene. About an hour later, I saw a man walking down the road toward us. We stopped in our tracks, stunned. It was the sergeant, who was a little bruised and shaky, but no broken bones.

Evidently, the ground was soft with so much snow

and grass, and the tank stopped before the full weight was on him. It was like seeing a miracle. I was so relieved, I laughed and cried at the same time. That night, I threw a beer party for the entire crew.

We were there through Christmas, and I had struck up a friendship with a bartender in the BOQ. There were a couple of attractive girls who were specialists of some kind at the camp. We decided that on Christmas Eve, we'd drive to a little town called Schmitmulen near the Czech border to their tiny church and listen to the choir.

We were just closing the bar when a first lieutenant made wisecracks about the " . . . movie star here in the BOQ bar." He was pretty obnoxious and decided he'd join us. I was holding my own with him in a nice way. No one wanted him to butt in, and he got rough and called me a half-ass movie star and said he was leaving.

I decided to help him. I picked him up, threw him into a sofa across the room, and we left for church.

By 6:30 P.M., we crested the last hill. Darkness had fallen, but to look down upon that little town about a mile away, with all the twinkling Christmas lights, was breathtaking. It was one of those nights and scenes you can't stage, they just happen.

We had a great night, and after breakfast, I saw the bar sergeant, who told me, "Did you know the lieutenant pulled a knife and was going to come after you? I caught him at the door and called the MPs, and he's in the cooler. They'll probably break him."

I asked to talk with whomever was in charge to see if I could help the guy. I'd hate for that to happen. The colonel and I had a talk, and he told me, "The man was out of line, and to pull a knife was too much to overlook. We don't want officers in this army who can't control themselves. He will be stripped of his position and dishonorably discharged."

I felt miserable, but there was nothing I could do about it.

* * *

I left early the next morning for Munich and bumped into Jerome Courtland, who had been Polly Bergen's husband when Polly and I made *Fast Company*. He was acting and directing in Europe. Jerry was a tall, handsome, young man who kept in good shape and was an expert archer. I told him I'd be leaving in a couple of days, and he invited me to join him and see Bechtesgaden and Dachau.

What an eerie sensation to stand in the spot where that monster Hitler stood. In the main room, all the windows were gone, and we stared at the majestic Alps. Breathtaking.

Dachau was unbelievable, and I walked it twice to make sure I wasn't having a bad dream. To stand in those gas chambers and see the spigots that were supposed to be shower heads. To think that one human being could do that to another human being is beyond reasoning. I couldn't wait to get on an airplane and head home to liberty.

The following day, I flew to London around 9:00 P.M. on a DC-8 and exited while they refueled and cleaned the plane. Another plane, a 707 bound for Los Angeles, landed. I waited in the lounge and then was told my plane wouldn't be ready for a while. The 707, however, was ready for the turnaround flight. I was asked if I'd like to take it, but I said I'd wait for mine.

We had delay after delay, then they told me they couldn't take off from Heathrow after midnight in a DC-8 because it was too noisy. They put me up at the Savoy. I called home and tried to explain to Helen, but she didn't believe me. I got bombed and left the next morning hung over. I knew our marriage had crumbled beyond repair.

36

They Call Me Mr. Roberts

★ ★ ★ ★ ★

John Kenley called me about playing the leading role in *Mr. Roberts* in Warren, Ohio, with the Kenley Players.

We'd play one week in Warren and one week in Detroit. When I arrived, they were performing *Pajama Game* with Anne Jeffreys and a young baritone named Robert Goulet. I went to see it because Anne is married to my good friend, Robert Sterling. She was great, and Goulet, who had terrific pipes, sang beautifully. An actor-comedian named Jack Goode had me in stitches with his humor.

After the show, we went out, I had one drink and went home. Goulet had a new Corvette, and he and Jack Goode continued to celebrate. Evidently, Goulet was driving pretty crazily. The local constabulary pulled them over, tagged them, and put them in the slammer. They called me to bail them out.

The next day, we went into rehearsals for *Mr. Roberts*.

Jack Goode was the captain and an amazing actor named Hazen Gifford played the best Ensign Pulver I'd ever seen and that includes David Wayne and Jack Lemmon. David Doyle, who later gained fame as Bosley in TV's "Charlie's Angels" was Dowdy. It was a very good cast. Because of Jack Goode's size, he's 5 feet 4 inches to my 6 feet 4 inches, all scenes were blocked with me either sitting or Jack on top of the holes on deck. At the end of the show, I'd sing "Some Enchanted Evening" and leave the stage.

Jack Goode, who was a very good golfer and one-time amateur champion of Ohio, and I decided we'd play golf when we reached Detroit. I called my friend, Walter Burkemo, who won the PGA when it was match play and was then the professional at Franklin Hills Golf Club, and arranged a game on Monday. When we arrived in Detroit, we checked out the geodesic dome theater, grabbed our sticks, and went to play golf.

We played as a threesome, and after a few holes, Jack's back went out on him, forcing us to quit for the day. Walter said they had a great masseur at the club who'd fix that back in no time. We took a sauna, and this huge masseur, who'd been a Polish wrestler, said he was ready for Jack.

Walter and I decided to stay in the sauna a while longer. After about fifteen minutes, we heard this scream from the massage room. We grabbed towels to cover our privates and ran to Jack's aid. Poor Jack was bent double in pain. When he tried to straighten up, his back would spasm, and he'd let out a kind of hiccup that sounded like the bleat of a poor little lamb.

Jack told me, "That son of a bitch tried to kill me. He pulled my legs so hard, it's a wonder they didn't come off."

We ate and arrived at the theater to get ready for opening night. One of the first scenes in the show is Mr. Roberts with the crew sitting around on deck. They know that Roberts has submitted a request to be transferred off the ship. They're waiting for the captain to see the request. The captain doesn't like Roberts and doesn't want to approve the transfer. The captain's aide comes out and calls attention, then the captain comes roaring out and hops up onto the deck for a face-to-face with Roberts.

When Jack roared out and hopped up on the deck, his back spasmed, he repeatedly hiccupped like a little lamb, and grabbed his back. The whole crew knew that Jack's back had been giving him trouble, but they hadn't seen the bleating act before, and they went crazy trying to stifle their laughter. That embarrassed Jack, and he started ad-libbing, "There will be no goddamn laughing on this ship." He continued to cuss and rave at me and grab his back and bleat when he tried to straighten up.

It was infectiously hilarious, and soon the audience was laughing as well. Jack made an exit shouting, "Roberts, you son of a bitch, you'll never get off this ship as long as I am captain."

How we worked through that play that night, I'll never know. I know we couldn't look at each other the rest of the week. Poor Jack. He wanted to be so mean as the captain, but he was the cutest captain ever.

In *Pajama Game*, he was as funny as Eddie Foy. He lived in Bucks County, Pennsylvania, near bandleader Paul Whiteman. Jack liked to buy old schoolhouses, refurbish them, and sell them as summer homes. In addition to being a damn fine actor and brilliant comedian, he was damned clever. Later he contracted hepatitis. They transfused him with bad blood, and it killed him. He was only forty-five or so and strong as a bull. I couldn't believe it when I heard about his death. He was just coming into his own as an actor, I loved him dearly and still miss him. He was beautiful!

37

Piss on the Triffids

I received a script and a book titled *Day of the Triffids*. John Wyndham wrote the book, Philip Yordan the script. I flew to London where Harry Friedman of MCA told me it'd be filmed at Shepparton Studios with Steve Sekely directing.

The money was up, and I had a nice flat just off Grosvenor Square near the American Embassy. Our sleek cast included Nicole Maurey, Mervyn Johns, and Janina Faye, a young actress who was fantastic as Helen Keller in the play, *The Helen Keller Story*. Steve Sekely was a lovely man with a thick Hungarian accent and a habit of offering a direction and walking away from you, so you caught very little of what he said. But somehow you knew what he wanted. We all loved him and his humor.

The script was awful and was rewritten by the producer and his wife, which only made it worse. The *Triffids* were a joke except for blind people. It became a cult classic.

Bing Crosby and Bob Hope were at the same studio filming *Road to the Moon*. What saved me from that dreadful movie was that on weekends, the three of us would play two golf courses and have dinner afterward. Bob won all the money with his phony handicap, but it was great fun.

One day, the producers simply announced that the picture was done.

I said, "We haven't filmed the lighthouse sequence where I learn to kill the Triffids with salt water."

We learned that the money men pulled the plug. A year and a half later, they added Kieron Moore and Janette Scott to the cast and filmed the lighthouse sequence. They could have saved a lot of money by having me pull out my tally whacker and peeing on the damn Triffids. Enough said!

★ ★ ★

A Columbia Pictures executive lived above me in London and told me the studio would be filming spaghetti westerns in Spain and I'd be great for them. But I was sick of the *Triffids* picture, and I didn't trust the guy in Spain. I went home.

That's when Clint Eastwood took the job, and his career took off. Timing! Timing! And life decisions. Ho! Ho!

★ ★ ★

With a completely new cast, I went to Chicago to do *Carousel* for Bill Rock's Theater in the Round in a tent. Inga Swenson, who had a nice voice and was one hell of an actress, played Julie.

We'd swung a little bit around England together, so

we were friends. I knew a musical version of *The Rainmaker* was being worked on, and I felt Inga would be great as Lizzie. I told her about it and that I wanted a shot at the role of Starbuck. I said, "I have a friend who has the Royal Poinciana Theater in Palm Beach, Florida. Why don't I call him and see if he would do the play with us?"

We closed *Carousel*, and I went home to make ready for Palm Beach. Inga went to New York, auditioned, and won the part of Lizzie in the musical, which was named *110 in the Shade*. Then I found out they didn't want Inga to do the play with me. There was no way that I could run out on my friend, Frank Hale.

N. Richard Nash, who wrote *The Rainmaker*, had planned to direct, but opted out. Strange! They cast Salome Jens, who could look like a farmer's daughter one minute and Helen of Troy the next. She moved like a beautiful panther, and Frank surrounded this great cast with a good director, Robert Moore. It was a tremendous success! Opening night at the Poinciana, diamonds glistened and gowns flowed over beautiful bodies. Those audiences were not known to stay for an entire play, but no one left.

When we closed, my agent, Abe Newborn, arranged for me to talk with the producers about the role of Starbuck in the musical. I arrived at the Imperial Theater where they were holding auditions, and we waited around for a while. Finally they called me onstage. No one said, "How are you, Howard?" Or "Good to see you." Or any damned thing.

The assistant director introduced May Muth, who had been with me in *Oklahoma* in New York, and said,

"They want you to go through from the top." So May and I did—from top to the bottom. Silence. Nothing. Someone asked, "Would you sing for us?"

I said, "No! Thank you very much." Silence. I thanked May Muth, the assistant director, walked to Abe Newborn, and said, "Let's go have a nice martini."

At Sardi's, I told him, "I know this business can be cold, but I never expected it from people I thought were old friends, particularly Gower Champion. I did three pictures with him. I don't think they know how wonderful this play can be. It's a very sensitive, warm, funny, and tender piece. I never knew what the role had until we put it together and played it. It surprised the hell out of me.

"I'll never understand what I did to Gower and Tom [Jones] and Harvey [Schmidt]. How they could be so cold? I think they're on the wrong direction if they think that any one person can carry this play. This play is the Star, and they better give Lizzie all the support she can get. It is a wonderfully knit play. I hope they don't fuck it up, but I think they will. Let's have another martini and wish them luck."

I was emotionally hurt by the audition. I had already played Starbuck with a terrific cast. I was a damn good Starbuck. They made a mistake.

★ ★ ★

In early 1962, the production company of Guber, Ford and Gross called me to do *Kismet* with a new company in West Springfield, Massachusetts. We rehearsed in an old tire factory that smelled to the high heavens. What a terrible place for singers. They hired an old man, who couldn't play the score, as the rehearsal pianist. He'd give us the keys, and we'd wing the music a cappella.

You're walking on dangerous ground when you try to wing Borodin's music. In fact, you're out of your cotton-picking mind. We moved to Westbury, New York, for dress rehearsals. We found a pianist who could play the score and discovered how far we'd gone afield. We tried to fix the musical errors and fit costumes, as well. What a mess.

Lee Guber showed up and whined about the delays. I explained our problems with the previous rehearsal pianist, but that went right over his head. He assured us that he had a good pianist for the opening that night. I suggested that we use the pianist we had rehearsed with. He whined again about the cost.

By this time, I wasn't in a very good mood, and Ole Hairbreadth Harry kicked in and said, "I don't give a shit who plays the opening. Why don't you save yourself some money and play the opening yourself? Now go away, and let us do our job."

We opened, and it was not a musical sensation. My most important costume, the one for "Gesticulate," had its first fitting during the first act. We worked through the show somehow, and after the audience staggered out, Guber announced he wanted to see everybody in the tent.

They came for me, and I said, "I will see Mr. Guber tomorrow and not until then."

That brought Guber backstage to my so-called dressing room, and I told him to stay the hell away from me the rest of the night. He did. Barbara Walters was Guber's wife at this time and had seen the opening. I understand she thought I wasn't very good in the part, and she was right. I hope someday I have a chance to tell her the whole story. Thank God the cast around me were all pros and did their best.

We moved to Camden, New Jersey, and continued to improve right along. During a matinee intermission, a tooth exploded on me. They found a dentist who specialized in root canals, and he did one on me between shows. I returned for the second show, and the whole right side of my mouth was numb from the Novocain. I started to sing my first song, which was "Rhymes Fine Rhymes" with all of those amazing lyrics, and I sounded like Elmer Fudd lisping and spitting all over the place. I couldn't sing the lyrics clearly. The cast went crazy trying not to laugh at me, and the audience, thank God, was understanding, if not questioning. I probably was the best singing Elmer Fudd ever. But the show must go on!

We played Painter's Mill, outside Baltimore, and finished in Shady Grove, near Washington, D.C. The show, by that time, had come together. Boris Aplon was the best Wazir ever, Marilyn Child played a sexy and funny Lalume, and Beverly Allyson sang and acted Marsinah beautifully. The whole cast were great troupers, and I loved them all. What we went through to do that show happens a lot in summer stock.

I believe summer stock people are some of the bravest people I know. It's damn the critics. Full Speed Ahead!!!

Another good thing about this tour was meeting Buddy Eig. He was a great golfer and tennis player, who stood about 5 feet 4 inches, was chubby, bright, funny, and wore thick glasses. The complete antithesis of an athlete. Yet, he designed and built two outstanding golf courses around his father's hotel, the Washingtonian. I called him Archimedes the Owl.

He's now gone to the great golf course upstairs. The games we had with David Wortman, who was a PGA lawyer, were some of the best times of my life. We were a great trio.

★ ★ ★

They called me about doing *No Strings* across country, and I went to New York to catch a performance. It is a strange show, ahead of its time. Diahann Carroll and Dick Kiley were the leads. The play had its moments, but they didn't happen often enough. Diahann looked sensational and sang well, but she always seemed to be standing in a model's pose. Kiley was a very good actor and sang beautifully, but I never felt any chemistry between them.

Working with director Joe Layton later, I think it was his fault. I found him arch and opinionated and hard to have a conversation with.

The costumes for the dancers were "How ugly can you get?" The orchestrations were exciting, and I would stand backstage in the second act to watch the wild orchestra.

Bernice Massi is an exciting actress, and I felt she was terrific in the show. She had red blood in her veins. We later did *Man of La Mancha* together, and she was the best Aldonza of all.

I asked, when we agreed on Barbara McNair as the lead, to let us go in together. But they cast her, and she became almost a clone of Diahann in the part. It must have been Layton because he did the same thing to me.

213

He tried to make me the same as Dick Kiley. We didn't get along.

We opened in New York for two weeks, then moved to Boston, where we did smash business. The show opener was a great song, "Sweetest Sounds."

In St. Louis, Barbara wasn't feeling well. I'd always check in on her after the show. One night, I knocked on her door, and her dresser, who was her half-sister, said, "Barbara is all doubled up on the floor. What shall I do?"

I told her to call an ambulance and locate her husband, who was a stagehand. I rode with her to the hospital. Thank God, the emergency doctor was a gynecologist. Barbara had an ectopic pregnancy, and if it'd gone much further, she would've died.

She was out for about three weeks and rejoined us in Kansas City. The first night she sang, she was a different girl: warm and delightful. I told her so. The next night, she was right back in the old Joe Layton mold.

We played in a barn in Kansas City where three thousand sat on one floor separated with three aisles: one in the center and one on each side. One of the nice moments in the show was the opening of the second act where we're lounging on a dock somewhere on the beach of Southern France and singing a lovely song, "Look No Further." We kiss deeply, then reprise the song.

We had a matinee audience of about three hundred in this huge auditorium. When we came out of the kiss, an elderly couple stood and walked slowly up this long center aisle. The timing of the reprise was just perfect. They neared the top and opened the door. The old guy turned to us, dropped his hat, and said, "Shame."

Barbara and I began to giggle. Whoever booked this

show surely did not think—a white man kissing a beautiful black woman. At that moment, we realized why the show bombed in Pittsburgh, Cincinnati, St. Louis, and Kansas City. We moved to Los Angeles and opened at the Orpheum, a nice old vaudeville theater, to a so-so review. We later received the same lukewarm reviews in San Francisco. I hated the part for other reasons. It was a dumb role, but it paid the bills.

I was driving downtown for a matinee when I heard on my car radio that President Kennedy had been shot. I'm no Democrat, but I'm an American who couldn't stop crying. I arrived at the theater in shock. We closed the show immediately and as did the entire world, watched the tragedy unfold on television. It was the most depressing and tragic thing I ever sat through.

Blissfully, the show closed soon thereafter. The only solace I had in the show was with an incredible dancer named Ann Hodges. We had a relationship that was worth the whole adventure. She was something else!

38

The 1960s Reprises

★ ★ ★ ★ ★

Camelot 1964. What an exceptional acting role that was more speechifying than singing, but great to perform. I had the best Guenevere of all, Constance Towers.

We had worked together in *Kiss Me Kate* in San Diego and Minneapolis. I adored Connie, but I knew her husband, and I never made a move. Once in a while, I could control myself. Bravo! I have a great deal of respect for her and her talent. She's a great gal.

We opened in North Tonawanda, New York. Laurie Main played King Pellinore, and Morgan Paul was Mordred. We were good individually, and as a unit, we blended into one great company.

I had recently purchased a new 1964 XKE Jaguar hardtop, which I would drive on the long trip to Ben Segal's in Wallingford, Connecticut. I suggested to Connie that we could leave after the show, drive for a while, then stop at a motel along the way and rest. We'd complete the drive the following day.

We drove for a few hours in a torrential rainstorm, pulled into a motel around 3:00 A.M., and parked under the motel's portraiture. The proprietor took one long look at us, a beautiful, statuesque blonde and a tall, handsome, burly young man, and said, "May I help you?"

We asked for two rooms.

He brought two keys to the counter: one in his left hand and one in his right. He placed them on the counter wide apart and slowly slid them together and pushed them toward us. We looked at each other and then at him. We each picked up our own key. I offered her my arm. She curled her arm around mine, and we marched out to our individual rooms and exploded in laughter.

* * *

There isn't a hotter place on earth than inside the Wallingford tent on a matinee day with all the lights on. It was so unbearable that during the first matinee, Connie became dehydrated completely and would walk off each scene, upchuck, and return to the stage. I was working with her, and I never realized she was so ill.

We did Buster's Semi Hardtop in Warwick, Rhode Island, and then switched to the Guber, Ford and Gross tents. Christopher Hewett was our new director. I'd known Chris briefly in London. He was with Hermione Gingold in *Sweetest and Lowest*. (After a long career that included movie roles in *The Producers* and *The Lavender Hill Mob* and on Broadway in *The Unsinkable Molly Brown* and *Peter Pan*, Chris became a recognizable face in America with his starring turn as TV's Mr. Belvedere.)

Chris said, "I have a couple of things you might not like, so let me lay it on you. First of all, we cannot get

217

the dog. Guber will not pay for it."

Knowing Guber's cheaper side, it struck me as funny, and I said, "With Laurie Main playing Pellinore, it will work out. What's the other one?"

He said, "The guy playing Mordred is strange and looks like he's on drugs or something."

I suggested, "Let's run our scene and watch him."

The young man walked down the aisle on his toes, as if he was tip-toeing through a minefield. We ran our scene, and he was wonderful. I had a ball watching him. His name was Jon Voight. We had a great time with our scenes, and he portrayed evil with skill. We became good friends.

Jon played a good game of golf. His father was a golf pro, which fit right in as far as I was concerned. Helen and I invited Jon to stay with us when he came to the coast. He stayed for several weeks then settled down. We were glad to give him a break. Years later, I saw him at a Los Angeles restaurant, and he didn't acknowledge me.

The dancer in the dog suit was fantastic. He and Laurie worked out their parts and had the audience in stitches. What a great summer: theater and golf.

★ ★ ★

In early 1965, I joined a production of *Camelot* in Mineola, New York, that had been on the road too long. I felt like an intruder in this company, but we worked through it. The actress playing Guenevere was an amazing copy of Mother Goose. I could hardly keep a straight face. Poor Lancelot! We paid her off and put in her understudy who was young, but showed promise. She had a great voice, wound up doing opera in Europe, and later played the diva who sang the aria in *Phantom*. Her last name was Munroe.

The summer of 1965, I did a production of *South Pacific* and directed it for Guber, Ford and Gross. I wanted Nancy Dussault, but Guber wouldn't pay her price, so we had a tough time. We auditioned and auditioned and finally a well-dressed young brunette, who could belt out a song, tested. Her name was Joanna Lester, and she turned out to be a damn good Nellie Forbush. Sylvia Simms played Bloody Mary, and my old friend, Dick O'Neill, was Billis.

Dick always said, "What do you do during the day when you don't have matinees?"

I told him, "I play golf. You wouldn't understand. It's a gentleman's game."

"Oh!" he said, "cussing and swearing and throwing clubs and calling oneself a stupid horse's ass, is that a part of it, eh? Then you must be a scratch golfer."

And that started thirty years of insults back and forth. He was delicious, and I loved him. He couldn't afford clubs on Guber's salary. I bought him a new set of MacGregor irons, woods and a putter and made him wear my size thirteen golf shoes. He cussed and swore and called himself a stupid horse's ass all summer. I told him golf would drive him crazy, but it would save his sanity.

Outside of insisting that he marry Jackie, teaching him golf was the next best thing I ever did for him. Jackie was a gifted pianist, and when Dick met her, he was crazy about her. They married and had three daughters. He was a true friend, one you either loved or hated, many times a day.

★ ★ ★

In the summer of 1966, Guber, Ford and Gross asked me to act and direct *Carousel* for them. I also had a production of *South Pacific* for Herb Rogers in Hawaii immediately after *Carousel*. We had very little time to rehearse, so we used Joanna Lester as Carrie in *Carousel* and Nellie in *South Pacific*. She wanted to play Julie, but I told her she'd have more fun doing Carrie, and she did. She was a perfect Carrie and was great with Igor Gavin, who played Mr. Snow. Willie Burke played Julie and almost had a Jan Clayton quality. It was a damned good cast, and the audiences ate it up.

* * *

Helen had been a very heavy smoker, and one day in 1966, she said she'd like to learn to fly.

I told her, "You quit smoking, and we'll both take lessons."

She quit smoking that day.

Adam Berg, who had been a Navy pilot and flew in the Battle of Midway and performed stunt flying in movies, became our flight instructor. He was a gruff, salty old bear, but had a great heart.

I had a deal with Cessna to pick up a Skylane 182 in Teterboro, New Jersey, so I could fly the circuit. I flew down to the Flying W Airport near Camden, New Jersey, where we rehearsed *Carousel*. I met the airport owner, Bill Whitesell, who was a great big former Pan Am captain. I stayed at the airport while we rehearsed and got to know Bill and his wife very well. He was an excellent pilot, and I learned a lot from him.

I flew between engagements, from Baltimore to West Springfield, Massachusetts, (where I played Ann

Corio's tent) to Cleveland with the family. On the way, we ran into bad weather and sat down in Buffalo. I caught a commercial flight into Cleveland. Helen rented a car and drove the kids to my opening, then drove to Buffalo and flew the plane to Cleveland. Later that week, she and the kids returned to the coast.

The next date was Framingham, Massachusetts. I found the nice cement strip and sat down. A while later, I decided to fly to an island off the Massachusetts' coast.

A friend of mine was playing golf there, and I thought I'd take a guy from Framingham and surprise him. We saw my friend, chatted, took off around 1:00 P.M. and returned to the airstrip around 2:30.

One strip was a little uphill, and I decided to use it. I set up for a short-field landing and made a pass, I didn't like it and went around. The plane set up again and rose over the trees nice and low. I cut the throttle, and it settled down nicely. It was pretty hot outside, and the plane floated and floated. I cut the flaps and landed, then hit the brakes. But the grass was slick, and it skidded and skidded. If I only had ten more feet, I would have been all right. But those stone walls that run throughout New England came to greet us—hard.

221

39

I Joined the A.C. Lyles' Players

★ ★ ★ ★ ★

Icussed a blue streak over the embarrassment, but we both walked away from the crash with very little damage to the airplane.

We finished the show's run. Joanna Lester and I flew from New York to Honolulu the following day. By the time we reached Honolulu, the left side of my anus was one massive hemorrhoid. They took me to see the best rear admiral in the islands, who wasn't available, and another doctor drew the assignment.

It's embarrassing to be put in a straddle and turned upside down and have a little Japanese doctor checking your problem. He had a thick accent and said, "Oh, Missa Kweewa, you have a large hemorrhoid. Muss operate right now!"

I told him I had to open a show that night.

He said, "Oh no, Missa Kweewa, we use anesthesia and operate right now. Be over shortly."

I told him, "What the hell, it can't hurt any worse than it does now. Go ahead."

When his snipping was done, he said, "We have you taped together now," referring to my gluteus maximus. "When you go back to the hotel and have to defecate, get your wife's sanitary belt and Kotex and pad up after defecation and wear a sanitary belt to hold the pad in place."

They unsaddled me. I felt fine and returned to the hotel to rest. Before going to the theater, I had to defecate. What a thrill. Wahoooo. I took Helen's sanitary belt and pad and put it on. By this time, the anesthetic was wearing off, and I was more than a little uncomfortable, you might say.

We drove to the theater, and I entered through the stage door. Streams of homosexuals from our chorus were all standing around inside the stage door waiting for me. They knew my condition and asked how I was feeling. I said, "Darlings, mother has the rag on this evening. All goosing and other frivolous play are taboo."

* * *

Waco, *Red Tomahawk*, and *Arizona Bushwhackers* were Westerns produced by A.C. Lyles, a prince of a man. Each film took seven days to put in the can, and except for a few shots in Agoura Hills, California, they were shot on the back lot at Paramount Studios.

A.C., as we call him, had been at Paramount forever. How he ever thought of me doing these pictures, I'll never know. I know I needed the money. When I talked with Eddie Traubner, my business manager, I said, "Eddie, I can't do this picture at that price. It will ruin my career."

He said under his breath, "What career?" and while he was probably right, that hurt. There may have been some truth to it, but the way that he said it was snide and uncaring. I had loved Eddie for twenty-odd years, and that was a shocker. I stayed with him, but it never felt the same. *C'est la vie*.

The actors made doing those pictures fun. In *Waco*, we had the most unpretentious, humorous, and beautiful Jane Russell.

We had a little trouble in the jail-cell scene, worked with the dialogue on our own, and were pleased with the final shoot.

The other actors in the A.C. Lyles' actor's group included Brian Donlevy, Wendell Corey, Terry Moore, John Agar, Gene Evans, Richard Arlen, Ben Cooper, Tracey Olsen, DeForest Kelley, Anne Seymour, Bob Lowery, Willard Parker, Jeff Richards, Fuzzy Knight, Red Morgan, and Reg Parton, my stand-in and double for years. They were all actors who'd been in the spotlight at one time in their careers and were excellent professionals.

We made *Red Tomahawk* simply because A.C. had reels and reels of Indians on the warpath. They rode from every direction, every tribe, wearing every type of feather dress, and howling every war hoot you ever heard. Plus he had a Gatling gun that could shoot faster than Brod Crawford could talk.

Originally Betty Hutton was to be my paramour, and I told A.C. she couldn't work that fast and would try to direct every scene. But he insisted, and we started.

The first morning for Betty Hutton was like Norma Desmond returning to Paramount in *Sunset Boulevard*. Her antics cost us three days the first morning.

In one-half day alone, we lost six full days of work. At lunchtime, Betty went to her dressing room, removed all her clothes and makeup, and took a shower.

J. Carrol Naish picked up a gun one day. She said, "Wait a minute. I'll show you how to use that gun."

He never picked up that gun again that he didn't go to Betty and mockingly say, "Am I holding the gun right, Betty?"

It was sad, but they had to replace her. Joan Caulfield assumed the role. I was in-between Broderick Crawford and Scott Brady all the time trying to explain the Gatling gun. By 9:30 in the morning, Broderick Crawford was about half-drunk and talking faster and faster. Scott Brady had his hair up his ass about me, and I couldn't figure out why.

I took him aside to find out what his problem was.

He said, "I see you signed off on the residuals on those pictures."

I sat him down and explained why the guild board set up the pension fund the way it did. I told him there was simply no way to document the record keeping. I said, "So we took a two-million-dollar lump sum, put it in a trust, and started one of the best Pension and Health plans in the whole world."

His reply was, "Oh, not a bad idea."

We became friends after he understood that there was no way that the monies could be distributed fairly to all actors.

In 1999, that fund was worth close to two billion dollars and growing.

★ ★ ★

Arizona Bushwhackers starred Yvonne De Carlo, John Ireland, Marilyn Maxwell, and most of the A.C. Lyles' players. I wound up in a brawl in a saloon and in no time at all, won the two lovely ladies. Tony Curtis always bragged about the fact that he seduced Yvonne De Carlo. But we had no time for any hanky-panky on the *Bushwhackers*. At the end of each day's shooting, I hitched up my horse and rode out of town like any honest cowboy would—alone.

When we completed that film, A.C. told me that James Cagney would narrate it and would I like to have dinner with Cagney and his wife at A.C.'s home. I was overwhelmed because Cagney was one of my favorite actors.

A.C. arranged a dinner party and said, "I'll send a car for you and Helen."

I told him not to bother, but he wouldn't hear of it.

"Oh no, my place is hard to find. The car will pick you and Helen up at 7:00 P.M."

Precisely at seven, the doorbell rang. I opened the front door, and there stood a little guy with a chauffeur's cap on. He said, "Mr. Keel, your car's here, sir."

That Cagney voice was unmistakable. I stood like a star-struck kid for a minute, then Helen and I laughed. Cagney and his wife, Frances, drove us to A.C.'s for a memorable evening. Cagney and Frances were like two lovely peas in a pod. What a privileged night for Helen and me. Cagney had also been a past president of the Screen Actors Guild, so we had a few stories to exchange. His great book, *Cagney by Cagney* is a mind opener.

Duke and The War Wagon

★ ★ ★ ★ ★

In 1966, my agent, Harry Friedman, called about a film called *The War Wagon*. John Wayne's production company, Batjack, would produce the movie, and it would star John Wayne and Kirk Douglas. Duke would direct. My part was a hep Indian called Levi Walking Bear. Sounded like a good part, and he was funny, so I agreed. The money wasn't bad, and I never paid too much attention about billing. I figured third billing. Ho! Ho!

They flew Robert Walker and me in a 180-Cessna tail-dragger from Mazatlán to Durango, Mexico. My original part went out the window when the Indians found the part insulting, and the writer changed it. We spent six or seven weeks in Durango, which is not the most exciting place in the world. Nice people and all, but not much to do.

I tried to stay sober. All the stunt men were serviced by hookers from a private house. I took off for home, then returned to the location. I told Duke, "It's been six, seven weeks. I've got to go home and get serviced or something," but the old boy became angry and cursed me over my leaving.

One night, I got bombed drinking with Bruce Cabot and John Wayne and a Mexican director who carried two six-guns all the time. Bruce left about midnight, and so did the director. John and I went on until about four o'clock in the morning and killed four bottles of their finest tequila.

There was a nice nine-hole golf course with two sets of tees, and I spent as much time as I could there. The next morning, I had scheduled a tee time. When the alarm went off, I was so hung over, they threw me in an open shower.

Duke wasn't a golfer. He was a chess man. Who would have thought? Duke asked me to appear with him in *Green Berets* later, so I guess he liked me. Duke was a no-bullshit man, a strong director, and a lot brighter than people thought he was.

★ ★ ★

We flew in a DC-3 to the location, which was about a twenty-minute flight out of Durango. The fantastic and unspoiled scenery was breathtaking. The Mexican crews loved Wayne and usually would do anything for him, except for one bad day. Duke was working with just one lung, and sometimes he'd get a little cranky. That one day, nothing they did was right. Duke blew his cork. They almost walked off the picture, but returned the next day as if nothing had happened.

We were getting near the end of the picture on location and were all a little stir crazy. After about four weeks, Montezuma's revenge struck me. I had to work through it because the scene was around the war wagon, which we crashed in a ravine. It was supposedly loaded with gold, and we were in a frenzy to get it out.

I did all my own stunts. The scene involved Wayne, Douglas, me, Keenan, and Bob Walker. We had the master and were doing the pickup shots. I was sick to my stomach most of the day, and in one place, I didn't move fast enough for Duke. He grabbed me and pushed me. I turned toward nearby bushes and threw up.

The following day, we got up at 4:30 A.M. and flew to the location. Al Jennings, the assistant director who was an old friend from MGM days, asked if I was all right. I told him, "Yeah! But Duke better not push me again, or he can shove this picture."

During a five-thirty breakfast, Duke sauntered toward me and said, "Hey, I understand I upset you yesterday."

I said, "I wasn't upset, Duke, I was angry. I think you are a damned good director, and I like you and respect you. But I don't like being pushed around. I'll do anything you like for you, but don't push me. I've got a bad temper. I'm not as good at brawling as you are. I only have one good arm, and if I lose my temper, I'll not brawl with you, I'll try to kill you."

He looked at me and said, "I'm sorry, kid. I understand."

We were fine from that moment on. I didn't have many scenes with Kirk, but I enjoyed all his tricks of the trade. We had a scene with Duke on horseback, and somehow I wound up between them. We pulled up, and they went for a shot of the three of us. The camera operator yelled, "Cut," halfway through the scene. Duke said, "What's the matter?"

The cameraman whispered something to Duke. He turned to me and said, "Did you look into the camera?"

I quipped back, "Hell, even in musicals, we don't look into the camera."

Kirk almost fell off his horse laughing. After we finished the shot, I walked to the cameraman and told him, "If you fuck up a shot, don't try to blame me, you miserable shit."

We had a big fight scene in a large saloon. Duke asked me about doubling for the scene, and I said, "No problem."

He said, "You'll have to go through the window at the end."

I said, "You take care of my stunt man, and I'll do it."

That would be my last shot in the picture and my last scene in a motion picture for theater viewing.

The contract system was pretty much over by then. It had been eighteen wonderful, exploring, and learning years.

41

Try to Remember

⋆ ★ ★ ★ ⋆

In 1967, they approached me about *On a Clear Day You
Can See Forever* that had a strong part for a woman and
an interesting role for the male lead, a doctor. Zev
Bufman produced, and Milton Katselas directed. Eddie
Roll was the choreographer while Richard Parrinello
conducted the orchestra.

Zev Bufman wanted me to meet and hear Karen
Black who lived in a small Hollywood apartment. This
was only a few years before she hit it big in *Five Easy
Pieces*. I listened to her small voice and told Zev that
she'd be terrific in the part.

We opened in Florida, and I stayed at the David
William Hotel in Coral Gables. The hotel had a restaurant called the Chez Vendome and a marvelous penthouse bar that featured Herbie Block, a blind pianist
who could play anything.

Al Sokolsky was the co-owner and was very generous to the cast, which included Karen, Lester James,
Francine Beers, Rowan Tudor, Leon Benedict, William

Coppola, and Jodi Perselle. We played three weeks in Florida to great reviews. But they kept insisting that Karen had to sing louder. Katselas continued to work with her, and I repeatedly asked them to just mike her. It got to the point where it affected her performance, and her voice gave out. They offered Karen singing lessons. I told them what they'd done to her voice couldn't be undone with a couple of singing lessons. We'd have to replace her in New York. I truly felt sorry for Karen. She was a wonderful Daisy.

When we arrived in New York, Barbara Lang assumed the lead role. She sang beautifully and acted the part splendidly. I called Burton Lane and said this girl is so good we have to give her equal billing above the title with me.

After the rehearsal, Milton took her to dinner. I don't know what happened or what he said to her, but her afternoon performance was dead. I felt like a fool, and Burton looked at me like I was out of my mind.

I asked Eddie Roll what happened, and he didn't know. I talked to Milton, and he assured me she'd be fine. We landed in Toronto, and opening night, they changed her hairstyle. She had long, blonde hair perfectly straight down the middle of her back, and she looked stunning. That night they piled it on top of her head, and she wasn't the same Daisy I saw in rehearsal. She made the same kooky faces, but her performance was gone.

After opening night, we had a meeting and dismissed Katselas. They wanted to bring in a new director, and I disagreed. I told them Eddie Roll could clean up the choreography, and I'd work with Barbara. I asked her what happened, but she wouldn't tell me. I started at the beginning, cleaned up all her wacky things, and the exceptional things began to return. We went to Chicago, and opening night, she started the same wacky things. The next night she was fine. I lost a lot of respect for Milton Katselas and what he did to those two girls. Barbara is a puzzlement, but I loved working with her.

I flipped when I first saw *Fantasticks* in 1960, when it opened in New York. I was stunned that so much could be done in the theater with so little scenery. Tom Jones and Harvey Schmidt had taken an old play called *Les Romantiques* written by Edmund Rostand in 1894, and created a two-act musical that was absolute magic. Tom Jones played the old actor when I saw it, and he was remarkable, but Jerry Orbach was the one who won me over.

I had seen him earlier in *Threepenny Opera* at the Delys Theater, and he had it then. There's a mysterious quality about Jerry onstage that's fascinating. Later, I bumped into Gower Champion when he was casting *Carnival!*, and I told him about Jerry and suggested him for the part. He got it.

Also, I had a recording contract with RCA records, and I begged them to let me make a single of "Try to Remember," but the producers didn't think the song had quality. Well, the song won an off-Broadway award. Ed Ames of the Ames Brothers recorded it, and that made him a recording star. It's still a great song.

★ ★ ★

Eight years later in 1968, Zev Bufman called me about doing a production of *Fantasticks*. I had a good close-knit cast around me with Susan Watson (who had starred as the ingénue in *Bye Bye Birdie* on Broadway), Jack Blackton, Dean Dittmann, Gwyllum Evans, Lionel Wilson, Edward Garrabrandt, and Don Miller. Bill

Francisco directed. I enjoyed his intelligence and humor and was glad we worked together again. He's the one who kept the audience in their seats at the Royal Poinciana Theater in Palm Beach.

It was a labor of love with all of us, and I think Susan Watson had a lot to do with that. She's a real pro and played the daughter to a tee. Frank Hale was ecstatic. The song "Try to Remember" has three verses, and should you sing the wrong verse, you get the show off to a strange start.

The story goes that one night, an actor playing El Gallo became so nervous, he froze when he couldn't remember the first line of "Try to Remember."

The stage manager kept cuing him whispering, "Try to remember. Try to remember."

The actor hissed, "I AM. I AM."

* * *

I planned for dinner at the Chez Vendome with Al Sokolsky and his wife. Al would always have a broad as our fourth, and I told him, "I have enough trouble without that."

He just laughed, but that night, he said, "I got a real nice girl for you tomorrow. I'll pick you up at six-thirty."

I had a few days off before we played Poinciana and arranged a tee time with a friend of mine, Clark Hardwicke, at Indian Creek. After golf, I returned to the hotel and cleaned up for dinner. I sat in the suite. Six-thirty passed with no Al. Then seven o'clock and no Al. I was getting bugged. At seven-fifteen, I'm sitting there, and the door opens. Al walks in and says, "Meet Judy Magamoll."

42

I Meet Judy Magamoll

★　　★　　★　　★　　★

There stood the most beautiful, well-dressed young blonde, with the most fantastic eyes I'd ever seen. I sat stunned, my mouth open. When I found my voice, I came out with, "You're late!"

She hit right back with, "Well, you've got on a seersucker suit, and I don't particularly like that, either."

I never met anyone like her. We had a fun dinner with Al and his wife and then went up to the penthouse bar and listened to Herbie Block. We closed the place, and I drove Judy a few blocks to a nice little Spanish home where she lived with a couple. I pulled up to the curb, looked into those enchanting eyes, and asked, "How old are you?"

She said, "I'm twenty-four."

OH SHIT! I exited the car and opened her door, all the while subtracting in my mind realizing that I was forty-nine; four from nine is . . . SHIT! Then I blurted out, "I'm old enough to be your FATHER." I walked her to the door and said, "You're a lovely young lady, and I can't get mixed up with you. Good night."

When I returned to my suite, I looked in the bathroom mirror and said, "Well, stupid, what are you doing? You are mad about a girl who could be your daughter. You are almost fifty years old, and you are out of your skull!!!! Grow up."

I played golf the next day. When I returned to the hotel, the phone rang. It was Judy. She said, "Would you come for dinner? My friends would like to meet you."

I told her I couldn't.

Judy said, "Please, Howard. Just have dinner and you can go. They would love to meet you, and they're very nice people."

I weakened and said I would. How could I say no to those eyes? When I pulled up in front of the house, there was a little trapdoor in the front door with a face in it saying, "It's him. It's him."

Al had told Judy that I was a doctor. When she went home so late and had to get up at six in the morning to go to work at National Airlines, they asked her where she'd been. She told her friends, "I was with a very nice doctor named Howard Keel."

They said, "He's no doctor. He's a movie actor."

So that's the scene I walked into. We had a nice dinner during which Judy put me on and was so funny, I couldn't resist her. We went to hear Herbie Block again, and I asked her if she would like dinner the following night.

I picked her up at National Airlines. She always had a get-well card or little present in her hands for friends and people she knew who worked in the shops. They all adored her. I told myself, this was a very special girl. We had dinner and then went to a club to hear a great group called the Impact of Brass.

Fantasticks opened the following night. I invited her and told her I'd leave a ticket for her at the box office. It was sold out, and she had to sit on a chair in the rear of the auditorium. That seat didn't impress her much, but she loved the show.

I drove to the David William Hotel with her and had one of the cast drive my car. I told her that I wouldn't see her until I finished at the Poinciana. I was absolutely smitten, absolutely crazy about her, but still hadn't made a move.

When the run ended, we got together for dinner. I told her I'd be doing *Pajama Game* in Houston in three weeks and if she wanted to come down and see the show to call me at the Shamrock Hotel.

Okay, so I kissed her a couple of times, then took off for California.

I hated to leave her, but what could I do? I was married with three children, not happy, but settled down and long ago had decided that was a marriage. I was in a serious quandary.

I worked on the part for *Pajama Game* and went to Houston for a couple of days in rehearsal. One evening when I returned to my room, the phone rang. It was Judy.

She said, "I can come down this weekend."

I said, "Great, but I want you to know there is nothing wrong with me. I'm a normal man, and if you come down, I may make a move on you."

She didn't say a word. She just hung up.

I didn't have a phone number to call her back and felt

237

stupid for threatening her. "Okay, that's it. That's the best way to end it."

She didn't join me, either. That was that.

★ ★ ★

In the summer of 1968, I did *Fantasticks* with Anna Maria Alberghetti. We did the Guber and Segal tent circuits. Bill Francisco directed again, and I told him about the idea of a nightclub act with Kathryn Grayson and me. He thought it was a sensational idea. I told him I'd contact Kathryn and let him know.

Anna was a real cute Luisa. Once in a while, she would smoke a little pot or something and wouldn't be totally there, but most of the time she sang beautifully. We were in North Tonawanda, New York, and when I was lonely, I would call someone I knew and chat.

I found Dee and George's number, the couple that Judy lived with when I met her. Dee was about four months pregnant when we met, so the baby should have arrived. I called with that ruse and woke them up.

They said, "What do you want at this hour?"

I said, "Was the baby a boy or a girl?"

"It's a boy. Why don't you call Judy? She has a nice apartment now. You want her phone number?"

I said, "No, the last time we talked six months ago, she hung up on me. If she wants to talk, I'm here."

About fifteen minutes from the time I hung up, Judy called. My heart pounded as I urged her to get on a plane right away and come to me.

Anna Maria loved Judy, too, and told me, "If you don't marry that girl, you're crazy."

November 1968, I asked Judy to come to New York where many stars worked on a benefit for the

Foundation for Crippled Children. I told her Judy Garland was in the troupe, had been drinking and on drugs, and it might be her last performance. Judy flew to New York and although Judy Garland appeared extremely intoxicated backstage, she walked onstage to uproarious applause, hopped up on the piano, and belted out songs that had the audience screaming for more. After that performance, Judy Garland left for Europe and died shortly thereafter.

My Judy flew up and sat with Bill Francisco while we had a music run-through, and I took her to the Judy Garland concert. We had such a spectacular evening. The more time I spent with Judy, the deeper I fell in love with her. I just adored her. Judy returned to Florida, and I flew to California to work on the act with Kathryn.

We found a couple of great songs, including "Bojangles" for me and a song called "Clouds" for Katie. Katie didn't like the songs. Bill Kronk sang "Bojangles" and had a strange voice, and I think that's what turned her off to it. Two months later, Judy Collins, who wrote "Clouds," recorded the song, and it became a megahit.

Katie and I opened to great reviews at the Fremont Casino in Vegas. The only song we had to take out was "Wunderbar" from *Kiss Me Kate*. Katie sprained her ankle while waltzing. (MY FAULT. OF COURSE.) She sat on a stool with wheels, and I'd push her on and off the stage. That worked out well. A lot of people thought Katie was paralyzed and how nice it was the way I handled her. Ole Hairbreadth Harry played the big hero and Katie the brave little diva.

After she sang *"Un bel di"* from the opera *Madame Butterfly*, I would come out and give her a little shove offstage. The stool moved beautifully. All Katie had to do was to keep her microphone wires clear. One night, she forgot and went kerplop on her fanny. The audience gasped, and I rushed to her. I picked her up, carried her offstage, and brought her onstage for her bow. I put her on the stool and moved her offstage, then returned for my bow.

After four weeks, we closed at the Fremont and traveled to Harrah's at Reno for two weeks, then the El Camino Hotel in Mexico City for eleven days, San Francisco for two weeks, and to the Coconut Grove in Los Angeles for two weeks.

During the engagement at the Grove, I moved out of the house on Coldwater Canyon, thus marking the end of twenty years of marriage with Helen. I tried to make it work, but I wasn't strong enough. For the previous ten years, I supported a lot of people. I had to do many things to keep life going for everyone, and nearly all of these things kept me away from Helen and the family.

A singing actor's life sounds exciting, and at times it is, but it's also a lonely one. To keep yourself fit, you have to control your social life to a bare minimum. Golf saved me during the day, but after a show or concert, I'd generally drink myself to sleep or seek debauchery. I've not only been blessed with a wonderful voice to work with, but I've been blessed with a very strong constitution to support it. No matter what I did with my life on the road, I was always very protective of my voice. As far as my sex life was concerned, I always tried to be discreet and honest about it and hide it from the press. I also was very selective and honest about it with my paramours.

I had a few close New York friends I could lean on, and Dave Tebet was an amazing press agent, as well as a personal friend. We spent a lot of time together making the rounds at Danny's and the Little Club and other New York hangouts. We parted during the *Saratoga* disaster. After that, I was on my own and only happy on the stage.

My meeting Judy was an act of fate, and the instant I saw her, I knew I was in real trouble. I tried not to pursue her. But she was there in my heart, in my head, and in my dreams.

During that six months, Helen's mother died, and we returned her to Lake Worth, Florida, for burial. I had to fly through Miami on National Airlines and walked through Miami International. I spotted Judy for a second in the National concourse, and it hurt to see her. I rushed to National's waiting room, and another special agent saw Helen and me on board.

It seemed that Judy and I were not meant to be. Well, you don't always control your destiny. It controls you. No matter how strong you might think you are, it will test you. I didn't have the strength to go against the flow and decided to go forward. I went to the mirror and had a chat with myself. Well Harry, what are you up to now? You're on a path of self-destruction. If you stay and go against destiny, you'll drink yourself to death like your father, and that won't do anybody any good, especially yourself. If you go with destiny, it will test your courage and fortitude and people will say you are out of your mind. Remember, you will have Judy to help you, and let's face it—you need help. You'll have a chance to build a new life for yourself and Judy and take care of your family. Chat over with!

43

I Have More Miles Than Most Pilots

★ ★ ★ ★ ★

The night we closed the Coconut Grove, I packed my three bags ending a twenty-year marriage and got bombed while doing it. I awoke the following day with one great hangover knowing I had to fly to Australia that afternoon. Katie and I had an engagement with Richard Gray to play the League Clubs, gambling clubs attached to different rugby leagues.

Upon arrival at LAX, I went to the bar to see if I could mend myself. The bartender asked, "Mr. Keel, what can I do for you?"

I said, "I don't know what I look like, but I'm badly wounded and need a survival kit."

He said, "I've got just the thing." He brought me a glass of what looked like black syrup and said, "Drink this. It'll either kill you or heal you."

I took a sip of the worst-tasting stuff ever to cross my lips and said, "What the hell is that?"

He said, "Fernet Blanca. It'll do the job every time."

I downed it without heaving and asked for one more, but he told me one was enough.

The bartender asked, "Where are you off to?"

I replied, "I've got to go to Australia."

A voice from the end of the bar to my right said, "You don't have to go to Australia, mate. We don't need your type."

Oh shit, I thought, that's all I need. I said, "Look I didn't mean to insult your country or you. I'm just not in very good shape right now."

He repeated, "We don't need your type. Is that clear?"

I said, "Yes. But I'm going anyway. At this particular moment, I'm a little depressed. I just walked out of a beautiful home and my kids, and I'm starting a divorce after twenty years. And I am lower than a crocodile's asshole, and I don't need any more shit from you. Is that clear?"

He said, "Right, mate. Let's have a drink."

After tossing back a couple, we parted friends. I caught my plane, slept through Honolulu, and woke up when we were landing in Fiji. The stewardess told me the captain wanted to see me up front. I sat behind him through the landing. What a thrill.

When we deplaned, I suddenly realized Katie wasn't around. She'd missed the plane. We planned to arrive early to adjust to the time change, so I thought she'd probably catch the next one. She didn't arrive until the day we were to open.

Richard Gray was one angry Aussie. Richard Parrinello, our conductor, had checked out the orchestra, and he and I did a rehearsal that afternoon. They were fine. Our curtain time was eight o'clock. Katie didn't make the rehearsal, which was strange because she was always so particular about tempos and such.

Richard knew her like a book by this time, so that didn't worry me. I stayed after the rehearsal and took a nap and was ready to go by seven. Still no Katie. We called the hotel and were told she was on her way. Finally at seven-forty-five, she flowed through the theater with a small entourage and went straight to her dressing room.

I asked her where she'd been. She looked at me with glazed eyes and said, "Everything is going to be fine, darling." She then started to apply eyeliner and hit her cheeks instead. She was bombed on something and in no shape to go on.

I said, "Katie, you go ahead and get ready, and I'll have a talk with Richard Gray. I'll be right back."

I told Richard Gray, "Lock the dressing-room door and don't let her out. She can't go on in her condition. She'll try, but don't let her out. I'll talk to the audience, and Parrinello and I'll wing a show somehow."

Fortunately, Richard Parrinello knew practically every show I'd ever done. I told the audience that Miss Grayson was not well and would not be able to do the show that evening. They were very disappointed and let us know it. But Dick and I did a show using my numbers that we'd rehearsed and added songs from shows that I'd done, and we got away with it.

After the show, Katie was on a tirade, but I calmed her down and told her we'd have an orchestra rehearsal the following afternoon and see how she felt.

Next day, she was still on something and sang so

244

badly that I started to cry. I went up to her and put my arms around her. She pulled away and took a swing along the side of my head. I grabbed her and said, "Katie if you want to hit me again, okay, go ahead. I'm not going to let you go on. Nobody knows about this. However, if you try to go on, they will, because you aren't well and not yourself."

I learned that the loss of her mother and brother was just too much for her. We gave her a two-week hiatus, dried her out, and she was fine. When she returned, she sang like a bird. The audience adored her.

Judy flew in for a couple of days. Katie and I finished out the run and returned to Los Angeles.

* * *

While in Sydney, an old friend, Peck Prior, called me with an idea for a TV show with me as host. I wasn't sure about it, but told him I'd think about it. Two days later, I called Peck, and we agreed to give it a try. We worked very hard at it. Mac Davis signed onto the project. Mac was excellent, and I sang very well, and the show looked like it had promise, but no one picked it up.

I fooled around for a while and played a lot of golf, and then Katie and I played the Cork Club in Houston for a week and the Fremont in Las Vegas for four weeks.

I worked on my golf game to get ready for the Crosby Pro-Am golf tournament at Pebble Beach. I thought we would close on a Tuesday, and I could fly up to the Crosby and have a practice session. Ho! Ho! We didn't close until Wednesday, and I had to tee off at Cypress at 8:15 A.M. Thursday with Roberto Bernardini, an Italian golf pro.

A huge storm struck Northern and Central California, and there were no commercial flights that would get me there in time to tee off. I talked to a pilot who had a Cessna-310. He agreed to fly me up there for a hefty price. We took off around two o'clock in the morning. The flight controllers asked us to continue talking to them as we maneuvered through and around the storm. They steered us around the worst part of the storm, and we touched down about six-thirty.

I caught a cab to the Lodge at Pebble, laid down for about fifteen minutes, popped a pep pill, and took off with Roberto at 8:15 A.M. He shot 70, and I shot 76, the best I ever played at Cypress. The next day, Roberto shot 70 at Spyglass, but my wheels dropped off, and I shot 85.

He led the tournament at the end of the day. The weather began to turn. I told him if he shot even par the next two days, he'd win the Crosby. Since neither one of us could speak each other's language, we conversed in sign language. He kept saying, "Beeg track. Beeg track."

I kept saying, "No! No! The weather makes the big track easier because there will be no wind." It was in his mind about the big track, and I couldn't persuade him. Without wind, I think Pebble is the easiest of the three. Unfortunately for him, I tied him the next two days. He shot 76, 76, and so did I. If he had shot even par the last two days, he would have easily won.

We placed third in the pro-celeb, and I was thrilled to death. Roberto is a very nice man and took his loss without any animosity.

★ ★ ★

I flew to Detroit and right into rehearsal for *Plaza Suite* with Betty Garrett. It was a hectic two weeks. Neil

Simon's brother, Danny, was supposed to direct the play, but failed to show up. I was directed by a stage manager who blocked the scenes.

I didn't want to see the show. I wanted to start with a clean slate and see what I could do. I worked the first week of rehearsals with Betty's understudy, then Betty performed in the second week every day, except for matinees. She was just terrific to me, and I sincerely appreciated it.

Forrest Tucker had been doing the show, and he was a very good actor, so I was stepping into some big shoes.

After a few rehearsals, I called Judy. We decided that she would quit her job at National Airlines and become my dresser. She was great, but the head of wardrobe wasn't happy with Judy because she was too particular how my wardrobe was cleaned and handled. I had to let Judy go. I didn't insist on keeping her because to lose the head of wardrobe in a traveling company can be disastrous.

At least we were together full time, and that healed a lot of tiny wounds.

Plaza Suite is a beautiful play for a man and a woman. Danny Simon showed up a day before opening and offered to make suggestions, but I was up to my ears and didn't need things changed that close to opening. It would have been nice if he could have hung around for a couple of days and make suggestions, but that did not happen. That's life. My character was a pretty wacky guy, and I had trouble finding the part in the second act. After a week and a half of doing *Plaza Suite*, I suddenly knew how to play him.

I had an impressive role model. I didn't tell Betty what I intended when I pulled it on her. Vincente

Minnelli had an annoying habit of pursing his lips as if he were washing his teeth. So in the second act when I open the door to let Betty in, I stood there with her offstage, pursed my lips, and said, "It's not."

Her line was "It is."

I say, "It's not. Well, come in, come in," and the scene goes on.

Well, I opened the door and looked at her and pursed my lips and said, "It's not."

Offstage, she's in hysterics. She knew immediately what I was up to and went crazy every time I did it. I would let her settle down a bit, then purse my lips again, and she would go off again. Afterward she hauled off, whacked me on the back and said, "Don't you ever do that to me again."

And I didn't, but I played Vincente for the rest of the tour. We closed in Detroit and went to, of all places, Central City, Colorado, to a historic little theater called the Opera House. We played four weeks and had a great time. I brought the kids up to meet Judy, and I bought a new 250 Yamaha motorcycle and taught myself to ride it in the parking lot of the theater to surprise Gunnar, who was a very good bike rider.

They arrived, and everyone was very open to Judy. I told Gunnar I had a chore to do and asked him to come along. We went to the garage of the rental house where I cranked up the Yamaha and said, "Hop on." He couldn't believe it. His bike arrived the following day, and we had a great time riding about.

Betty's kids and her husband, Larry Parks, arrived, and all the kids meshed well together. Betty and Larry had nice children who were as bright as new coins.

We had warm family times while we were there, and I got to know my children better. Gunnar and I would take the bikes and pile Kirstine or Judy on the back and ride through the mountains. Judy was wonderful with the kids. It was a trying and awkward time for us, but we did a good job with my children. They went home softened a little to both of us.

We closed the show in Central City and opened September 1 in Toronto at the lovely Royal Alex Theater. Larry Parks entered the show, and Judy and I went to L.A. to brush up with Kathryn so we could play the Houston Cork Club from September 19 to the twenty-seventh, then into *Plaza Suite* on the twenty-ninth in Toronto. Judy and I left Toronto on the nineteenth, and Kathryn and I opened at the Fremont for the Christmas season in Vegas. We rushed to join Betty in *Plaza Suite* on January 26, 1970, in Philadelphia. Boy, what a whirligig! Judy was getting a real taste of what our life together might be.

The show didn't do too well in Philly, and I remember calling Mike Douglas hoping to get publicity for the show. No one returned my call. We stayed in a small hotel right across the street from the "Mike Douglas Show." How soon they forget, the people who helped THEM get started?

We closed the show on February 14 and were ready to move on when the phone rang. I picked it up and said, "Yes?"

A voice with a slow Southern drawl said, "Hoerd?"

I said, "I beg your pardon?"

The voice said, "Is this Hoerd Keel?"

"You mean Howard Keel?"

"That's what I said."

"Well, I guess I am."

He said, "Now you don't know me, but my name is Cowboy Clement, and I'm down here in Nashville, Tennessee. I went to see one of your motion picture shows the other night, and you could be a good country western singer."

I said, "Well, I hadn't thought much about it."

"Well, you ought to give it some thought. Now why don't you come on down here to Nashville and see me and do some thinking about it?"

We talked for a while, and he had a great sense of humor. I discussed it with Judy, and we decided to drop by Tennessee to see him. We hopped in the Volkswagen bus, drove to Nashville, and gave Cowboy a ring. He picked us up twenty minutes later in the longest limo I had ever seen. The back door opened and out stepped a gentleman all dressed up in a suit and tie. He walked up and said, "Hoerd, Jack Clement."

We shook hands, and I introduced him to Judy.

No kidding, he said, "Pleased to meet you, Ma'am. Come on you two, hop in the old limo. I want you to see something."

We rode through a lovely suburban neighborhood to a very nice home that he had remodeled, adding an office and a recording studio with a huge Gillespie board and a large room where he could seat up to sixty musicians at one time. It was a beautiful setup, with special lighting for setting the mood of whatever you wanted to record.

Cowboy wasn't pompous nor did he brag about all this. It was just his, and he was proud of it. He told us he was a songwriter and sat down with a guitar and played and sang a couple of songs for us.

I asked, "Hell, Cowboy, you sing the hell out of those songs. What do you need me for?"

He said, "I don't like to perform in public. I just like to write them." He was a fine country western singer: voice and all. He also was about half in the bag on something, all the time, but an absolute joy to be around.

We met a lot of people around his office who were awfully nice and busy doing something all the time. His girlfriend and Judy got along great, and everything was going along smoothly, except that I wasn't doing anything.

I asked, "Cowboy, when do I start doing some songs and things? I'm getting restless."

He said, "Look. Here are some simple scales and a guitar. You go into that room there and see what you can do."

I said, "Hell! I don't want to learn to play a guitar. I just want to sing something."

He said, "That guitar's a new Gibson, and it's yours. Now go in there, and go to it, but close the door 'cause we don't want to listen to you."

I went into that room and practiced for about an hour. My fingers became sore, so I put down the guitar, picked up a newspaper, and read for a while. I read an article in the paper about Andre Segovia. At the age of seventy-eight, he'd just fathered a brand-new spanking baby boy. I picked up that guitar and kept right on practicing.

The next day, musicians fooled around with some of Cowboy's songs. There were no orchestrations at all.

251

They'd simply call out numbers and play, and I mean they were incredible musicians. The piano player, who was called Pig, was blind. Every once in a while, I would let the voice out, and Cowboy would say, "Hoerd, I don't want that educated sound."

I told him, "Cowboy, that's just me. That's my voice when I let it out, unless you want me to sing softly all the time."

We tried and tried, but I didn't want to sound like a hillbilly with my voice. They went so far as to take me down to Memphis where Elvis recorded a few of his first songs. I even smoked a joint and tossed back a few Scotches to try and loosen up, but all I sounded was drunk.

It was a great adventure, but I'm not a singing cowboy. I could have been a good opera singer, but I didn't particularly like opera. Actually I wanted to be a serious concert singer, then was sidetracked into musicals. I loved doing *Carousel* and *Oklahoma* and *Kiss Me Kate* and *South Pacific* and *Kismet* and many others.

Country western is a style and a select group that's hard to break into, and I always felt I was intruding into something I was not right for or meant for. I love Cowboy and the things that he does, but it wasn't for me. I love country western songs and singers and admire the songs they write. As I told Willie Nelson when I met him, "You are something else!"

44

Can I Settle Down?

★   ★   ★   ★   ★

Judy and I thanked Cowboy for his hospitality and the opportunities he gave us. We hopped in the Volkswagen camper and took off for California. I wanted to see the kids again and play golf and find a place where Judy and I could take it easy for a while. There was also a short run of *Man of La Mancha* coming up, and I had a lot of work to do on that.

Two old friends, Bernice Massi and Earle MacVeigh, would appear with me. Bernice played the role of Comfort in *No Strings* in New York and helped us out when Kit Smythe became ill in Boston. (A little trivia on Kit. She played Ginger in the "Gilligan's Island" pilot, only to lose the role to Tina Louise.) MacVeigh played Jud in the London company of *Oklahoma* during the second half of the 1947-48 season. The role in *La Mancha* is a difficult part to find, and Bernice had played Aldonza before and helped me a great deal with Don Quixote. The production was performed in San Bernardino, California, by the Civic Light Opera Association.

During rehearsals, Judy and I stayed in my business manager's Palm Springs home. The secluded backyard had a high wall completely surrounding the grounds. It was near the season's end in Palm Springs when the area was quiet and getting hot. One afternoon, I'd been going through the blocking of Quixote in the backyard. It was very warm, so all I had on was a pair of shorts. I was cavorting around going through all the craziness of the part over and over, yelling and extending myself as much as possible with the madness.

After about an hour of this, I had worked up a sweat and literally fell down exhausted. I looked up, and there on top of the wall were three little kids watching me. Talk about getting caught with your pants down! I instinctively gave them a Don Quixote yell and charge, and they fell over each other trying to get down. What a sight I must have been.

They must have felt I was out of my mind because they didn't return. Maybe it was foreboding the lousy reviews I received in San Bernardino. We had a rough opening, which can happen with a short rehearsal period. We then closed and played the Lindy Opera House in Los Angeles. Bernice Massi, in my mind, is the best Aldonza I have ever worked with. Her performance was perfection personified, both vocally and dramatically. I hated losing her when we finished.

One night, the popular actor, Pat O'Brien, came backstage to meet me, and that absolutely floored me. He was overwhelming with his compliments about my performance. It was so encouraging at a time when I really needed it. I felt that I was beginning to give a good performance, and it was a great shot in the arm to have someone of his accomplishments and respect as an actor come back and pay his respects for what I was trying to do. I walked on air for days. During the run at the Lindy, I felt that I was truly finding Quixote.

Director, Jack Bunch, who I loved as a person, left me on my own and said very little to me about the part. I wasn't happy with the Sancho, but I tolerated him and worked around him. Lou Monica, the Padre, was absolutely awesome and sang beautifully.

I insisted that he play the part in the Guber, Ford and Gross production, and they acquiesced. I wanted Bernice and Earle MacVeigh, too, but the producers wouldn't meet their salary.

We closed at the Lindy. Judy took off for Orlando, and I went to Valley Forge, Pennsylvania, and rehearsed for a week with a new cast. From the very beginning, we got along terrifically. Lou Criscuolo, as Sancho, was a wonder and so giving as an actor. Jacqueline Alloway, as Aldonza, was close to Bernice Massi in her rendition, and I was very happy with the rest of the cast. Lou Monica fit in perfectly. Eddie Roll did an outstanding job of adapting *La Mancha* to the round, and I had someone I could talk to as an actor. My old friend, Richard Parrinello, conducted.

La Mancha is a killer role physically, and in the round, you'd better be in shape. The weekends were tough, with matinees on Saturday and Sunday. I found that at the end of every performance of *La Mancha*, I was physically, emotionally, and vocally beat up. I always took care of myself before any performance, and with *La Mancha*, I was doubly careful. In all the years and places I did *La Mancha,* I never missed a performance.

We always played to a sold-out audience, except in Phoenix. It took me about six weeks to get comfortable in *La Mancha*, and from then on, it was like playing a harp.

It's the most demanding and satisfying role I've ever done. It's a great piece of work. I never had the pleasure of meeting Dale Wasserman, Mitch Leigh, and Joe Darion, but I'm so grateful to them for having put together this wonderful musical.

We opened at Valley Forge on June 2, 1970 for three weeks. The audiences were exceptional, the show came together, and we spent the whole summer traveling with it. From Valley Forge, we went to Latham, New York, for two weeks, then Springfield, Massachusetts, for one week, to Baltimore at Painter's Mill for two weeks, then to Shady Grove near Gaithersburg, Maryland, for three weeks and stayed with our good friends, Buddy and Jackie Eig, at the Washingtonian. The Eigs threw a fabulous party for us after the last show. Lastly to Westbury, New York, for three weeks.

We played to packed houses the entire tour, and the company never let down. Jacqueline Alloway only sang better and stronger. Fred Major, as the Innkeeper, was charming.

The whole cast fell in love with Judy, and it was one of the happiest tours I ever made. During the last week in Westbury, I had meetings with Bill Francisco about my solo act for Australia. We had a party at the closing on October 4. It's an emotional trauma to leave a wonderful cast like that, and it hit Judy and me hard. We talked about it for years.

The following morning, we hopped in the

Volkswagen camper and drove to Orlando, Florida, to Judy's parents. We sold the camper to Judy's dad for a nominal fee, and I flew to Los Angeles. Judy joined me later.

During the next couple of weeks, I looked for a place to live and visited with my mom. I also looked into the divorce procedure. Eddie Traubner, my business manager, told me I'd have very little left after the divorce. I also found out that Mrs. Rhodes, who ran the home where my mother had been living for the last few years, was planning a move to La Jolla. I spoke with Mrs. Rhodes, and she agreed to have my mother move with her. My mother just adored Mrs. Rhodes, and I knew she'd be in good hands.

Judy flew to L.A., and we checked around for a house to settle down in. We looked at boats in the marina.

I also tried to work in golf at Bel-Air and have rehearsals with George Annis, our conductor. George was a bright, soft-spoken little Greek with a dry sense of humor. We got along famously.

The rehearsals were going fine. Judy and I found a beautiful new forty-two-foot Chris Craft Connie still sitting on blocks. It boasted a wooden hull and two Lincoln engines. We had to have it, and Eddie Traubner went crazy over the expense.

We left for Australia the next day with George Annis and a brochure of the boat.

★ ★ ★

We arrived November 2, and opened on the fifth at the South Sydney Junior League Club. It was great to be with Richard Gray again. He looked after us and played a pretty mean game of golf, too.

We stayed at the Cosmopolitan Double Bay Inn. Judy and I went to see Orson Bean in *Promises Promises*, and he was, as usual, charming. He invited us to have lunch with he and his wife, Carolyn, the following week. Orson is a very special person. We arrived at Doyles Restaurant in Double Bay for lunch. It is world famous for John Dory fish and Australian wines. We enjoyed a nice lunch and laughed a lot.

We were just finishing up with coffee when Carolyn said, "What's the date today? Oh my God, Orson this is the day we were to have lunch with the elite of Sydney!!!"

They went into a frenzy on how to handle the embarrassing situation. We drove them home, then called the following day. Someone answered and told us the Beans had left for the U.S. Judy and I felt terrible about it, but it must have been very important for the Beans to just pack up and leave. I guess they were trying to make friends in Australia feel more comfortable.

Fortunately for me, my show was a big success and an extra week was added. We left for home December 7 and arrived the eighth. My divorce was final on the tenth, but my bachelorhood didn't last long.

Judy and I went to the Chris Craft pier to pick up our boat. A cute little salesman named Ernie Ball took us for a demonstration to show us how to handle it. He had me move the boat away from the pier. We took a spin around the marina, and I docked it.

He said that's all there was to it and wished us a bon voyage. Handling the boat is not as difficult as flying an airplane or driving in traffic in Los Angeles. But common sense and good manners are involved. We received permission to leave the boat there until after our marriage and honeymoon in the Virgin Islands.

Judy went shopping with Del Noland, a friend of ours, and bought our first piece of furniture—a love seat—and we moved in.

While we were in Sydney, we had looked at the boat brochure so much, the pages became frayed. We tried to find a name for the boat and couldn't agree on one. One morning around three o'clock, I lay in bed thinking about it. I tried to make a name using our names. "Hey Judy" came to mind, but that didn't work.

I thought "Howard and Judy," but that was too ordinary. Then I combined part of the two—"How" and "Ju," but that didn't work. Then being a complete Anglophile, I remembered the English saying the greeting, "Howjudo." I said, "That's it! Howjudo."

I woke up Judy, "I have a name for the boat."

"What's that?"

"Howjudo."

She said, "Swell," and went back to sleep.

Nobody could understand the name, but we did, and we loved it! We closed in Australia and hurried to our floating home.

We loaded the boat with all our belongings, the divorce was finalized, and we took off for the Virgin Islands to meet Buddy and Jackie Eig to tie the knot. When we deplaned, we were met by Pie and Nita Branch, who were very close friends of Buddy and Jackie's. Pie, a big husky man with a welcoming grin from ear to ear, held two magnums of Taittinger Champagne, one under each arm.

Buddy and Jackie's plane was late, so we popped the

Champagne and waited for them. By the time their plane arrived, we had almost consumed the two magnums and were feeling no pain.

Buddy and Jackie's home, situated near the straits of Tortuga, was a magnificent sight, especially at night. The full moon lit up the water, we sat on the verandah and gazed across the straits. Something to behold.

We made arrangements to get married on the twenty-first. That was the only time we could get the town's mayor to perform the ceremony. We spent the rest of the twentieth drinking Champagne and shopping around the town with Buddy and Jackie. That night, we dined at Pie and Nita's home. They were a beautiful and charming couple. Judy and I fell in love with them and more in love with Jackie and Buddy.

We exchanged vows the following day around noon and had the most memorable honeymoon and Christmas you could ever imagine. Buddy and Jackie gave us our wedding as a gift. We will always be grateful to Buddy and Jackie and Pie and Nita Branch for being so generous to us. It was an unbelievable time in our lives.

We left on the twenty-eighth and flew up to Orlando in a DC-3 to meet Judy's family. After we landed in Orlando and were taxiing into the gates shortly before noon (it was only a small airport then), I looked out the window and saw a large number of people lined up along the fence line near our gate. I said to Judy, "Golly, there's a lot of people meeting our plane."

She said, "That's my family."

I couldn't believe it. There must have been fifty or sixty people waiting for us. Judy's mom and dad held a party at their home. Her uncles offered me a special drink they wanted me to try, and by one in the afternoon, I was playing drums in the band. I'd never played drums in my life, but there I was banging away and not doing too bad a job. The concoction they gave me was evil. Man, I didn't have a clue the rest of the day.

I had more damned fun with her aunts and uncles and all the kids. They welcomed me with open arms, and by the end of the day, I felt like a Magamoll. By the way, "Magamoll" is a German word meaning "Stomach One Time."

★ ★ ★

The following day, we flew to Los Angeles and the *Howjudo*, our home.

January's typically cool weather drew colder and dank in the evenings. We invited Eddie Traubner, my business manager, to see the boat and have dinner. We made a six o'clock reservation at a pleasant restaurant in the marina. We ate early because by eight-thirty, Eddie'd normally be in bed. With all his peculiar traits, you couldn't help but love the guy.

By the time we finished dinner with him and his girl-friend, it was already around eight-thirty. Eddie, who stood about 5 feet 4 inches and always impeccably dressed in a suit, shirt, and tie, walked with us down the pier to the boat. Because we didn't have steps to get on board, I would always grab Judy and lift her onto the deck.

The slip adjacent to the *Howjudo* was empty, and there wasn't a breath of air that night. The water shone like a mirror, it was that still. Dock lights provided the only illumination, and the yellow hue cast a mysterious spell over the marina. Outside night air had become colder, but I'd left the heater on inside the boat to take the chill off the night.

I helped Judy and Eddie's girlfriend onto the boat and gave Eddie the old heave-ho, too. Once inside, we opened a bottle of wine and gave Eddie a Cook's tour. He sipped his wine for only a few minutes, having warmed to the idea of us living on a boat, when he abruptly said, "Well, it's great, but I have to go home."

I hopped onto the pier and helped Eddie's girlfriend down and reached up for Eddie. He said, "I'll just hop down."

It was only about a five-foot drop so I stepped aside and Eddie jumped down to the pier—right into the water of the empty slip. Eddie always wore glasses, and he popped up from the murky water, still wearing them and treading water puppy-dog style.

I laughed like hell and tried to lift him onto the pier. He kept reaching out for me and spit water everywhere. I kept laughing because he looked like he was trying to imitate Shecky Greene. It was just one of those mad, mad, funny, goofball scenes.

I pulled him onto the pier. We somehow poured him inside the boat and took his clothes off. He shivered so hard, he couldn't talk. I wrapped him in one of my robes, and he downed hot coffee. I said, "Eddie, what in the hell were you trying to do?"

He said, "The empty pier looked like it had a black covering on it, and I was going to make the jump easier."

You had to know Eddie to know that jumping into cold water wasn't his style. Imagine him dressed in my long robe, walking his girlfriend down the pier. What a night.

The following morning, the phone rang, and a voice said, "Johnny Weissmuller here."

I fell out of bed laughing. Eddie was something else.

★ ★ ★

We eventually located a boat slip in the Venice Yacht Club. One night not long after, while we were having dinner on board, the boat gave a list to one side. I looked outside, and a guy who looked like a vagrant was on board. I yelled at him to get his ass off the boat, and he did. I watched him as he walked down the pier toward the end, and I asked Judy to call the police.

He continued walking down to the end near a sixty-footer that was tied up there and started unzipping a tarp that covered the entrance to the boat. I hit him with a big flashlight I had and told him to get off the pier. He zipped the tarp closed and ambled away. I held the light on him all the way to the gate. By that time, the shore patrol arrived, picked him up, and that's the last I heard of that.

A couple of mornings later, I was dead asleep when the boat gave a big list and rocked violently back and forth. Judy and I bounced out of our bunk and looked around. Water sloshed around us, but no one was in sight, so we returned to bed.

I had just about fallen asleep again when the phone rang. My mother said, "Harry, did you feel the earthquake?"

I said, "Hey, that's what it was! I thought somebody was trying to get on board the boat. Are you all right, Mom?"

Mom replied that she was fine.

The 1971 earthquake in Fillmore, California, caused

a lot of damage in the San Fernando Valley. I called my daughter, Kaija. Her house in the valley took quite a beating. There was no damage to the Coldwater Canyon home.

★ ★ ★

Judy and I attended the Crosby at Pebble Beach, my favorite pro-celebrity golf tournament, and stayed at the lodge. I didn't play too well, but we loved the trip and meeting old friends.

When we returned, Ralph Edwards's office called. They were going to revive the "Name That Tune" television program and wanted to see me. They suggested I might be the man to emcee the show. It sounded like a good idea. We went into a two-week rehearsal beginning February 1 and shot the pilot.

Everything seemed to go well, and I felt good doing it. They had a party after the show for which I bought all the Champagne. The overall feeling was that the pilot was great. It seemed that I'd found a new, exciting adventure. What a dreamer I was. I heard nothing for a couple of days. Then I was out, and they hired another emcee. I received no explanation from Ralph Edwards. What a snake charmer.

★ ★ ★

One day, I hit some balls at the Bel-Air and by late afternoon, went into the men's grill for a drink. The room was empty except for a gentleman sitting by himself. I introduced myself to him and asked if I might join him.

I had seen him around the club a lot, but had never met him or knew who he was. His name was Tom Arthur. We hit it off at once. We found out that the club was sort of a home away from home to both of us. He asked me where I lived, and I told him we lived on a boat in the Venice Yacht Club at Marina Del Rey.

He said, "Hell, I lived aboard a forty-foot sloop in the marina for years. My divorce came through, and I got married again and moved into an apartment on Panay Way."

I said, "Well, I got divorced and married again and happy as a lark aboard a forty-two-foot Chris Connie."

We seemed to have a great deal in common. He invited Judy and me to have dinner with him and his wife, Skip, that evening at Donkins, a marina restaurant. Skip and Judy hit it off immediately, and we became fast friends.

The following day, he called me, "How would you like a slip right on the main channel?"

I said, "Where and when?"

"Call me tomorrow morning."

We were assigned to a slip adjacent to the Arthurs' *Whynot* at the end of Panay Way. This was February 21, our second-month anniversary.

★ ★ ★

A couple of days later, my old English friend, Leslie Grade, called and invited me to perform a Night at the Palladium followed by a two-week date at the Talk of the Town.

Judy and I dusted off our passports and were off to London. My brother-in-law and sister-in-law, Pete and Cookie Magamoll, baby-sat our home/boat.

I added a couple of numbers to my regular show: "Raindrops Keep Falling" and "My Way." Sinatra had retired, and I felt someone had to keep that wonderful song alive. I changed a few lyrics and made it "His Way," as my tribute to Frank.

My daughter, Kirstine, joined us for a few days to watch her old man and get to know Judy a little better.

My dresser, Bill Linton, was a live Andy Capp and the funniest Cockney I ever knew. His wife was head costume mistress and always on his ass about something. His response would be, "Bugger off." Now that's a true love-hate relationship.

One night early in the run, I didn't have a ride to my room at the Savoy Hotel. Bill offered me a ride in a Rolls-Royce. I thought the vehicle was a courtesy car provided by the Talk of the Town producers.

We walked out front, and there stood a Mini Minor, the size of child's toy automobile. He said, "Your Lordship, your carriage awaits."

I said, "Your Cockneyship, Grassyass."

I crammed my long, lanky frame into that tiny car night after night, and for the show's run, he drove me to and from the Savoy before and after each performance.

When Talk of the Town closed, we journeyed north to play a week at the Wakefield Theater Club. I played golf with a terrific singer, Martin Dale, returned to London to rest and have a new tuxedo made. We dined with the artist, Walter Keane, and his wife. His paintings are famous worldwide, especially the breathtaking Little Girl, the one with the huge eyes standing on the long stairway. When I met Walter in San Francisco, that picture took up the entire wall of his foyer.

The following night, we dined with Christopher Lee and his wife, Gitte, and the next morning flew for home and the *Howjudo*. It had been a fun tour, and I was in good form, but it was nice to get home.

As we walked down the pier and turned at our slip to climb aboard, a brand-new set of steps greeted us, along with a sign that read, "Welcome to the Kruntz." That was the secret order of the Keels and Arthurs. They remain a special pair in our lives.

Tom and I would play golf at Bel-Air, and whoever had less to drink would drive. Then we'd cruise and have dinner, usually at Donkins. Friends thought I was slightly touched when I moved to the marina, but some of our happiest moments were the times we lived aboard. The people around us, the Arthurs, Montgomerys, Randalls, and Fig Newton and his family were all great fun and good friends.

One great weekend, we took my daughters Kirstine, Kaija, and her actor husband, Edward James Olmos, and my son, Gunnar, to Catalina for the weekend. As we passed the entrance to the marina, both engines died. I had miscalculated the gas consumption and luckily cruised to the marina. I called the Coast Guard, and they towed me to the gas dock for a fill-up. That was an embarrassing lesson about topping off the tanks before any voyage.

We also motored south to La Jolla to see my mother, who was eighty at the time, but still very sharp. She didn't get seasick and enjoyed the little cruise. She also used that opportunity to get to know Judy and absolutely fell in love with her. How could she not?

Mother and I adored Mrs. Rhodes, who had taken great care of mother for almost eight years. She was an incredible lady, and I knew mom was receiving the best care I could possibly procure for her.

Our cruising ended. I had to go to work.

45

I'm a Most Happy Fella

Judy and I cruised to the marina, and I began rehearsals with Jack Metz on *Most Happy Fella*. When I spoke with John Kenley about the production, I made arrangements for Gunnar to spend the summer at Kenley Players doing whatever he could to learn about the theater. He's a great dancer, and Kirstine has a beautiful voice.

We flew to Cleveland, then drove to Warren, Ohio. The wonderful cast included Karen Morrow, Catherine Christensen, Terence Monk, and Dean Dittmann. In a couple of songs, I had to lower the score. The F-sharp in "Mama Mama" was a challenge for me, but I managed to squeeze it out. I had seen Robert Weede, who was one of the few baritones and also a very good actor, with the original cast in New York. Nobody sang Joey like Art Lund. Mona Paulee was great in a thankless part. Catherine Christensen sang "Rosabella" beautifully. Opening night was an exciting, moving evening in the theater.

Minutes before my first entrance from stage right, a brief electrical fire sparked directly above my head. That startled my adrenaline for the entrance.

Later in the performance, when they pushed me out in the wheelchair, it cut loose and almost dumped me headlong into the orchestra pit. My experience from doing *Sunrise at Campobello* saved me from going over.

We played Columbus and Dayton, then closed. Gunnar stayed with me the entire run and along the way fell in love with a very pretty girl from Pennsylvania for the summer. I don't think he ever got over her. When Judy and I left Ohio, Gunnar stayed on to finish the season at Kenley Players.

★ ★ ★

I had received a script of the musical, *Ambassador*, and heard the lovely score that Donald Gohman and Hal Hackady wrote. The producers were Nancy Levering and Miranda D'Ancona. I had reservations, but the Grades in London liked it so much they put Leslie's son, Michael, on it.

I had played quite a bit of golf with Michael and found him to be very bright with a good sense of humor. Stone Widney would direct, and he had a long association with Lerner and Loewe. They also signed Danielle Darrieux, the beautiful French actress whose reputation suffered during the Nazi occupation of France. I didn't know her, but thought they were taking a big chance with her. I thought, what the hell, I have nothing else coming up. I love England, so let's do it.

Judy and I went down to see my mother and told her about our trip. She seemed more frail than during our

earlier visit, but Mrs. Rhodes assured us not to worry.
Mother had a few operations the previous summer and
never did completely recover. I hated to leave her, but I
had to do something to keep solvent. I had a lot of family to support.

On August 7, Judy and I left for London, rehearsals
started the ninth. I was a little late the first day, which is
not like me, but I had received word that Gunnar had a
bad accident on his motorbike and was in the hospital at
UCLA. I had trouble getting through on the telephone
to check on his condition.

It would be the beginning of a very tough expedi-
tion. I met Danielle, who was a lovely, delightful, and
charming woman, and the balance of the great English
cast. Bill Linton was my dresser once more.

The London apartment was a mess, but livable. Two
weeks into the show, Mrs. Rhodes called, and I spoke with
mom's doctor. He told me that mother needed another
operation, but he couldn't assure me her medical problems would be resolved. Mrs. Rhodes told me mom had
suffered a lot after a previous surgery, and she didn't think
another operation would help. My mother was very frail
at eighty-two, and I didn't want her to suffer through
another operation if it wasn't going to help her.

I told Mrs. Rhodes, "I don't want to put this decision
on you, but I think we should let mom go peacefully and
naturally. I don't want to put her through another futile
operation. Let's control the pain and let her go. I wish I
could be with her, but I can't. She's been a wonderful
mother to me and a true friend to many people on this
earth. I think it's time to let her go to the heaven she has
always talked about."

270

That was the twenty-third of August, and on the ninth of September, Mrs. Rhodes called to tell me mom didn't have much time and wanted to talk to me. Her weak voice whispered, "Harry, you have been a good boy. Now you must go on with your singing and study hard. Don't let anything stand in the way of your career. I love you, son."

That's the last thing she ever said to me.

I had to smile a little because for the last thirty years of her life, she was retired, and I took care of her. She handled my fan mail, and I gave her a new car every two years, until she had a stroke and could no longer drive. Then she spent the rest of her life with Mrs. Rhodes, who cared for her better than I ever could. Here I was a grown man, and she still worried about me and treated me like the little brat she remembered. That was my mom. And what a great mom she was.

She passed away a few hours later. Aunt Rea and I made arrangements to lay mom away in Aunt Rea's cemetery near Collinsville, Illinois.

46

The Show, Like Life, Must Go On

★ ★ ★ ★ ★

On Sunday the nineteenth, we traveled to Manchester to try out at the Palace Theater. During the drive, something hit my cords, and I told Judy I was in trouble. We arrived at the Midlands Hotel in Manchester where I tried to contact a throat doctor. But it was Sunday, and no one was available. Monday, we tried to rehearse, but the voice wasn't there. The cords were swollen and wouldn't pronate. Even though the house was sold out, we were forced to cancel the rest of the week. The Manchester doctors didn't have a clue.

I remained in my hotel room and breathed in hot steam and a mixture called tincture of benzoin. The press wanted to come in and take pictures, but I wasn't in the mood for that. There is nothing more terrifying for a singer than cords that refuse to pronate. I couldn't understand what happened to me. I'd been singing very well and feeling strong.

Sure, I had emotional things that I had to handle, but I didn't think that had anything to do with it. Before her death, mom had been very ill, and we had tried to get her to England to be near us. We even rented a new flat that had a bedroom for her.

They closed down *Ambassador* for the rest of the week. By that time, I was singing very well again and never experienced anything like that again.

We opened to average reviews. I had a fabulous opening number that had the word "waiting" in it. Unfortunately, one of the critics' headlines read, "Waiting! Waiting!"

The show was opulent and beautiful, but scenery and costumes do not a hit show make. They help, but the story needed help. For examples, I wondered why Danielle and I didn't have a romantic scene? Why was I a cuckold the whole show?

Alan Lerner saw the show and met with me and Stone Widney. We expressed our concerns. Alan agreed.

They worked out the small kinks and gave Danielle a new song. They took "All of My Life" out of the beginning and moved it to the end. The show in my mind was just too soft and lovely with Danielle having a lovely affair with a younger man and me running around like a doting CPA. It was pretty funny, but all wrong.

From Manchester, the show moved to Her Majesty in London. A clip of Danielle on a train with "Göring in Paris" was run on the news, and it hurt the box office. It didn't surprise me, but I was shocked when they did it. I never knew her very well, but she was a trouper and didn't flinch an inch. She and her husband were very French.

During the London rehearsals, we were in this apartment I didn't like. The apartment was arranged with a living room in the center, and on one side, there was a kitchen and dining room, on the other side the bathrooms and bedroom. There was a wide opening in the middle of the living room and an entrance to a hallway to the left and right and an entrance in the middle to the front door. Judy and I were entrenched in our work on my dialogue, when out of the corner of my eye, Henri de Toulouse-Lautrec walked across the wide opening of the living room and into the bedroom. I thought I was seeing things, so I asked Judy, "Did you see that?"

She asked, "See what?"

With that, Lautrec walked across the opening again from the bedroom to the dining room and kitchen. We both exploded in laughter, and Lautrec walked back, took a bow, said something in French that sounded terribly dirty, and stood up. It was Bill Linton. He had spent a few years with the Crazy Gang in Variety, and Lautrec had been one of his specialties. He was amazing.

I told Bud about it and suggested that they write in a few entrances for Lautrec to add humor in the dull spots. Nothing ever came of it.

We rented a lovely little home in Islington, a newly renovated section of London. It had been the home of an English actress, Noel Dyson. Perfectly situated, each day I'd hop a double-decker bus that took me practically to the stage door of Her Majesty.

I had very fast costume changes as Lambert Strether in *Ambassador* and could never have made them if it had not been for Bill Linton. He was incredible, and we never missed one change. The whole company was in love with Bill, and the spirit of the company and the backstage crew was always up for every performance. It might not have been the greatest show, but we gave them every ounce that we had.

The show closed after three months or so, and there was already talk of going to New York. I said I'd go only if Bill Linton was my dresser, and I meant it.

It wasn't easy to leave all the friends we made. There is nothing tougher than the closing of a show, whether it's a hit or not.

★ ★ ★

On January 3, we returned to the *Howjudo* and spent a couple of months relaxing with the Arthurs, playing golf, and playing with our boat.

A pilot named Robey Smith, who had once been married to a girl I knew from Gillespie, had a Cessna dealership at the Van Nuys Airport. I made him a deal to fly a 182 and pay only for gas and oil. Judy and I would fly around with him and help him with sales pitches. I also trained on the new 421-Cessna, a twin-engine airplane. I took lessons in an Airabatic airplane called Citabaria (Airabatic spelled backward). It was a tail-dragger, and I had a lot of fun with my old trainer, Adam Berg.

Fun aside, I worked in Vegas at the Fremont for four weeks, then rehearsed for *La Mancha* for the Meadowbrook Dinner Theater in New Jersey, also starring Lou Criscuolo, Gaylea Byrne, and Jack Dabdoub.

A dinner theater is another animal, and about half the time, you perform for your own amazement. Near the end of the run, which was ten weeks, we had a sold-out dinner show for a group of nothing but ladies. It was

275

a very tough show. More like performing in a chicken house. It seemed they never stopped yakking. After the scene where Don Quixote and Sancho get beaten and robbed by the Arabs, they return to the Inn, or Castle as Quixote saw it. They walk to the entrance, and the Innkeeper played by Jack Dabdoub sees them coming and says, "This inn is closed."

Quixote says, "Thou wouldst deny entrance to a knight dubbed by thine own hand?"

The Innkeeper repeats, "This inn is closed."

A lady in the audience said, "Oh. Let him in, let him in!"

I turned to her in character and said, "Shut up, you miserable old broad!"

I had a hell of a time keeping things going for a while, but I had had it with the ladies that performance, and I couldn't resist responding. It was the only quiet program I performed because that shut up the audience.

★ ★ ★

One day, I bumped into Reginald Owen, a terrific character actor and a delightful human being, who had been an old golfing buddy of mine from Bel-Air Country Club. I invited him to see the show. He loved it and like Pat O'Brien, carried on and on about my performance. That gave me a great lift. At the end of the run at the Meadowbrook Dinner Theater, I was voted the best male performer of the season in a musical. It was my first award in the theater.

We closed June 25, and flew home to the *Howjudo*, worked on the boat, played golf with Tom Arthur, and had a nice time in Catalina. I did a Christmas show for

NBC and also appeared on the "Sonny and Cher Show."

On July 30, we rehearsed in Camden, New Jersey, and opened an eight-week run of *La Mancha*. After Camden, we toured in Albany, New York, then Shady Grove, and Gaithersburg, Maryland, followed by the Storrowton Theater in West Springfield, Massachusetts, and Westbury, New York.

The producers wanted Lainie Kazan to play Aldonza in Westbury. Like a boob, I said, "No problem." Ha! Ha! She was scheduled to be at the Storrowton Theater on Wednesday to rehearse with the cast, but didn't show until late Friday afternoon. Eddie Roll, who directed the show and played Sancho, warned me she was a fistful, but I never expected anything like this. She was the size of a baby whale. We didn't start rehearsals until Monday because we had matinees Saturday and Sunday.

Monday morning, she insisted that we adapt to her way of playing the Queen Aldonza. Right, that sat well with me and the cast. It usually would take only one musketeer to carry Aldonza off after the rape scene, but it took six to carry her. She was over the moon as Aldonza, and when it came to singing the "Impossible Dream" in the final death scene of Quixote, she sang like a diva in a Wagnerian aria from *Tristan and Isolde*.

I sat up and said, "Where are you going, Lainie?"

She said, "Howard, you are embarrassing me."

I said, "No Lainie, you are embarrassing you. This show is the *Man of La Mancha*, about a man named Don Quixote, and you are to play a supporting role and a damned good one named Aldonza. Not the Queen of Sheba."

Guber was offstage. She ran to him, and I followed

her. She screamed that she'd never been treated like that before and I said, "She brought it on herself. She showed up two days late in West Springfield. We waited for her for two days in that tent, and she missed two days' rehearsals. We couldn't rehearse Saturday or Sunday because we had matinees. Now here we are, and she has been nothing but trouble.

"My advice is to call in the other Aldonza and let her see how the part is played for a few days before she assumes the role. Or pay her off, and I will split the cost with you. I think that would be the best way because I am sick of her and her complete rudeness to a good company. She hasn't a clue what the part is about.

"Or you can get another Quixote." I walked away.

After Guber talked to her for a while, we started from the very beginning. Eddie Roll worked her butt off the rest of the day and part of the next. I love the theater, and I can't understand the lack of respect for other actors that she showed.

We played Westbury for two weeks and Valley Forge for another. We were on her ass the whole three weeks, and she was becoming a fairly decent Aldonza. But she's a tough cookie.

During the Westbury run, I learned they wanted to try *Ambassador* in New York. When we closed *La Mancha* in Valley Forge, Judy and I scampered to L.A., checked the *Howjudo*, and packed for New York. We arrived at the Wyndham Hotel and started rehearsals.

Bill Linton was there for the first rehearsal, and most of the major roles were the same as those in London. Andrea Marcovicci, a young girl who was so special that she brought her own spotlight to the stage, was the only real change. We rehearsed four weeks. The media ran the same pictures of Danielle as in London. I sang the same songs and made the same changes and had a great time with Bill Linton.

We opened at the Lunt-Fontanne Theater on November 19, 1972, to poor notices and closed the twenty-fifth. I never understood who or where the producers, Miranda D'Ancona, Gene Dingenary, and Nancy Levering, were.

★ ★ ★

We flew home on November 27, had dinner with the Arthurs, and played a little golf. I received a call that weekend that they were having trouble at the Coconut Grove Playhouse in Florida with Robert Horton in *La Mancha*. I said I'd fly from Washington to Miami to do the play for them. Even though they told us we weren't needed, Judy and I flew out to Los Angeles Monday morning. Tuesday morning they called. They wanted me. Judy and I flew across country to Miami and with no rehearsal at all, I walked onstage in a totally different environment and opened for them that night. It was maddening.

It was wild, and thank God I had Lou Criscuolo as Sancho. I knew *La Mancha* like the back of my hand, but the rest of the cast had never worked with me. The roles were harder for them than me. The audience was very understanding and demonstrative, and the critics were also positive and understanding.

Judy and I stayed at the David William Hotel where we first met. We played two weeks and saw Judy's mom and dad and spent Christmas with them, then flew home.

For three blissful months, January, February, March,

Judy played house, taking care of the *Howjudo*. I played golf at Bel-Air and enjoyed seeing friends. On April 1, we leased a one-bedroom apartment above the Arthurs and moved in. We had a glorious view of the *Howjudo* and the marina's main channel. We purchased a small Porsche 914 to scoot around town in.

Break over! April 23, it was back to work in *La Mancha* in Jacksonville, Florida. It was a dinner theater and had a producer/director who decided that *La Mancha* should be done with a thrust stage. I told him it wouldn't work and made them tear it out, which was no big job, and build a proper proscenium-type stage with the stairway into the dungeon going up and down. The production was all right and had a fair cast. After six weeks, we left for Cohasset, Massachusetts, to rehearse *La Mancha* with Patricia Marand. We played South Shore Music Circus and Cape Cod Music Fair one week each, then onto Shady Grove, Maryland, for rehearsals of *Molly Brown* with Tammy Grimes. It was a good cast of professionals, and I enjoyed them, but I didn't enjoy the role at all. Musically, it was written for a tenor like John Raitt, and I think it lost a lot in my keys.

We played Painter's Mill in Baltimore; Shady Grove, near Gaithersburg; Camden, New Jersey; Westbury, New York; Valley Forge, Pennsylvania; Cleveland, Ohio; and West Springfield, Massachusetts.

Josh Logan attended one performance in Westbury. Tammy knew he'd come to see her, and she gave a spectacular performance. After the show, I asked her where that came from or where have you been. I lost all respect for her after that.

She had a wonderful cast around her and up to that

time hadn't given us a performance anywhere near that one. I could hardly wait to get out of that show. I've never met Josh Logan, but I know who Tammy Grimes is now.

★ ★ ★

We arrived home Sept 2 and rested. We cruised to Catalina for a couple of days, saw our friends, played golf, and raised a little hell. During these rest periods, I wouldn't sing at all for about two weeks. After which, I'd do my soul fedge and move it every day for fifteen or twenty minutes. It helped keep the voice in shape. Soul fedge is nothing more than a group of scales using all the vowels with different consonants to warm up the voice. Papa Rossi gave them to me, and I've always used them.

September and October, I appeared several times on the "Merv Griffin Show" although I never felt comfortable on those talk shows and eventually stopped doing them.

Bill Francisco visited us the last two weeks of October to work on a show for the nightclub at Disney World. He and I have a wicked sense of humor. Judy can sing very well, but I wouldn't put her in because she'd steal the show. She has a superb comic sense, and I've always felt that given the chance, she would be great.

We told Judy we needed a singer to back me up with "tra la las" in the first number, which was "Sing, Sing a Song." We told her when to come in, and she was fine. So fine in fact that once she started, she would have to do more. After about a week, we confessed that we were just kidding. Well, she had worked very hard on her part, and that hurt her. The joke backfired, and she didn't speak to us for a couple of days.

We opened at Disney World, and she stayed with her parents for a few days before forgiving us. She's very talented, but I didn't want to start something that might get us into entanglements. I was selfish and loved her too much for that. I just adore her, always have, and always will.

After Disney World, I went to Houston for *Kismet*. I played a little golf with Jackie Burke and Jimmy Demaret at the Champions Golf Course when I could. I'd met Jackie Burke years before at the Los Angeles Open at the Riviera Country Club, and it was fabulous to play golf with he and Jimmy Demaret again. They were very kind to Judy and me while we were there and made us feel right at home.

Kismet had a lady director. Her husband was a good singer and played the Caliph. In the first talk-through, I learned she wanted to finish the show with the lovely song "Night of My Nights," which her husband sang.

I locked horns with her and said the show finished with "Princes Come, Princes Go," which I sang, and I wouldn't stand for that cut. That didn't sit well with her.

We started rehearsing with "Rhymes Fine Rhymes" and came to the word "onomatopoeia." She stopped me and said, "The word is pronounced 'onomatopia.'"

In front of the entire company, I corrected her. "No, the word is a cornucopia of vowels, and you sing every vowel." I added, in a very polite way, that I wanted no more shit from her. She never said another word to me, which was fine. It had nothing to do with her being a woman. She was just a bitch. I have worked with lots of women directors and found them to be very good. I just don't like being pushed around by anyone.

The management also put me in a lousy motel even though my contract said, "suite at the Shamrock." So I checked into the Shamrock, took a large two-bedroom suite, and had Boris Kaplan, who played the Wazir, move in with Judy and me.

I had a lot of fun onstage with the cast and all, but I don't think I made too many friends with the management.

★ ★ ★

Back at the marina, I brushed up on my nightclub act. Jane Powell was supposed to do a date in Hobart, Tasmania, and couldn't for some reason. Her husband, James Fitzgerald, asked me if I could fill in for her. It was for four weeks, and it would help pay the bills, so I said yes. The only problem for me was that it cut me out of playing the Crosby at Pebble Beach.

That hurt. I sat down and wrote Bing a letter and told him that I had a job in Tasmania and couldn't pass it up. Bing wrote me immediately. He said, "Sorry, Howdy, that you can't make the clambake, but Hobart, Tasmania, can't be all bad. Merle Oberon was born there. See you next year."

Gunnar needed a little spending money, so I took him along as my tour manager. He did a damn good job. Dick Parrinello agreed to conduct. The flight to Tasmania is twenty-seven hours, and we arrived the day before New Year's Eve when we were supposed to open.

We were beat and needed a good rest. My diplomacy suffers when I'm tired. We walked to the desk at the

Westpoint Hotel Casino and was told that our suite wouldn't be ready until the following day. I said, "Hold the limousine, we're going back home."

Silence from behind the counter.

I added, "If my suite isn't ready now, then I'm going back to the United States, and someone else will have to do the show. Now make up your mind. I'm tired, and I'm not in a very good mood."

The suite suddenly became ready. The Swiss, who are a bit strange and cold, ran the hotel.

We had a nice orchestra and a beautiful room to work in, good sound and lights. Gunnar and Parrinello played tennis while I played golf. Poor Judy was sick the entire time and didn't leave the suite. She was pregnant, and we didn't know it. Later, we were ecstatic when we heard the news.

The casino only allowed two-dollar betting, so there was no big money around. After our sold-out run, we were followed in this beautiful room by a sheep-shearing contest that was also sold out.

We stopped in Sydney before returning to L.A. and had dinner at the Coachman, one of my favorite restaurants.

★ ★ ★

In the middle of August, Barry Freed, with the IFA agency, called me for *I Do, I Do* in Seattle at the Cirque Dinner Theater. The theater was actually a converted bowling alley, but it worked out very well. Bowling alleys are built on a slant with the pins at the low end and the retrievers for the bowling balls and the bowlers at the high ends. Acoustically, it holds the noise of the balls hitting the pins to a bare minimum. Put the stage and music at the high end, and the sound bounces off the ceiling on down to the low end, and it's amazing. Acoustically for a theater, it works out well. No sound equipment is needed at all.

I had met a terrific singer and actress in New York named Alice Evans, and we brought her out to play the Mary Martin part. An awesome lady with a great sense of humor by the name of Mary Levine directed, played piano, and conducted the small orchestra.

The audiences were very sharp and made it a pleasure to perform for them. We opened August 25. At the end of the first week, Judy entered the hospital. I caught a Western Airlines to L.A. I had called Art Kelly, president of Western, who was a friend of mine at Bel-Air Country Club, and they held the flight for five minutes for me. They closed the doors, and I sat down exhausted after two shows. I no sooner sat down than a hostess approached me and said, "Mr. Keel, you're a father of a little baby girl."

Art Kelly got word to the pilots of the flight. They gave me a bottle of Champagne, and we toasted Judy and the baby. Tom Arthur picked me up in L.A. I had to see my two beauties. Judy never looked more beautiful, and Leslie was a gorgeous baby. I was over the moon. I went to Bel-Air, passed out the cigars, and lifted a few drinks with my buddies.

Judy experienced no medical complications. She, the baby, and her mother joined me in Seattle after a couple of weeks. The show was very successful, and after five weeks, we closed.

★ ★ ★

The rest of 1974 was spent at home in the marina watching Leslie grow and Judy becoming a wonderful mother. In November, I did one week of *South Pacific*. It was not a good production, and I was glad when the show's run ended.

In January 1975, we realized we'd outgrown the boat, and the Panay Way apartment managers didn't allow children. Judy found us a two-bedroom-plus-den home in Sherman Oaks with a beautiful view of the valley only twenty minutes to nearly all that we needed and ten minutes to the Bel-Air Country Club.

We settled in, sold the *Howjudo*, and I played more golf. In the middle of July, we went to Australia again and played a lovely spot up on the Great Barrier Reef for six weeks.

Back home, we had a three-month run of what was called *Gene Kelly's Salute to Broadway*. He was supposed to direct it, but became ill. Ron Field assumed the role and did a brilliant job. We had an awesome cast that included Ken Berry, Mimi Hines, and Lainie Nelson. Norman Geller conducted a great band of young guys. Not one hophead in the whole group. We were a happy group of strolling players on a three-month run of one-nighters. I never missed a performance.

I drove the whole tour with Judy and Leslie in a big Lincoln Continental. We started in September and wound up late in November. We felt that the irresistible Norman Geller was largely responsible for the group's esprit de corps. To have a cheerleader like him in the orchestra pit made each performance a pleasure.

The balance of 1975, we stayed home and rested. We needed the time off and took it.

47

Stranded in a Blinding Snowstorm

★　★　★　★　★

In the middle of May 1976, the Theater Guild asked me to join a touring company called *Musical Jubilee*. The Guild was partly responsible for starting me on my career, and I felt that I owed them. The cast was all great, starting with Patrice Munsel, Eartha Kitt, Larry Kert, and Milo O'Shea. We toured from Wilmington, Delaware, to Pasadena, California. In a few places, we would play a week and in others, only two or three days. It wasn't an easy tour, but it paid the bills, and the cast again became one big happy family. We closed at the Ambassador Auditorium in the middle of August.

★ ★ ★

During *Musical Jubilee* when we were in Michigan, I received a note that Rebecca Pratt of Gillespie, Illinois, would like to see me. She stood about 6 feet 2 inches tall and walked like a sidewinder down the aisle. She had been a great choir teacher and a strong role model, always going out to the baseball and football teams to grab players to be in her glee club.

As a teenager, I had tried out for the quartet, but she refused to hear me sing.

She walked down the theater aisle toward me and said, "Harry, damn you. I've never been able to live down the fact that you tried to get into the glee club and I wouldn't let you."

"I didn't say glee club, Mrs. Pratt. I said the 'quartet.' And I don't blame you for not putting me in the quartet. But you thought it was the glee club."

She said, "I thought it was the glee club."

"No. It was the quartet."

"You've turned into a really handsome man," she added.

I was stunned to see her. She stood tall and proud before me and looked wonderful. Her hair had grayed a bit since we last met. More importantly, she had waited all those years to apologize to me—thirty years or more. She had great dignity and was a very sharp teacher and gracious lady.

* * *

In the early fall, I got a call from Australia about doing *Annie Get Your Gun*. I agreed, but only if I could pick the actress for Annie. I asked Lainie Nelson, who brought her daughter, Heather, with her. Heather, who was about eleven years old and brilliant, was disabled and confined to a wheelchair.

Lainie and I played the clubs and sang beautifully together. She made a big hit with the Aussies. Heather and Judy and Leslie developed a lasting friendship. The trip paid off in many ways. After four weeks, we were home for Christmas.

In January, I went into New York for rehearsals of the *Shenandoah* road show. When this show opened on Broadway, it took me by surprise because I didn't know it was being done. The producers had wanted Robert Ryan and Jack Palance, but for some reason, it didn't work out. Why my agents didn't put me up for consideration, I'll never know. They simply never called me. I always thought Jimmy Stewart was wonderful in the movie role, but I thought John Wayne would have been perfect. He had the size and strength for the role.

When Zev Bufman offered me the role, I jumped at it. I did it for a price to try it out, and I think I was right. It's a very emotional role, and the first couple of days, I kept breaking down in tears. I got a hold of myself and started performing the role. I kept getting ahead of myself emotionally. I simply had to play the part page by page.

Joel Zwick was an insightful director who let me go at first, then took me aside and suggested that I hold back on the emotion.

The cast was all young professionals, and the chemistry was there. There was not one weakness in the casting. *Shenandoah* is a very moving story. It grabbed you by your throat, and you'd find yourself laughing and crying at the same time.

We opened in Florida and played to packed houses for six weeks, closed on March 4, and left for Idaho Falls and played Ricks College for a week with their students. That was a nice and different experience.

Zev Bufman called about playing the Kennedy Center with *Shenandoah*. I said fine, but not for the same money. I received a substantial raise and the Presidential Suite at the Watergate. We rehearsed, and opened to great reviews and packed houses for three weeks.

I brought my Aunt Rea, who was eighty-two at the time and still sharp as a tack, to Washington for a week. She had never heard me in a theater, and she saw every performance that week. At one time, she had a terrific voice and opted to marry my Uncle Don, thus giving up any thought of a career.

President Jimmy Carter came to a performance, and the cast was very excited. The house was smothered with guards, and we thought he might come backstage. But he didn't, nor did he send a message to the cast. I guess he found out I'm a Republican.

We closed on April 30, and Buddy and Jackie Eig threw a big party for the cast. We flew home the next day. Judy ordered new furniture for the place on Longbow in Sherman Oaks, and I bought us a BMW. Our Porsche had been stolen, and it took a long time to settle with the insurance company. Our Steinway piano had been completely redone, and it arrived, too.

We flew down to Fort Worth, Texas, and rehearsed a week and played a week at the Casa Manana Playhouse and worked again with my old friend, Jack Bunch.

My daughter, Kirstine, married David Borges. Not one of my favorite people, but I returned for the wedding.

Jane Powell and I went into rehearsals of *South Pacific* in Tulsa, Oklahoma, for an extensive tour. We opened in the middle of June and finished the first part of the tour in the middle of September. We then refurbished the show in L.A. and opened in San Diego for a week, two weeks at the Pantages Theater in Hollywood, then Kansas City, Missouri, at the Lyric Theater, and onto St. Louis for a week, then closed November 20.

On January 29, 1978, Jane and I flew into New York to rehearse *South Pacific* again and opened at the Fischer Theater in Detroit the following week. The day we were to leave New York, a huge snowstorm hit and closed down all the airports. I rode in a taxi driven by a Russian. He told me, "We don't even have snowstorms like this in Russia."

The producers decided to bus us to Philadelphia then fly us into Detroit.

The bus didn't pick us up until around two o'clock and what was actually an hour or so trip from New York to the Delaware River took us four hours. The driver drove us through huge snowbanks, and when we reached the bridge, it was closed.

We came to a dead stop behind huge semitrucks and automobiles. I exited the bus and walked ahead to see what was holding us up. The whole gap had been blocked by falling snow. No one could get through. It was an incredible sight. I returned to the bus and told them we were lost. No one knew where we were.

Meanwhile, Judy received a call from a Detroit reviewer who told her, "They've lost Howard and Jane and the cast. We don't know where they are."

I called the National Guard and said, "Look, I'm Howard Keel. Jane Powell and I and a whole cast of *South Pacific* is stalled here on this bus with no food or anything. We need to get to Detroit so we can open tomorrow night at the Fischer Theater. See what you can do to help us out."

In about four hours, the National Guard and two

trucks reached us somehow and took us to a big armory, fed us, and put us up for the night. We managed to get to the Philly airport the next day, but couldn't make the opening in time. The National Guard tried their damnest to help us, but it just wasn't possible. We opened the next night, played two weeks, then on to Chicago in a huge theater. It didn't work well, and we closed in a week. That's show business.

In the middle of May, Jane Powell and I went into rehearsals for a run of *Seven Brides for Seven Brothers*. We rehearsed for two weeks and then opened June 6 in Dallas for two weeks. I wasn't too happy with the casting, and the show itself, I felt, didn't adapt well to the stage. We ran until August 7 and closed. It did well financially, but I found the part of Adam a bore to play night after night.

The barn-raising and dance scenes didn't adapt to a stage at all, but it paid the bills. The whole show was on a stock contract, and after opening, nothing could be changed. It was my understanding that it was to be a trial run.

In January, they hired a new director. Again they tied our hands with a stock contract. We closed shortly, and I said good-bye to the whole thing.

★ ★ ★

In September 1979, I played the Barrier Reef in Australia again for a couple of weeks. In February 1980, I flew to England and did a hit musical series, *Song by Song*, for a week. In April, Barry Freed came up with a job in Washington State at a place called Moses Lake. I was to do *South Pacific* with a group of townies. That was something else, and there's no way to explain it. They had a good golf course, and that helped, and I met a fan and her mother who were very curious as far as fans go.

For a lark, I took them to dinner and the fan said she had looked up my horoscope and would send me good news.

To keep my interest up and my boredom down, I'd watch 747s do touch-and-goes at the local air base. There were as many as four or five, all Japanese air carriers, in the air at one time. It was the same air base that tested the Boeing B-29s that dropped the atom bombs on Japan.

When I returned to L.A., my fan sent me a letter saying that I was going through a bad time, but that not too long into the future, I would hit the jackpot and become very well off financially. Thank God for Moses Lake.

On June 3, 1980, Jane Powell and I opened in *I Do, I Do* at the Pantages in Hollywood. We played there, closed July 6, and took the show to San Francisco and Seattle with great box-office success.

In September 1980, I did *Camelot* for four weeks at the Cirque Theater. They had put in the scene where Arthur gets caught in an invisible cage and cannot get out. I guess I played it a little too well because when Leslie, who was only six years old, saw it, she became so upset at seeing her daddy in the predicament that Judy had to take her backstage to see that I was all right. What a lovely sensitive child she was and still is. We had a nice run and returned home.

Around this time, Prince Rainier of Monaco arrived in Los Angeles and contacted Charles Bernold, manager of the Bel-Air Country Club. Bernold called and asked me if I could play golf with the prince. We played eighteen holes at the club, stopped for a lunch break, then played another nine. He's a fine man and competitive golfer. I told Prince Rainier the story about Lt. Douglas Bader and King George. He fell apart laughing. He invited me to play in his local tournament, but I had a conflict for that date. Kismet.

New shows weren't being written, new songs not being scored, no new or original roles were being developed for quality musical shows. That saddened me, and I talked with a friend of mine in Oklahoma City about their oil boom. He suggested that I move to Oklahoma, and he'd introduce me and see if I could become an ambassador of the boom and get on the bandwagon.

Judy and I discussed it and decided to sell everything and move. Kaija's husband, actor Edward James Olmos, and my son, Gunnar, and other friends packed our belongings in a U-Haul truck and trailer, and on Thanksgiving day, we headed for Oklahoma.

Tom Arthur packed us a delightful turkey dinner that we ate at the first rest area short of Palm Springs on Interstate 10. A bittersweet move and a low point in our lives.

We arrived in Oklahoma in three days and settled into a little home. On January 5, 1981, I flew into L.A. to do a "Love Boat" appearance with Jane Powell. On Monday the nineteenth, I received a message. "They want to see you for 'Dallas' at MGM."

Big D, Little A, Double LL AS saves my ASS

★ ★ ★ ★ ★

48

"**D**allas" wasn't just a series. It was a phenomenal event … the most incredible piece of television to hit the airwaves in that century. The whole world watched it and still does today. To become a part of the cast was beyond my dreams. I didn't know why they wanted me, but I felt this would be the biggest turn around of my career, and it was.

I'd been working in show business for more than thirty-five years. I was sixty-one and all but dead broke, on my ass, no jobs, no money, nothing. We placed our Sherman Oaks home on the market and moved all we had left to Oklahoma to a little home owned by Maurice Woods.

There was an opportunity for a new job there in a new life away from show business. Later the oil wells busted, and the banks caved in. Meanwhile, Judy unpacked. When my manager called with an offer to appear in a "Love Boat" episode with Jane Powell for Aaron Spelling, I packed in minutes. Judy rushed me off to the airport. On her way home, the car stalled dead four blocks from home. The driver's window slid down into the door frame never to be seen again. Did I mention it happened in a driving snowstorm?

In L.A., came word that Leonard Katzman wanted to see me at MGM. He wanted to take a look at me. He liked me right away and offered me a role in "Dallas."

I flew back to Judy. We again rented a U-Haul, packed up, and returned to Sherman Oaks. Thirteen days later, we partially packed for a summer move for filming.

We filmed two episodes, and they asked me to return the following year for ten more. My first scene in "Dallas" was with Linda Gray. It was well written and played easily. We were on the same stage set at MGM where the horse fell on me many years prior. Linda is a beautiful, warm, sexy lady, and a very good actress. We had a mutual admiration society going full blast. Irving Moore, who was a quiet man with great taste, was my first director on "Dallas."

The first scene took no time to shoot. Leonard Katzman came down to the set and said he liked what he saw. The whole afternoon was filled with professionalism.

Parts of the show were filmed near Dallas on Southfork, an enormous ranch; the rest was filmed on an MGM sound stage in Los Angeles. And what déjà vu. That first scene was shot on the same stage for my first entrance in *Annie Get Your Gun* when the horse slipped, went down, and broke my ankle. That was 1949. This 1981 scene became the rebirth of my career and an introduction to a whole new life that would be both exciting and successful.

★ ★ ★

I knew Jim Davis casually, but I didn't see him while I was working on the two episodes of "Dallas." During the show's hiatus in 1981, Jim passed away and left a huge hole in the cast. He had an inoperable brain tumor that, after a long illness, took his life. Fate can be so cruel sometimes. Jim had been around the business doing lesser movies at MGM, and he considered the part in *Winter Meeting*, a movie with Bette Davis, his big chance.

The director misdirected the picture, and it was a flop. They naturally put the blame on Jim, and he was more or less buried in the business doing small parts. This was in 1947-48. But Jim had guts and determination, and nearly thirty years later, he won a part that fit him perfectly—Jock Ewing.

Jim made his career mark in that role and no one could replace him. I never knew that Jim was sick. When I received word that he'd passed away, I was dumbfounded. I couldn't believe that this big incredible man had been taken away when he was beginning to reap the rewards of his life's work.

There was talk that I'd replace him as Jock, and I said, "That's impossible."

I guess the powers of "Dallas" agreed, and I stayed on as Clayton Farlow. As soon as I finished the first two scripts, I hopped back to Oklahoma City. Poor Judy. She had just finished unpacking all those boxes and trunks. We'd been walking on pins and needles for so long, trying to make ends meet. We had large responsibilities and being able to handle them looked awfully dim until "Dallas" came along.

We'd been together ten years, and in spite of all the

297

places I dragged her, Judy never complained once. My Judy is something else!

★ ★ ★

I never felt I was part of the "Dallas" family. Always an outsider. That's the way the role was written, and that's how I was treated. Judy and I were flown to Dallas and arrived at the hotel. There was no itinerary. We were told that helicopters had taken the stars from the hotel to Southfork for a big gala. Steve Kanaly and I scrambled to get a taxi or a ride out to the Southfork Ranch in time for the Willie Nelson show. We made it on time, but barely.

They asked us, "Where the hell were you two? How come you didn't make the trip with us?"

They flew out without us.

Then the electricity went out. Fortunately, generators had been provided. We were seated on a dais with a table in front of us. A white substance in a dish was passed to Judy, and she passed it to me. She whispered that it was Sweet'N Low and I was supposed to pass it to the next person at the table. Cocaine at my first party on "Dallas." I drank my Scotch and passed on the white stuff.

On May 18, I flew into Dallas to start working on the next ten episodes and moved into the Doubletree Inn. I stepped in the elevator, and there stood the tiniest, pretty little girl I ever saw. I thought, "That's all I need, to be caught on an elevator with a juvenile."

She looked at me and smiled, and I gave an awkward, silly grin and begged to get off the elevator. When the elevator stopped, she smiled again and walked out. I breathed a big sigh of relief when I reached my floor. This all happened around five o'clock, and as soon as I entered my room, the phone rang.

Leonard Katzman said, "Welcome to Dallas. Come on down to the bar, and have a drink."

He introduced me to a couple of "Dallas" crew members, and I told him about my little ride on the elevator. They all laughed like hell. I said, "Okay, let me in on the laugh."

Leonard told me, "That little juvenile happened to be Jock Ewing's granddaughter in the show. Her name is Charlene Tilton."

I actually never had time to watch the show and didn't have a clue about the Ewing family. I breathed a sigh of relief and said, "I'll have another double Scotch."

From then on, "Dallas" was a cornucopia of surprises one after another. Everything was done to make me feel comfortable on the show and working on the lot at MGM made me feel at home, too.

Judy and I had dinner with Leonard and LaRue Katzman on the first night, and Judy let her own character out of the bag. She and LaRue hit it off right away. After dinner, Judy wanted a banana split, and Leonard ordered an extraordinary large-sized one on a huge silver platter.

When he reached over to take a scoop, Judy pulled the plate away. Leonard couldn't believe it. He tried and tried, but Judy wouldn't share the split with him. LaRue was in hysterics and rooted for Judy.

Through the years, we shared many great dinners, vintage wines, and lots of spoon fights over Judy's dessert. It became an inside joke, Leonard swiping a bite from Judy's plate. Dinners ended with a fine cigar and brandy.

LaRue is a tall, elegant woman, who has exquisite

taste in clothes and walks like a model. She's not only a great cook, but a home decorator, and in her spare time would knit beautiful sweaters for all the girls in the show and all the wives of the main actors.

Leonard was the finest producer, director, and writer I ever worked for. His door was always open to discussion about the slightest thing. You could talk to him while he was directing, and if he saw something he didn't like, he'd always tell you about it without pulling any punches.

Judy and I love the Katzmans and cherish the wonderful years we've spent together.

Lenny stood by me through twelve seasons and had the balls to take me to lunch when he had to let me go at the end.

* * *

Larry Hagman and Pat Duffy would sometimes get bored at the dinner-table scenes. They'd kid about and would be terribly funny. Word would get out that they were at it, and Leonard would merely walk onto the set to settle them down.

Nothing was ever said. It didn't have to be. They simply settled down to the work at hand. You didn't fool around with Leonard. With him, there were no histrionics, only his look.

Working with Larry Hagman was quick, precise, and always a pleasure. We only had one day of what you might call "testing" who Clayton Farlow was. Larry didn't seem to be in a great mood, and he yelled at me, "Hey, asshole, get the hell over here."

Now I don't like being called an asshole or being

yelled at. So I said, "All right, Mr. Asshole, what do you want this asshole to do?"

He looked at me and said nothing. I said, "Come on, asshole, what do you want me to do?"

He chuckled. "Well, asshole, you're standing in my key light, so move over, please."

"With pleasure, sir."

We got along fine from then on. Larry is one hell of a fine actor.

★ ★ ★

He had a dinner-table scene one day when he had to apologize to the entire family. It was an extended scene and to lay it out, or "block it" as they say, he did it a little limp wristed. Well, he had us in hysterics. He was incredibly funny. The whole scene ran about four minutes, and he never missed a beat. He had us all on the floor. Even Barbara Bel Geddes, who hated fooling around during a scene, was beside herself.

He turned right around when it was time to shoot it and had us all in tears at the end. He moved around that table to everyone and did it in one take. What an incredible actor.

He stopped, looked around the table, and walked off the set. They left the scene the way he did it and never cut in for closeups on anyone.

★★★

Let's talk about sex. I ain't no Clayton Farlow. He never had sex with anyone. Not even with Miss Ellie. I was crazy about Sue Ellen, and there was something there. Linda Gray is one of the sexiest women I know. Priscilla Presley and I added renewed interest with viewers, too.

301

That is one gorgeous lady. If I hadn't really loved Judy, I know I'd have gotten in trouble.

"Dallas" was a funny show. Every year, they added a new beauty, and everyone hopped in and out of everyone's bed, mostly to have sex with J.R. or Bobby. Even Cliff Barnes rolled in the hay with Sue Ellen.

Clayton Farlow only fantasized about sex, and as a stepfather of J.R., wanted to beat the crap outta him or beat some sense into him. For some reason, I was only allowed to get mad, raise my hands, leave that dinner table, and never stand up to the biggest shit in television.

There was one scene with Sue Ellen and Clayton. She's sleeping off another drunk wearing Clayton's pajama tops. I'm this close, arms on her shoulders, face to face, lips to lips in a hotel room. It looks like I'm going to kiss her crazy any second. The doorbell rings, or someone knocks on the door, I forget which. Miss Ellie's on the other side of the door. It's Clayton's last chance to bed Sue Ellen. Instead, CLAYTON GOES TO THE DOOR. WHAT A SCHMUCK! Should have kissed her. Hard. It wasn't in the script, but what the hell. Linda and I could have had some fun with that scene and gotten away with murder. Who knew where that story line might have gone? Stepfather beds stepdaughter-in-law. It's no wonder I got a two-way bypass later.

Clayton became a second-rate character. In most of the cast photos, I'm one step lower. (I'm taller than J.R.) Or seated shorter, or in the background, or off the photo entirely. That's okay, I came in late, a couple of years late. And it was Larry Hagman's show. No one worked harder than he did. No one. J.R. was the show. But Clayton was the biggest wimp I've ever played. You only have to watch me on the golf course to know what a bull I am.

Phil Capice, the producer, wanted me to sing to Miss Ellie in bed. They wouldn't let us make love, but wanted me to sing. I declined as only I can.

★ ★ ★

Barbara Bel Geddes. What can you say? I wondered how she'd feel working with a singer since she was basically a stage actress. She gave a tremendous performance in *I Remember Mama* and had received an Academy nomination. She starred in other films, but her performance in *Vertigo* was the best. She seemed happier onstage than in films. I happened to see her in *Cat on a Hot Tin Roof* opening night on Broadway, and she was amazing.

She had a quality all her own and was a marvelous Miss Ellie. We never met the first year that I worked on "Dallas," as I recall, which was usual.

I was concerned with Sue Ellen and Dusty, my supposed son. We first met at one of the big parties that CBS threw for all the affiliates throughout the country. While waiting around to be introduced, you might have a drink or two, then sit down to a dinner afterward. The "Dallas" cast sat at one table, and I was placed beside Barbara.

We had a couple of martinis, didn't eat very much, and when the dinner was finished, the cast mingled and dispersed to smaller parties. Barbara moved her chair to get up, and being the gentleman I was, I stood to assist her. We both tripped on something and not having the greatest balance because of the martinis, I fell on my ass taking Barbara with me. We were both embarrassed and laughing at the same time. When we stood, I gave her a great big kiss and said, "Thank you, Madam. I enjoyed that very much."

She replied, "So did I."

We dusted ourselves off and walked off, as gracefully as two potted ones could, with great aplomb. She could be adorably cute, and it was amazing to work with her. I found her to be a complete enigma at times and wide open at others. I think Barbara thought I didn't like her much, but I did. But she was a New York-trained actress and probably didn't think I knew a thing about acting. Listen up, folks. It didn't take a fucking genius to act the part of that milquetoast, Clayton Farlow.

We only had one little tiff early in our relationship during a scene. I was off-camera for her closeup and was nodding and reacting to her. She suddenly stopped and said, "Stop that."

I said, "Stop what?"

She said, "That nodding and humming that you're doing."

"Oh. Are we giving acting lessons now?"

"Oh no. No. I'd never do that."

I said, "Thank you," and that was the end of that. We never had another dispute.

Barbara loves her profession. In a series like "Dallas," there are so many ways to do a scene that you sometimes have to do scenes that are projecting the story. They can be very trying and dumbfounding at times. You can't say the things that are written. They must be interpreted.

I think after the sadness of losing Jim Davis, me coming in, Leonard Katzman leaving the show, Bobby leaving the show, and all the physical problems she had,

Barbara decided to leave, too. I asked her what she was going to do.

"Howard, I'm going home to my beautiful farm in New York and retire and work on my pottery and sculpting."

They immediately replaced her with Donna Reed. I don't know who made this decision. At the beginning of the new season, I walked into the show, after a wedding had occurred somewhere, with a new Miss Ellie. It didn't work for us. Don't get me wrong. I enjoyed working with Donna and loved her, but it didn't work. Everything was against her, poor doll. I began to hear the rumblings and ignored them. I told Lenny that Donna was all wrong for Miss Ellie. She was too sweet, too pretty, too set. But he really liked her. I had suggested Nancy Olson, Alan J. Lerner's wife, to fill in when Bel Geddes left.

The soap led to concerts and recording contracts that revitalized my career. During one concert in England, I fielded questions from the audience. One question was "Will Donna Reed be back next year on 'Dallas'?"

"Yep, sure," I replied.

Then boom. I read in the London papers that Miss Ellie's Barbara Bel Geddes had returned to the soap. They fired Donna. Egg on my face.

Playing the stepfather to that family was not the easiest thing to do. They never discussed anything with me. So I stepped aside. Then Leonard returned to the show, Bobby did, too, and so did Barbara. We settled back into the saddle, as they say, and the show's success skyrocketed again.

Golf and Balls, I've Got 'Em All

★　★　★　★　★

Funny, after twelve amazing years in "Dallas," I thought I'd be hot again: in Vegas, Broadway, do another series, get a Tony, something. Wrong.

Goodbye, Clayton Farlow. I scrambled to pay the bills, appeared in a few guest shots for practically no money. The phone stopped ringing.

In 1984, after a concert in Liverpool, England, I sat in the Adelphi Hotel bar getting drunk. I had seen a little guy, Willie Morgan, playing football (or soccer, as it's known on this side of the pond), and he walked in with some folks. They sat down, and we all got bombed together. One of them asked me, "Have you ever thought about doing a golf tournament here?"

I quickly replied, "I'd love to."

Two weeks later, I received a phone call suggesting that we do one in Manchester.

I said, "Fine."

And that's how the Howard Keel Invitational Golf

Tournament started. The NSPCC (National Society for the Prevention of Cruelty to Children) is the tournament's beneficiary. Princess Margaret headed the program. Since her passing, they believe Prince Andrew will assume the NSPCC reins.

The tournament is held in September of each year, and since 1984, has earned more than a million dollars to help England's children. Jack Lemmon was among the celebrities who join me annually for this sold-out event.

* * *

In December 1985, I was in Los Angeles and went to the country club to play golf. I had a little chest pain, but ignored it and played a round. As the pain increased, I sat down to lunch when Dr. Nick Panagiotis joined me. I said, "Hey, Doc, I got some chest pains."

He said, "Your car or mine?"

Judy and I had planned a fifteenth-wedding anniversary party and dinner that evening. Dr. Panagiotis called Judy to tell her I was in the hospital.

Judy said, "Oh, Nick. You're joshing me. It's our wedding anniversary."

They conducted tests and discovered some heart blockage. They tried the balloon thing, then hauled me off to a Northridge hospital for more tests that included an angioplasty.

I was on the table about half-bombed for three-and-a-half hours before they realized the procedure wouldn't work. Now to find out what's wrong with you, they do an exploration called an angiogram. Afterward they put a ten-pound bag on your groin where they entered the artery, and you have to lie on your back for ten hours while you heal up. It's very uncomfortable.

When they went in to do the angioplasty, it was the second time they entered the groin. When they put the ten-pound bag on again, my back ached after about four hours. A male nurse asked me how I was doing. I told him my back was killing me. He said, "Let me give you a little shot of morphine to help you with the pain."

I asked, "Dope?"

"It won't hurt you, and you won't get hooked."

"Okay, what the hell?"

He returned about five minutes later and asked me how I was doing? I told him, "It still hurts, but I don't give a shit."

I was flying high. Wow, what a flight! In early 1986, they performed a double bypass on me, and I returned to work thirty pounds lighter three weeks after the surgery. It was quite an experience that I don't want to go through again.

* * *

The support I received during my hospitalization was incredible. The first call I received was from Sinatra. Remember now that they'd checked me into the hospital under a fake name so the media wouldn't get hold of it.

He said, "Hey, pal, how you doing?"

I said, "I'm in good hands, Frank. I'll be fine. It's great of you to call."

"Just checking in, old pal. You need anything, let me know."

"Thanks, Frank. I really appreciate that."

I hadn't seen Frank or talked to him for maybe ten

years, and how he found me or learned of my medical problem, I don't know, but that was Frank. God bless him.

All my friends and family were terrific. Judy was a solid brick. Her mother and father and brother flew to California to help her and helped finish the house we were rebuilding.

Gordon MacRae called, and he seemed fine. A couple of days later, he passed away. Donna Reed and her husband, Grover Asmus, called. I knew she was under the weather, but I couldn't believe it when they told me she, too, had passed away three days later from cancer.

I looked up to the Almighty and said, "Not me, pal. I'm not the third one. I'm not ready. I ain't going. No way!"

Judy attended Donna's funeral, and my manager took me home from the hospital on the same day.

It may seem strange, but I never worried about the whole damn thing. I wanted to get it done with and get on with my wonderful life.

★ ★ ★

I never worked much with Pat Duffy. It seemed the only times we had any connection at all was at the dinner table, or he might step in between me and J.R. when we disagreed and came close to blows.

We ate dinner a few times with him and his wife, Carlyn. Met his two sons, who were very bright and idolized their mother and father. They were a great family. Pat was also a fine director. He directed a few episodes, and I enjoyed working with him.

Steve Kanaly and Susan Howard, who played Ray and Donna Krebbs, were always easy to work with. We were sort of the outcasts of the Ewing family and would get together and sort out our troubles. I enjoyed working with both of them. There was an understanding and sympathy between us that worked.

I knew that Ken Kercheval and I had a connection years before when we were in San Francisco. He was in *Virginia Woolf,* and I was doing *No Strings.* The two theaters were adjacent to each other. I never paid any attention to him, and he never noticed me, either, even though we both spent our after-theater hours at the same bar directly across the street from the theaters.

We talked on the set one day, and the subject of San Francisco came up. We discovered that we had been there at the same time. In the second act of *No Strings,* the band had a wild jazz session during a ballet, and I used to stand in the wings and listen to them. I told him about it, and he said, "That damned band was so loud, you could hear it in my theater, and it happened every night before my most important scene in the whole show. I hated that damned show with a passion."

We weren't a smash in San Francisco and closed after two weeks. Ken and I crossed like two ships in the night and met twenty years later to find out that I was part of a thorn in his side and never knew it. I got to know Ken and his new wife, and Judy and I had great times with them.

Being on "Dallas," I met a lot of exceptional people, and during the ten-and-a-half years, I never saw anyone get out of line. They're a group of special, talented, and very professional people.

I never had any scenes with Victoria Principal, Charlene Tilton, or Priscilla Presley, but seeing them occasionally was very easy on the eyes. They were a beautiful talented trio with no pretense about themselves.

George Kennedy was a multitalented actor. There was a rumor around that he and I would do another version of *The Odd Couple*, and while the idea was interesting, the timing was wrong. Hmm. It would be interesting to see what they could do with two spoiled, physically big men in that situation. . . .

Clean Heart, Fresh Balls, New Fans

★ ★ ★ ★ ★

Twelve seasons on "Dallas" introduced me to a new generation of fans and revived my singing career. I had an opportunity to do concerts.

I did one concert tour in England where they put a comic and a girl singer with me who were much my junior. Now my audiences' hair looks like a field of cotton balls—all white and fluffy. Mature people who had a tough time figuring out the comic and singer's acts. I did, too.

My next tour, I'd be alone. I'm a trained singer with a gifted voice, and after an hour of singing, I'm just getting warmed up. To do an extra hour was no sweat. I put together a tour, and we were on the road again. I did about thirty-four dates in England with an awesome fourteen-piece band and Richard Holmes, our conductor.

I learned their names during the afternoon rehearsal. In the middle of the concert that night, I introduced them all by name and made them each take a bow. They worked with me during all my concerts in England,

Scotland, and Wales. The big cities in England are close together, and we performed thirty-four dates in thirty-six days. I had a wonderful time, even more wonderful because Judy and Leslie traveled with me.

During my years on "Dallas," I did five concert tours during the spring hiatus.

★ ★ ★

I sang in the greatest concert halls in Great Britain that comfortably sat from 1,700 to 5,000 patrons. There is nothing more incredible than British audiences. After every concert, I'd sign autographs, sometimes fans would wait in the theater foyer for an hour to see me. I had two extraordinary tour directors, Don Archell and Tony McGrogan.

★ ★ ★

During my tenure on "Dallas," I spent a lot of time in and around Dallas. The last few years, I stayed at Las Colinas Hotel, which boasted two golf courses and a good practice area. I also met Eddie Chiles at Bel-Air through my good friend, Bob Sterling, and he put me up for a nonresident membership at Shady Oaks Country Club in Fort Worth.

Eddie was a very successful oil man. He introduced me around Shady Oaks, and I played a lot of golf with a character named Bill Flynn. The first day I went to Shady Oaks, I approached the pro shop and saw a man practicing on the putting green. He had on a flat hat à la Ben Hogan. He turned out to BE Ben Hogan.

I had met Mr. Hogan the first time I played in the Crosby at Pebble Beach, thirty years earlier. I had played Pebble that day with Bob Sterling, and when we completed our round, Bob said, "How would you like to have dinner with Ben Hogan and his wife, Valerie, tonight?"

I couldn't believe my ears. I said, "You're putting me on."

"No! Meet me and Anne at seven o'clock in the foyer of the lodge."

I was walking on air. Never in my life did I ever expect to meet Hogan, let alone have dinner with him. I remember I didn't have much to say. I listened. Hogan and his wife were so open and gracious and easy to be with.

Now thirty years later, I was walking up to the pro shop at Shady Oaks, and there was Hogan practicing on the putting green. I said to myself, "I have to go and say hello. I just have to."

So I strolled over and said, "Mr. Hogan."

He looked up and said, "Hey, Howard. I heard you were in town. Gosh, the last time we met, we had dinner at the Crosby. How are you?"

I was flabbergasted that he'd remember me.

I said, "I'm fine. My golf hasn't improved much, but I'm fine."

He said, "Well, my putting hasn't improved much, either, but I'm out here every day working on it."

"I can give you a singing lesson, I guess. But I don't think I can give you a putting lesson."

He laughed and replied, "You work on your singing, and I'll work on my putting. You never know what might happen. I'll see you around."

As I walked away feeling 10 feet tall, I thought to myself, he's not only a great golfer, but a great guy.

314

I had the best time at Shady Oaks and played a lot of golf with Bill Flynn. I used to watch Mr. Hogan practice. He'd go out with a caddie, hit about twenty balls, then move to another area, and practice with another iron. The caddie hardly moved to pick up the balls. I would sit off about thirty yards to watch him.

After a couple of years, Bill Flynn and I were having a cocktail with Mr. Hogan, and he invited us to play nine holes with him. "Let's tee off around 10 o'clock tomorrow, and we'll have lunch afterward."

Play golf with Hogan? WOW! I didn't sleep much that night. We stood on the tee box that morning, and I want to tell you, I have been through some pretty trying experiences in my lifetime, but I really had a dry mouth on this one. I was to be Mr. Hogan's partner. I hit off the tee pretty well and managed to par the first four holes.

Then my wheels flew off, and I started spraying a bit. After a couple of holes, Ben, we were calling him Ben by this time, gave me a tip and straightened me out. To play with Ben Hogan and have him give you a tip is something you don't forget.

Hogan always sat at the same place in the men's grill. He could watch the first tee, the tenth tee, and the practice area. One day, I'd been on the practice tee for about thirty minutes and entered the men's grill and asked if I could join him.

He said, "Sit down. Sit down. I've been watching you on the practice tee. You never cock your hands in your backswing. Let me show you something."

He stood and gave me a demonstration. "Now you have to do that, or you will never get your full power potential. Have you got that?"

315

I said, "Yes, sir," and I showed him.

He said, "That's it."

"Thanks, Ben, I really appreciate that."

That afternoon, I must have hit two hundred balls when I began to feel the difference and hit the ball like I'd never hit it before.

I had an early afternoon call on the set for "Dallas" the next day, but I had an opportunity to play with a guy named Mike Dunaway, the longest ball hitter I ever played with. After twelve holes, I was two under par. I was hitting the ball with great confidence, both the woods and the irons.

I had to quit because of the early call on "Dallas," and it killed me because I was playing so good I didn't want to quit. We closed the location shooting on "Dallas" the following day, and I had to return to L.A.

I called Ben before I left and told him how much he had helped me. In the next couple of months, I went from an eight handicap to a three and nearly shot my age when I was sixty-eight.

Howard: On Life and Golf

★ ★ ★ ★ ★

One day, I was coming into the sixteenth hole at my home course at the Bel-Air and was two under par on a par seventy. It suddenly occurred to me that I could shoot my age. I stroke-choked and shot the next three holes bogey, bogey, bogey, and shot seventy-one.

I played well the next few months, then had a brief period where I couldn't play golf. When I could play again, my swing was gone. That's golf. It'll drive you crazy, but it'll save your sanity.

I've been playing golf now for more than fifty years, and I've never been bored with the game. I've been pissed off with the game and sometimes with a couple of people I have played with, as I'm sure they have been pissed off with me in my earlier days.

It takes a while to learn there's someone else on the course beside yourself, to learn good manners, good sportsmanship, and the game of golf itself. This is not a simple game. It's the most maddening, exasperating, self-deprecating, mystifying game in the world.

It's a lot like learning to sing properly. You are given the gift, but to sing properly and extend it, stay on key and be understood, takes the same maddening, exasperating, self-deprecating, mystifying, contortions.

When I first started to learn the art of singing, I couldn't afford to pay to make a recording to hear myself sing. Being a bass, I had to learn to extend my voice upward. The low tones were natural, but the upper voice was another thing. When I could make a recording, it was awful.

I've had the same nightmare over the years. We're at Carnegie Hall. Huge stage. Big applause. I come out dressed in a tux. I say to the conductor, "What are we doing tonight?"

He says, "I don't know."

There's no sheet music.

* * *

It's like when I saw my golf swing on film that I thought was so graceful and smooth, I wanted to throw up.

Without the help, patience, and knowledge of George Houston, I'd never be the singer I am today.

I learned more about the golf swing in my early days of golf with the help and patience of Robert Sterling. In golf, you can feel a good swing, but not see it.

In singing, you can feel a good tone, but not hear it.

In golf and singing, little things can sneak in. All of a sudden, your golf swing and your singing production are not working. You can't feel it or hear it. But it's gone. It can be badly demoralizing. You need someone who knows you to look at your golf swing. Someone to listen to you sing that knows you. They also must be good teachers and know how to straighten you out. There are as many theories about the golf swing as there are about voice production. I've been lucky in singing to have met Papa Rossi and Leon Cheparo and a baritone named Richard Fredericks.

But my golf swing is around the bend. Young muscle is better than old muscle. Fortunately, I still can sing pretty well. I still do my arpeggios that Papa Rossi gave me years ago. He and Cheparo were my two favorites.

★ ★ ★

In 1994, Judy and I had a home in Sherman Oaks, and I played a lot of golf in Palm Springs. Then the earthquake hit in January 1994. An 8.4 struck our recently rebuilt home, and that terrified Judy. We decided then to move our permanent address to the Coachella Valley near Palm Springs.

★ ★ ★

On February 10, 1995, I was playing golf on my home course in Palm Desert, California, when an announcer and a cameraman approached our foursome on the greens and said, "This is your life." I had told Judy a hundred times I never wanted to be embarrassed like that. Like she listens to me.

Thames TV in London had flown to America to film their BBC episode. I showered, changed into a tux, and a limo drove us to Hollywood where our family and friends had traveled from around the country to surprise and roast me.

My friend from Gillespie, Chuck Gibbons, broke me up with his memories of our youth together. "Gillespie, Illinois, where the girls were."

Kathryn Grayson, Jane Powell, Ann Miller, who remembered her "Too Darn Hot" number from *Kiss Me Kate* when her bracelet caught on Kathryn's blonde wig.

Leonard Katzman who said, "For *Kiss Me Kate*, we were looking for a romantic leading man, and we thought immediately of Howard." George Sidney who told the audience MGM had three great dancers whom MGM called KAK; Gene Kelly, Fred Astaire, and Howard Keel.

From the cast of "Dallas," Ken Kercheval and George Kennedy, reminisced. "We sat on the floor with a Scotch. I got me one, too, and that's the last I remember of that night with Howard."

Charlene Tilton and Linda Gray surprised me. Jane Wyman told the story of me losing her to Van Johnson in *Three Guys Named Mike*.

Robert Stack, who called me the best shot in Hollywood. I had won the West Coast championship in skeet shooting after practicing with him for three months. Robert is a world-renowned Olympic shooter himself.

Russ Tamblyn remembered when, during the filming of *Seven Brides for Seven Brothers,* the seven brothers, all with dyed red hair, jumped into a Cadillac convertible and drove to a nearby drive-in for lunch. We stopped the lunch crowd.

Dolores Gray said appearing in *Kismet* was the biggest thrill of her life. "Howard was a consummate genius and an angel to work with."

Judy wore a white pantsuit and sat smugly on the edge of her chair and smiled that she pulled something this big over on me. She'll never trick me like that again. I'm onto her now.

My children and grandchildren attended, as did many close friends and family members.

The BBC ran the show in England on February 22, 1995. "This Is Your Life" captured a record breaking 45-percent market share that night, reaching more than 11.7 million viewers. Prime Minister Margaret Thatcher missed the viewing and asked that it be rebroadcast. She also requested and received a copy of that tape for her personal library.

* * *

In 2000, we had an *Annie Get Your Gun* reunion in Hollywood. The movie had been out of circulation for years. The new colorized version premiered that evening. Lou Calhern, who'd been like a father to me, had passed away.

We reminisced that Frank Butler was a real person, a mean drunk and not a pleasant character. Actually he was a bit of a shit, bigheaded, and had a way with the ladies. Annie Oakley was very smart to give up her career to marry Frank. She spoiled the hell out of him, and in the film, he returns the favor with a wonderful song, "My Defenses Are Down." I loved that song. For the high keys, I squeezed my buns to hit the note. The movie had a $3-million budget.

I've been invited to the White House and to Buckingham Palace, but never been to either. Paying the bills always got in the way. No regrets.

I always took good care of my mother, paid all my alimony checks on time, and have never been late to an appointment.

Ah, memories. . . .

* * *

If you're ever in the market for a trombone player, a pool shooter, dancing fool, a fighter, skin fitter, a mechanic, horseback rider, gun handler, fast-draw artist, bullwhipper, airline or boat pilot, motorcyclist, actor or singer, call me. I'm available.

The timing of my life has had some wild and curious ups and downs. But the timing of my meeting Judy has been one of constant joy and love. She is the love and joy of my life!

What's the best part of me? My singing. I can still peel the paint off the walls.

Epilogue
November 2004

We packed for our nineteenth annual NSPCC golf tourney in Manchester, England, the one event Howard loved so much, when I suggested we have a few vitamin drips before our flight. The doctor gave Howard a complete physical and said, "CAT scan tomorrow at the hospital."

The tests revealed Howard needed immediate surgery. After his operation, the surgeon stepped into the waiting room and told me Howard had advanced colon cancer (the same sickness that took Howard's mother). He said Howard had maybe six months, but he couldn't look at me as he left the room.

Little did we know he had sixty days left.

No spouse is prepared, no matter what, to face the end of a long beautiful journey with his or her loved one. And although there was a twenty-five-year age difference between us, I was the one who struggled to keep up with his energy and the fight he gave to everything he faced in life.

September 7, he wanted to go home, be with his family, say goodbye to those he loved, and watch the golfers play on the course behind our house.

At home, we were guided by visiting nurses, who taught us how to offer aid for a loved one. Then they slowly and quietly stepped back, and hospice enabled us to prepare for the next stages. He had the warmth and support of his family, who cared for him dearly and lifted his spirits: visits with his grandchildren and great grandchildren led by his beloved daughters Kaija and Kirstine, and Howard's greatest comfort, his son, Gunnar, who drove in from Los Angeles to stay with us. Gunnar remained by his father's side massaging his pain and caring for his every need.

My parents, sister, our daughter, Leslie, and her friend, David, joined us, and that made our family complete. Leslie would remain long after Howard's passing to support me. I love you, Leslie, so very much.

Kurt Hach, a world-renowned faith healer, joined our extended group to ease Howard's pain. The prayer circle widened throughout the world as news of his illness spread.

Alas, our love story on earth came to an end too swiftly. His robust life of 1,027 months ended with two horrible months of pain.

He cared for his voice his entire life, and that in itself was a tremendous burden to carry on one's shoulder. As a perfectionist, he tried never to disappoint an audience.

"Give 'em everything you've got," he'd say, and he meant it. I know how much his fans loved him, and he loved them just as much.

I met a wonderful man who loved me so much more

the day he died than on that first blind date almost thirty-six years ago. And I was given the gift to love and care for him in the brilliant winter of his life.

At the end, he was surrounded by his children and my family who loved him so much. In the wee hours of November 7, 2004, at the time of his passing, the lights in the bedroom dimmed for just a second or two, came up again, then dimmed a second time, just like the house lights at the theater. We thought it was his last encore. Oh no, not Howard.

That morning, when the hearse left with Howard, we stood in the front yard and waved as they drove toward the side gate of our neighborhood. The driver discovered they couldn't exit there, so they turned around and drove past the house again. So damn you, Howard, you got another encore.

I prayed we've have more time together, but it was not to be. He was a giant of a man, so strong, but some signs were there. We should have noticed the weight loss and the lessening of energy.

If we are able to help just one person from this experience, we'd say, "Go and pick up a phone and set up a colonoscopy TODAY. It takes so little time, is painless, and you could save your life and/or someone you love."

Remember Howard with great fondness. Play his music often. Rent his movies, and smile as his beautiful voice fills your heart. It was a life of great happiness and much charitable giving to others. Thank you all who loved him as much as I did and always will.

—Judy Keel

Filmography

THE SMALL VOICE
(Constellation Films, British Lion 1948)
This psychological drama marked the screen debut of Howard Keel. A British film, it concerns the victims of a car crash who turn out to be escaped convicts and hold captive their rescuers.
Cast: Howard Keel, Valerie Hobson, James Donald.
Producer: Anthony Havelock-Allan
Director: Fergus McDonnell
Writer: Derek Neame

ANNIE GET YOUR GUN (MGM 1950)
This great Irving Berlin Academy Award winning musical tells of the young female hillbilly, Annie Oakley, who joins up with Frank Butler.
Writer: Sidney Sheldon

PAGAN LOVE SONG (MGM 1950)
A musical romp as an American schoolteacher marries a Tahitian beauty.
Cast: Howard Keel, Esther Williams, Rita Moreno.
Producer: Arthur Freed
Director: Robert Alton
Writers: Robert Nathan, Jerry Davis

SHOWBOAT (MGM 1951)
Glorious screen version of the Broadway smash musical, with music and lyrics by Kern and Hammerstein.
Cast: Howard Keel, Kathryn Grayson, Ava Gardner, Joe E. Brown, William Warfield, Marge and Gower Champion, Agnes Moorehead.
Producer: Arthur Freed
Director: George Sidney
Writer: John Lee Mahin

TEXAS CARNIVAL (MGM 1951)
A sly fairgrounds showman is mistaken for a millionaire and runs up huge debts.
Cast: Howard Keel, Esther Williams, Red Skelton, Ann Miller, Keenan Wynn, Paula Raymond.
Producer: Jack Cummings
Director: Charles Walters
Writer: Dorothy Kingsley

CALLAWAY WENT THATAWAY
(MGM 1951)
Engaging comedy with great charm tells of an old movie cowboy whose career is revived by television but by then he is a hopeless drunk. An actor is engaged to pose as him for public appearances.
Producers: Melvin Frank, Norman Panama
Directors: Melvin Frank, Norman Panama
Writers: Melvin Frank, Norman Panama

ACROSS THE WIDE MISSOURI
(MGM 1951)

In the 1820s, a weary trapper marries an Indian girl and lives with her people.
Narrated by Howard Keel
Cast: Clark Gable, Ricardo Montalban, John Hodiak, Adolphe Menjou, Maria Elena.
Producer: Robert Sisk
Director: William Wellman
Writer: Talbot Jennings

THREE GUYS NAMED MIKE
(MGM 1951)

A stewardess who is accident-prone finds herself with three suitors. A romantic comedy.
Cast: Howard Keel, Jane Wyman, Van Johnson, Barry Sullivan, Jeff Donnell, Phyllis Kirk.
Producer: Armand Deutsch
Director: Charles Walters
Writer: Sidney Sheldon

DESPERATE SEARCH (MGM 1952)

A suspense drama about the search for two children, lost in the Canadian wilds.
Cast: Howard Keel, Jane Greer, Keenan Wynn, Jeff Richards.
Producer: Matthew Rapf
Director: Joseph Lewis
Writer: Walter Doniger

LOVELY TO LOOK AT (MGM 1952)

Film version of the hit Broadway musical *Roberta* has three Broadway producers inheriting a Paris fashion house. The music and the fashions made this Jerome Kern musical a long awaited hit.
Cast: Howard Keel, Kathryn Grayson, Ann Miller, Red Skelton.
Producer: Jack Cummings

CALAMITY JANE (Warner Bros. 1953)

While helping a saloon owner friend find a star's attraction, Calamity finds and wins the heart of Wild Bill Hickok. This western musical became one of Hollywood's greatest. The outstanding score contained "Secret Love," which won the Academy Award (Oscar).
Cast: Howard Keel, Doris Day, Allyn McLerie, Phil Carey.
Producer: William Jacobs
Director: David Butler
Writer: James O'Hanlon

FAST COMPANY (MGM 1953)

After inheriting a racing stable, a girl uncovers chicanery.
Cast: Howard Keel, Nina Foch, Polly Bergen, Marjorie Main.
Director: John Sturges
Writer: William Roberts

KISS ME KATE (MGM 1953)

A bright, brisk screen version of the Broadway musical hit, it tells the story of the wedded stars of a musical version of *The Taming of the Shrew* who led a riotous backstage life.
Cast: Howard Keel, Kathryn Grayson, Ann Miller, Bob Fosse, Bobby Van and James Whitmore.
Producer: Jack Cummings
Director: George Sidney
Writer: Dorothy Kingsley
Music and Lyrics: Cole Porter

I LOVE MELVIN (MGM 1953)

A high-born chorus girl is pursued by a photographer's aide.
Cast: Howard Keel, Donald O'Connor, Debbie Reynolds, Una Merkel, Allyn Joslyn.
Producer: George Wells

RIDE VAQUERO (MGM 1953)
After the Civil War, ranchers move and settle in New Mexico, causing some natives to become bandits. An outstanding cast added to this colorful western.
Cast: Howard Keel, Ava Gardner, Robert Taylor, Anthony Quinn, Charlita.
Producer: Stephen Ames
Director: John Farrow
Writer: Frank Fenton

SEVEN BRIDES FOR SEVEN BROTHERS (MGM 1954)
Set in the old west, seven hard-working brothers decide they need wives, and carry off young women from the villages nearby. Distinguished by a great score and brilliant dancing.
Cast: Howard Keel, Jane Powell, Jeff Richards, Russ Tamblyn, Tommy Rall, Marc Platt, Jacques d'Amboise.
Producer: Jack Cummings
Director: Stanley Donen
Writers: Frances Goodrich, Albert Hackett

ROSE MARIE (MGM 1954)
A Canadian Mountie gets his man—and a lady. This backwoods romance from the Broadway success was very well received.
Cast: Howard Keel, Ann Blyth, Fernando Lamas, Bert Lahr, Marjorie Main, Ray Collins.
Producer: Mervyn LeRoy
Director: Mervyn LeRoy
Writer: Ronald Miller

JUPITER'S DARLING (MGM 1954)
As Hannibal advances on Rome, he falls under the spell of the dictator's intended bride. A glorious example of the higher lunacy, with colored elephants adorning this musical about the fall of the Roman Empire.
Cast: Howard Keel, Esther Williams, George Sanders, William Demarest, Richard Haydn, Marge and Gower Champion.
Producer: George Wells
Director: George Sidney

Writer: Dorothy Kingsley

DEEP IN MY HEART (MGM 1954)
One of MGM's great musicals, it is the life of Sigmund Romberg, one of the theatre's great writers of musicals. A large and outstanding cast and a far above average script made this a visual treat.
Cast: Howard Keel, Jose Ferrer, Merle Oberon, Paul Henreid, Walter Pidgeon, Helen Traubel, Gene Kelly, David Burns, Tamara Toumanova, Jane Powell, Ann Miller, Rosemary Clooney, Cyd Charisse, Tony Martin.
Producer: Roger Edens
Director: Stanley Donen
Writer: Leonard Spiegelgass

KISMET (MGM 1955)
A lavish period musical with outstanding costumes and sets, embroidered with the music of Borodin.
Cast: Howard Keel, Ann Blythe, Vic Damone, Dolores Gray, Monty Woolley, Sebastian Cabot.
Producer: Arthur Freed
Director: Vincente Minnelli
Writers: Charles Lederer, Luther Davis

FLOODS OF FEAR (Rank Films 1958)
Four people are trapped by floods in a remote house. A melodrama with impressive performances and production.
Cast: Howard Keel, Anne Heywood, Cyril Cusack, Harry H. Corbett.
Producer: Sydney Box
Director: Charles Crichton
Writer: Charles Crichton

THE BIG FISHERMAN (Centurion 1959)
Simon Peter, disciple of Jesus, meets an Arab princess and convinces her not to kill her stepfather King Herod.
Cast: Howard Keel, Susan Kohner, Alexander Scourby, John Saxon, Martha Hyer, Herbert Lom, Beulah Bondi.
Producer: Rowland V. Lee
Director: Frank Borzaga
Writers: Howard Estabrook, Roland V. Lee

ARMORED COMMAND
(Allied Artists 1961)

As the Battle of the Bulge begins, a ravishing Nazi spy infiltrates an American army base.

Cast: Howard Keel, Burt Reynolds, Tina Louise, Earl Holliman, Marty Ingels, Carleton Young.
Producer: Ron W. Alcorn
Director: Byron Haskin
Writer: Ron W. Alcorn

THE DAY OF THE TRIFFIDS
(Allied Artists 1962)

This engaging film has become a cult favorite worldwide. Meteorites blind populations of London, Paris and Spain, activating giant mobile plants.

Cast: Howard Keel, Nicole Murray, Kieron Moore, Janet Scott.
Producer: Philip Yordon, George Pitcher
Director: Steve Sekeley
Writer: Philip Yordan

THE MAN FROM BUTTON WILLOW
(United Screen Arts 1965)

An animated western, it is filled with derring-do. With the voices of Howard Keel, Ross Martin, Herschel Bernardi, Verna Felton, Dale Robertson.
Producer: Phyllis Bounds Detiege
Director: David Detiege
Writer: David Detiege

WACO (Paramount 1966)

A knowing gunfighter is brought in to straighten out a badly corrupt town in the old west.

Cast: Howard Keel, Jane Russell, Wendell Corey, Brian Donlevy, Terry Moore, Richard Arlen, Gene Evans.
Producer: A.C. Lyles
Director: R. G. Springsteen
Writer: Steve Fisher

RED TOMAHAWK (Paramount 1967)

After the battle of Little Big Horn, the small town of Deadwood gets caught up in the aftermath.

Cast: Howard Keel, Joan Caulfield, Broderick Crawford, Wendell Corey, Scott Brady, Richard Arlen, Tom Drake.
Producer: A.C. Lyles
Director: R. G. Springsteen
Writer: Steve Fisher

THE WAR WAGON (Universal 1967)

Exhilarating action western, tells the story of two cowboys and an Indian who plan to ambush the gold wagon of a crooked mining contractor.

Cast: Howard Keel, John Wayne, Kirk Douglas, Bruce Dern, Keenan Wynn, Bruce Cabot, Gene Evans, Robert Walker.
Producer: Marvin Schwartz
Director: Burt Kennedy
Writer: Clair Huffaker

ARIZONA BUSHWHACKERS
(Paramount 1968)

A western town takes a Confederate prisoner and makes him a sheriff.

Cast: Howard Keel, Yvonne De Carlo, Brian Donlevy, John Ireland, Marilyn Maxwell, Scott Brady, Barton Maclane, James Craig.
Producer: A.C. Lyles
Director: Lesley Selander
Writer: Steve Fisher

Discography

45 Records

"American Dream" (March 1956)
"Annie Get Your Gun" (MGM 1950)
"I Can Do Without You" (Columbia 1953)
"I'll Stay With You for a Lifetime"
  (Warner Bros.)
"Lovely to Look At" (MGM 1952)
"The Most Exciting Night"
"Pagan Love Song" (MGM 1950)
"The Right Girl for Me" (MGM 1954)
"Rosemarie" (MGM 1954)
"Seven Brides for Seven Brothers" (MGM
  1954)
"Show Boat" (MGM 1951)
"The Touch of Your Hand/You're
  Dreaming" (MGM 1952)
"Whoa Emma/Young Folks Should Get
  Married" (MGM 1951)
"The World is Mine Tonight/My Magic
  Heart" (MGM 1951)

Albums/Cassettes/CDs

Ambassador of Song (RCA British 1971)
And I Love You So (Warwick British 1984)
Annie Get Your Gun (MGM 1950)
Annie Get Your Gun (Sandy Hook 1981)
The Best of Howard Keel (British 1993)
Calamity Jane (Columbia 1953)
Deep in My Heart (MGM 1954)
An Enchanted Evening with Howard Keel
  (British 1991)
Film and Musical Favorites (Germany)
The Great MGM Stars (MGM British 1991)
Howard Keel: Close to My Heart (British 1990)
*Howard Keel: A Selection of His Screen
  Successes* (MGM)
Just for You (British 1988)
Kismet (MGM 1955)
Kiss Me Kate (MGM 1953)
Kiss Me Kate (RCA 1984)
Live in Concert (British 1991)
Lovely to Look At (MGM 1952)
Oklahoma/Annie Get Your Gun/Carousel
  (1947)
Oklahoma/Annie Get Your Gun (1947)

Pagan Love Song (MGM 1950)
*Reminiscing with Howard Keel: His Stage &
  Screen Favorites* (British)
Rosemarie (MGM 1954)
Saratoga (RCA 1959)
Seven Brides for Seven Brothers (MGM 1954)
Show Boat (MGM 1951)
Show Boat (RCA 1958)
That's Entertainment (1974)
That's Entertainment Part 2 (MGM 1976)
That's Entertainment III (1994)
With Love (1984)
With Love from Howard Keel (1988)
With Love Howard Keel (1989/1990)
You Needed Me (1989)

Compilation Records

Classic Movie Musicals of Sammy Fain
Collector's Show Boat
Dallas: The Music Story (1985)
*Doris Day Sings Songs from the Warner Bros.
  Pictures: Calamity Jane and Pajama Game*
  (British)
Golden Age of Movie Musicals (MGM 1972)
Great Duets from MGM Musicals (British)
Great Singing Screen Stars (1991)
The Great Victor Duets (RCA)
Hollywood Sings Volume 2: The Men (RCA)
Hollywood Years of Harry Warren (1930-1957)
International Stars of the Talk of the Town
  (British)
Kathryn Grayson: Let There Be Music
MGM Years
Original Movie Soundtrack Hits
Original Soundtracks (MGM British)
Theatreland Showstoppers (MGM British
  1943-1968)
*25 Years of Recorded Sound 1945-1979 from the
  Vaults of MGM Records* (MGM 1945-1976)
Very Best of Cole Porter (MGM 1964)
Very Best of Irving Berlin (MGM 1964)
Very Best of Jerome Kern (MGM 1964)
Very Best of Motion Picture Musicals (MGM)
Very Best of Sigmund Romberg (MGM 1964)

Index

332